Healing and Being Healed
By Our Compulsions

Liz

You are such
a joy —
May Life reveal
its deepest treasures
Mary C 2003
May 2003

By
Mary O'Malley

Cover art by Diane Solomon

Printed in the United States of America by Thomson-Shore, Inc.

Library of Congress Control Number: 2002095022

Published by
Awaken Publications
Kirkland, Washington 98033

ISBN 0-9720848-1-9

Dedication

This book is dedicated to the Wellspring of deep wisdom that resides within every single human being. May each of us discover its truth and in that discovery, live from its clarity, love and support. In this living, the world will be healed.

Acknowledgments

A book is a living process funneled through the mind and heart of the author with much assistance from many different directions. This was certainly true in the creation of this book. So many wonderful, committed, and inspired people supported its birth and they have my deep gratitude for the parts they played. A few of them are as follows:

❖ MarySue Phillips – The midwifery of your deep wisdom and your unfailing commitment to this work is appreciated beyond words.

❖ Virginia Howell – Your feedback took this book to a whole new level. Thank you for being there in so many ways.

❖ Vaughan and Lyn Mason – This book wouldn't have happened without your support in ways that are too numerous to mention.

❖ Nancy Murray (my sister!) – Your razor sharp ability to cut the superfluous parts in a way I could handle is amazing! I am so glad we are together in this life.

❖ Nancy Hutto, Barb Yamasaki and Dee Smethurst – Your sharp eyes and understanding of language along with your resonance with the heart of this book brought it to a higher level of clarity and professionalism.

❖ The Compulsion Groups – The feedback you gave after reading the first manuscript was invaluable and I am so thankful you are all in my life.

❖ Mark Ricker and Patrick Hill – You kept me up and running when the world of computers would bring me to my knees!

❖ And for all the people who have read parts of this book, adding your perspective in the process – Thank you!

INTRODUCTION

To some degree, we are all compulsive. By compulsion I mean any recurring activity we use to manage our feelings that eventually ends up managing us. We can get compulsive about almost anything – over-spending, over-eating, over-working, over-planning, over-worrying, over-exercising, over-drinking, over-computerizing, or just over-overing. Many people are compulsive without even knowing it. It isn't until the computer crashes or the credit card is canceled or the doctor says you can't eat a high fat diet that it becomes clear how much any particular activity controls your life.

Ultimately, *our core compulsion is to struggle.* We live in a story in our heads that is always trying to *do* life. It feels that we need to make ourselves and our lives better or different than what they are. In our endless trying, we have forgotten how to *be*. We have forgotten how to open to the marvelous and magical adventure that is Life. We have forgotten how to trust ourselves, trust our lives, and live from our joy. *So we turn to our compulsions to numb ourselves out from all of our struggles, only to find ourselves struggling with our compulsions.*

Our compulsion to struggle causes such havoc in our lives. What would our lives be like if we could move beyond struggle and, instead, reconnect with the joy, the wonder, and the vitality of being truly alive? And how would it feel not only to heal our compulsions, but also *be healed by our compulsions*. By healing I don't just mean that they no longer overtake our lives; I mean being healed to the point that we experience again the deep peace that comes from being comfortable in our own skins, knowing that we are okay, life is okay, and everything is going to be okay.

It is possible to be healed in this way. That is what we will be exploring in this book together – a new approach to working with compulsions that not only heals our compulsions, but also allows us to be healed to our core. In order to do this, we need to learn how to be in relationship with our compulsions in a new way. We have been taught to dominate them, only to have them dominate us. And if we do control one, another seems to take us over. We stop smoking and we find ourselves over-eating. We let go of drinking and we end up shopping. We try to think positive thoughts to stop our worrying and we find our To-Do lists taking over our lives.

Controlling our compulsions promises that it will hold back these powerful urges, *but controlling never brings us the lasting healing that we long for. Instead, it actually fuels the compulsive cycle.* The U.S. Surgeon General reports that 98% of all of the weight that is lost in the United States is gained back within a year and a half! In fact, people usually gain more weight! *What we fight controls us. What we resist persists!*

There is another way of working with compulsions, a way that will heal our compulsions and bring us back home to ourselves, opening what has been closed, reclaiming what has been hidden, and remembering what has been forgotten. This new way moves us beyond seeing our compulsions as enemies needing to be conquered, to seeing them as guides back into a deep and abiding relationship with ourselves and with our lives.

This new way is about being curious rather than controlling and *responding* rather than *reacting*. Our compulsions thrive in *reaction*. They heal in *response*. They won't let go until they teach us how to *respond*, giving every part of us the attention and the compassion it needs in order to heal. In the light of our compassionate attention, compulsions not only lose their power over us, but they also become a doorway into the healing that we long for.

In learning the art of being curious rather than reactive, we will be exploring in this book what could be called alchemy. In the Middle Ages, it was thought that alchemy was about turning base metals into gold. Some people believed this so deeply that they spent their entire lives pursuing this fantasy. True alchemy is much more powerful than that. *It is about using the light of human attention to transform the dense, dark clouds of our forgetting into the aliveness and joy of our remembering.* It is about cultivating curiosity and compassion in order to transform the holdings in our minds, bodies, and hearts back into the free flowing aliveness that we truly are.

Our explorations in this book will bring us to three simple questions that we can use to heal our compulsions, and at the same time, be healed to our core. These questions clear up the struggles in our minds, open the healing of our hearts, and put us into direct contact with a wellspring of deep knowing within us that will guide us back home. As we learn again how to partner with the wellspring of wisdom within us, we will know the true and lasting healing that we have always longed for.

The wonderful thing is that as we allow our compulsions to be a guide back into ourselves and into our lives, we will not only be healed, we will also become a part of the healing of our planet. When we learn how to listen to our compulsions, they will teach us how to be conscious, compassionate, loving and wise human beings. Living from our inner wellspring of wisdom, we will find ourselves relating to our friends, our family, and all the other people we meet in our lives from a wiser, more compassionate place. And then, no matter where we are or what is happening in our lives, we become a healing presence in the world.

Let us explore together how we can heal and be healed by our compulsions.

Table of Contents

Section 4: Treasure Hunting

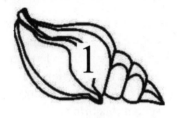

The Healing Journey

✦ MY JOURNEY, OUR JOURNEY ✦

I trust myself.

It may have been a long time since you have really known what I am talking about. So take a moment and imagine what it would be like to really trust yourself. It is about loving yourself from the inside out, accepting every part of the community of your *being*. It is about living in your body, connected to a wellspring of deep wisdom within you that supports and guides you in every moment of your life. And it is about living in a responsive mind, one that is passionately curious about what is happening right here, right now.

I also trust my life. I know how to wake up each morning and open to the unfolding of my life – both the easy and the difficult – living from a grounded center within me that knows that whatever shows up is a part of my journey into an ever-deepening connection with Life. I am much more fascinated with showing up for *what is* than with trying to make it into what I think it *should be*. The joy that this brings is beyond words.

How have I found a deep and wondrous connection with myself and with Life when most people live in minds that are always struggling, always wanting themselves and their lives to be different? How do I know a deep love affair with myself when most people not only don't love themselves, but they think that if they do, they are being selfish? And how did I discover the joy of living in my body when most people live almost exclusively in their heads, believing that their bodies are just vehicles for maneuvering through their lives rather than a wellspring of wisdom, clarity, and support? The amazingly wonderful thing is that it was my compulsions that brought me to a deep and abiding connection with myself and with Life.

It wasn't always that way. As a child I lived in a family where nobody was really there, a familiar experience for many of us. There were people going through the motions of living, but there was no real human-to-human contact. There were no playful eyes, no loving arms, no listening hearts that welcomed me into the world and also let me know that I was valued exactly as I was.

> *There is a wellspring of deep wisdom within you that supports and guides you in every moment of your life.*

In order to stay connected to themselves, children need a sense of connection and support from their caregivers. Being deprived of this essential 'nutrient' of Life, I left the world of *I am!* for the world of *I am not/I should be*. I became a human *doing* rather than a human *being*, and the further I got away from my own authenticity, the more I lived from fear. I tried to make myself into the *right* kind of person in order to get the connection that I so desperately needed, but it was never enough. By the time I was a teenager self-judgment and despair filled me to my core and my life was a never ending maze of pain.

> *The amazingly wonderful thing is that it was my compulsions that brought me to a deep and abiding connection with myself and with Life.*

I became vulnerable to anything that promised it would make me feel better and compulsions topped the list. I discovered that they could temporarily free me from the deep unease, struggle, and heartache that was my inner life. When my cravings were satiated, I could relax all of my trying, and for brief moments, I could taste a bit of the deep joy I had known before I disconnected from myself. But quickly the self-hate and despair (that always came after a wave of compulsion) would devour my peace and I would tumble back into that familiar place of struggling with myself and with Life.

For almost half of my life, I both hated my compulsions and I desperately needed them to survive. They numbed by heartache enough so that I could at least function in my life. I was taught that my compulsions were bad, and yet they relieved the pressure of always trying to make myself better or different from what I was in order to get the connection that I needed. Sneaking forbidden food is one of the strongest memories of my childhood as I desperately tried to ingest the love I craved. I can remember when I was 12 years old, coming home from school, putting two pieces of toast in the toaster, and as soon as they popped up, putting two more in. Quickly buttering the finished toast, I stuffed them into my mouth so I would be ready to butter and eat the next two. On and on I went until the fullness in my stomach temporarily numbed the emptiness in my heart.

I then went on to discover the mind-numbing world of prescription drugs, alcohol, busyness, and even some street drugs. Over time, most of those dropped away, but my core compulsion—overeating—stayed. My descent into eating hell had many twists and turns over the years, all accompanied by great self-hatred, deep despair, and a sinking feeling that I was just too weak-willed to take control. Every failure at being in charge only fueled more self-disgust, which brought on more eating. After years of failed diets, counseling, shots, pills, hypnosis clinics, fasting, and anything else that promised a way out of this descending spiral, I gained enough weight to top out at 220 pounds. I, like everyone else, was trying to heal my compulsion using the only method that was around at that time—*control*.

> *...lasting healing comes from being curious rather than controlling. It comes from mercy rather than manipulation and from responding rather than reacting.*

Thank God that controlling my compulsion didn't work for me! Stripped of any illusion that I was powerful enough to be in charge of these deep forces that would come roaring through me, I began to hear, like listening over a very fuzzy phone line, a *knowing* inside of me. This *knowing* said that *lasting healing comes from being curious rather than controlling. It comes from mercy rather than manipulation and from responding rather than reacting.*

I began to work with a woman who deeply understood these truths, and like a comet returning from the depths of outer space, I began the journey back to myself. One of the first things she invited me to do was to let go of the violence of dieting. This was like asking me to jump off the end of the world. I *knew* that I would gain a thousand pounds in a month. But after a small weight gain, things began to settle down. As the clouds of my controlling mind began to lift a little, I could see that it was in listening to what was going on inside of me when I was compulsive, rather than living in the endless cycles of reaction, that I would be healed.

So I began to *listen*.

Even though the Compulsive Eater within me would still rage through my life, leaving great devastation in its wake, I was becoming curious about exactly what was going on when I wanted to overeat. Slowly and surely, rather than hating my compulsion, I began to feel a bit of respect for it.

Watching my compulsion in action, I realized that it was an old survival tool that I had learned when I was young. This survival tool truly believed that if I ignored, denied or ran away from anything unpleasant in my life, then everything would be okay. When I finally began to truly listen, I could see that, not only did this not work, but the exact opposite was what was happening. When I felt anxiety come, I would numb out by overeating and then I would feel more fear. (I will never be able to control myself and I will just get fatter!) When I felt self-judgment, I would overeat and then I would then feel deep shame. (You are such a failure for not being able to control yourself!)

Noticing that my compulsion never brought me the deep peace that I longed for; and noticing that trying to control it only made it worse, I began to truly become curious. *Slowly I was learning how to respond rather than react to both my compulsion and the feelings that were fueling it.*

Even just a few moments of being curious when a wave of compulsion came dramatically lessened my compulsive urges, and for years these bouts of uncontrolled eating calmed down. *I was no longer fighting them, so they weren't fighting me.* My body discovered the weight it was comfortable with and I ate mostly what I wanted, when I wanted. I can still remember the first fall when sweets didn't look interesting. All of the soccer candy, Girl Scout cookies and Halloween junk didn't capture my attention. I was gloriously amazed!

There were times where the urge to eat everything in sight—and then some—would return, but it was more like a big ocean wave passing through than the devastation of a *tsunami*. Sometimes I could be curious for a moment or two during an eating storm, but most of the time I could not bring any curiosity to bear until after the Compulsive Eater had left. Even though I had received so much healing from learning how not to fight my compulsion, I hadn't yet learned how to meet and explore all the hidden feelings that fueled my periodic binges.

That was soon to change. After a number of glorious years of living in a balanced way around food, my health began to deteriorate in my late *30*'s. My doctors began to suggest some fairly heavy dietary restrictions and I began to re-experience all of the feelings that were frozen inside of me from being on a restricted diet when I was young.

I had been born highly allergic to wheat, eggs, chocolate, and dairy products. If you think about it for a moment, you will realize that I couldn't eat 'kid food' – no birthday cakes, cookies, hot dogs, sandwiches, or Hershey Bars. In other words, I was always on the outside looking in, whether it was at birthday parties, the school cafeteria, or eating with my family. All the feelings of isolation, the rage at being left out, and the sense that there was something wrong with me were a core part of my childhood and a hidden part of my adulthood.

Now the doctors were telling me I had to go back to the food restrictions of my childhood! The Compulsive Eater inside of me woke up again and it was having none of this. It didn't want to experience again all of those agonizing feelings that come from a severely limited choice of foods. When I was told that wheat was poison to my body and that I should never eat it again, I went out and ate lots and lots of wheat! I was

> *Even just a few moments of being curious when a wave of compulsion came dramatically lessened my compulsive urges...I was no longer fighting them, so they weren't fighting me.*

> *Our core compulsion is to struggle.*

again locked in a battle with forces that were a lot stronger than my attempts to control them.

In reaction, I desperately tried to hold on to control, even though I knew somewhere deep inside of me that it would only make it worse. This time I didn't use diets. Instead I used healthy eating programs that were supposed to be good for me. The intent for doing these programs was more benevolent than my previous intention to lose weight in order to be *acceptable*. Yet I still was looking for somebody else's ideas about how I should eat rather than learning how to listen to myself. I hadn't yet discovered that only *my* body can tell me what I need in order to maintain balance and health.

After a time of living the devastation of trying to control these urges only to have them control me, curiosity kicked in again. I could now see that my core compulsion was to struggle, and my other compulsions had all been an attempt to numb out from the chaos, confusion and despair that came from struggling with myself and struggling with my life.

So rather than struggling with my compulsions, which only created more struggle, I began to listen when the old urges would come. I began to listen so deeply that I was able to see what I was trying to run away from when I was compulsive. And (big surprise!) all of the feelings of being left out, defective and hopeless that had been buried deep inside of me since I was young were there when I wanted to binge. I could finally recognize *why* I was overeating. That was pay dirt, because it isn't in trying to control our compulsions that we will be healed. *It is in becoming aware of the feelings that fuel them that we will know the peace we long for.*

I began to learn how to develop a relationship with the feelings that were fueling my eating binges. What I was doing with these feelings was probably different than anything I had tried before. I wasn't so much *feeling* these feelings as I was *meeting* them. There is a huge difference between *feeling a* feeling and *meeting* a feeling. In *feeling* a feeling you can get lost in the middle of it. *Meeting* a feeling is about standing with the feeling and giving it the attention and understanding that it needs in order to be transformed into free flowing energy again. As I met each of the old, frozen feelings that were fueling these binges, touching them with my compassionate attention, they lost their power over me and everything began to calm down.

> *It is in becoming aware of the feelings that fuel our compulsions that we will know the peace we long for.*

> *I became partners with my compulsion. I committed to being present for my compulsion in a nonviolent way and it showed me all of the parts of myself that needed the healing of my curious and compassionate heart.*

Through this willingness to listen to my compulsion and all of the feelings it was trying to take care of, my Compulsive Eater and I became partners in my healing. I became partners with my compulsion. I committed to *being present* for my compulsion in a nonviolent way and it showed me all of the parts of myself that needed the healing of my curious and compassionate heart. As I met my feelings, I no longer needed to numb myself. The Compulsive Eater became less and less a part of my life as more and more parts of myself were healed through my compassionate attention.

If you have ever been taken over by something that you cannot control—whether it is over-eating, over-drinking, over-carousing, over-worrying or over-working—you will understand the intense gratitude I felt in learning how to come back into balance again. At the time, I believed that was the extent of my healing. Little did I know that I had just begun to taste the joy of coming back to myself!

As I was able to be present for myself during a wave of compulsion, I began to be present for myself during the rest of my life. Rather than the heavy, constantly struggling mode of existence that I had lived most of my life, I began to feel lighter. The tiny flicker of joy that used to be hidden deep inside of me began to grow into a flame and then eventually into a warm and toasty fire that warmed me from my core.

I was becoming myself – not an idea of what I should be, not an ongoing project that always needed to be better or different than what I was, but truly and authentically myself. I was moving out of the *I am not/I should be* way of living Life, back into the *I am*! The *I am* is the place of pure *being* and it is alive, joyous, trusting, and full of Love. It connects us to a wellspring of deep knowing within us that supports and guides us in every moment of our lives, whether we are aware of it or not. I finally saw that it was never my compulsion that I was hungry for. What I was really longing for was a deep and

> *I was becoming myself – not an idea of what I should be, not an ongoing project that always needed to be better or different than what I was, but truly and authentically myself.*

> *As we come back to ourselves, we discover that we are okay, Life is okay and everything is going to be okay.*

abiding relationship with who I truly am.

This felt totally new to me, for even though all children know a rudimentary form of this kind of connection when they are young, as an adult I have no memories of it. Very early on I had lost connection with myself, pulling myself up and out of my body and becoming lost in my head. Being that disconnected, I lost trust in myself and in Life. I even lost the knowing that I had lost anything!

Being present for my compulsion peeled back all of the layers of contraction and hiding and took me step-by-step back into myself. I now live in a mind that doesn't war with itself; I know the joy of loving myself from the inside out; and being connected to my body again puts me in contact with the wellspring of joy and wisdom that resides there. Every once in a while, I still get scared and my compulsion looks interesting, but in a very gentle way. And because these little waves of compulsion always take me another step into a deeper connection with myself and with Life, I now even trust them!

I am telling you this story because it isn't just my story. I am not just one of the lucky few that have healed and been healed by compulsions. More and more of us have reached the place of having learned all that we can from trying to manage our compulsions, finally realizing that controlling our compulsions will never bring us the deep healing we long for. We are now ready for the next step – ready to heal and be healed by our compulsions. We are also beginning to comprehend that it is our birthright to make the journey back home – back to ourselves, back to our essence, which is the wellspring of joy, peace, and trust that is within us. This wellspring has never left us. It has supported us every step of the way, even if we have not been aware of it and it has been orchestrating our return home.

As we come back to ourselves, we discover that we are okay, Life is okay and everything is going to be okay. This depth of healing doesn't come from fixing, changing or rearranging our lives; for what we resist persists. It comes from *responding* rather than *reacting*; from connecting rather than contracting. It comes from finally understanding that we are enough and Life is enough, right here, right now.

The wonderful thing is this type of healing, where you reclaim the truth of who you really are, doesn't just affect you. It affects the whole world. As you heal the war inside of you, you heal the world. For the style of mind that fuels our compulsions and then fights with what it has created is the same style of mind that has caused such heartache all over the world. This compulsion to struggle with Life shows up in the sense of incompleteness and isolation that is the undercurrent of most people's lives. It shows up in the power games that are the hallmark of most relationships whether it is between people, businesses, or countries. It also shows up in the political, religious, and ideological confrontations that are rampant on our planet.

This discontentment in which we live extends all the way from the struggles with our compulsions to the rise of terrorism in the world. Even though you are not a terrorist, how you use your mind makes a difference. When you hate and fear compulsions and when you judge yourself for having them, that aggression spills out into your world, adding to the unconsciousness of humanity. When you learn how to be curious and merciful with yourself and your compulsion, you bring equanimity and kindness to all that you are and do. In this new way of relating to yourself, you become a part of the healing of this planet.

As more and more of us move beyond our compulsive need to *do* Life – always trying to make it be different from what it is – and instead we allow ourselves to *be* Life, just like drops of water filling a pond, one day the pond of human consciousness will overflow and the Earth will know the deep peace it longs for. You are reading this book because you are ready to ripen into a full and deep connection with yourself and with your life. You are ready to heal at your core and in that healing, become a part of the healing of our planet.

This book is about changing your relationship with compulsions so that, rather than being the enemy, they become your guide, taking you step by step back into the place where you feel that everything is right with yourself and your world again.

So let us commence the journey of healing and being healed by our compulsions.

Core Ideas in My Journey, Our Journey:

❖ It is your birthright to trust yourself and trust your life enough so that you can be healed to your core.

❖ Trusting yourself and trusting your life is about knowing you are okay, Life is okay, and everything will be okay.

❖ Healing is about becoming yourself again, not an idea of what you *should* be nor an ongoing project that always needs to be better or different, but truly and authentically yourself. Instead of always trying to *do* life, then you can *be* life.

❖ When you connect to your *I am!*, the essence of you that is alive, joyous, trusting and full of love, you can live from the wellspring of deep knowing within you that is waiting for your return.

❖ Healing is about opening what has been closed, reclaiming what has been hidden, and remembering what has been forgotten.

❖ Compulsions are a skillful guide on this journey back to again being at home within yourself and with your life.

✦ RECONNECTING WITH YOURSELF ✦

There was a time that you absolutely loved being you.

In your early childhood you hadn't yet learned how to second-guess yourself. Not needing to be any different than what you were, you lived in your body and in your heart, and whatever you were was enough. In fact, it was more than enough *for it was you*. Even if you have no memories of this, your body does. It remembers the time when you were completely connected to yourself, open to the adventure of Life. Your enthusiasm for living was felt in every cell of your body and it was wonderful just to be alive.

All of us—some for a very short time and others longer—knew this timeless place where there was no separation between us and ourselves and between ourselves and our lives. Before we pulled back from Life, we were unshakably attuned to the truth that we were okay, that Life was okay, and that everything was going to be okay.

Centered in ourselves, Life was a magical adventure. We hadn't yet become caught by the world of time, and nothing was more important than being fully ourselves, connected to whatever was happening in that moment. We were present for the heartbeat of a puppy, the magic of the butterfly's dance, and our fascination with having a belly button.

A friend told me a wonderful story of a walk through the woods with a three-year-old girl that reveals what it was like for us when we were connected to ourselves and to our lives. Coming to a bridge over a stream, the little one became completely enamored by the flow of the water, so enamored she had to lie down on the bridge, hanging her head over its edge to see more clearly. Every once in a while she would look up at my friend and simply say, "Wow!" Three times they headed down the path beyond the bridge and three times the little girl turned around and went back to the wonder of the flowing water. With no separation between who she was and what she should be, there were no filters clouding her pure experience of *being alive*.

You also knew, as children the world over know, how to keep the joy of Life alive by hugging and snuggling, swinging and twirling, dancing and running. Shelby, a three-year-old niece of a friend, was at a theater watching a movie full of dancing and singing. There was no way she could sit in her seat! Luckily they happened to be in a row of seats with a space in front of them for a wheelchair. Since it was not occupied, Shelby danced her way through the movie. She was okay with herself and with her life. Can you feel her vitality and joy?

Hopefully these stories will bring up a memory, no matter how faint, of what it is like to love yourself from the inside out, staying open to the magical adventure of your life. Even if there are no memories, before the world of *shoulds* and *ought-tos* dimmed your love affair with yourself and with Life, you too were authentically *you*. The river of Life flowed through you, sometimes in torrents, sometimes in stillness, full of the peace of being connected to Life and of being comfortable in your own skin.

This connection with yourself and with Life was a rudimentary form of the full connection that is possible for you as an adult. When you were young, you were awake to Life. As an adult, you can not only be awake, you can be aware – curiously and compassionately present for your life. It is possible to wake up in the morning with an abiding love for yourself, a deep apprecia-tion for the gift of Life and a wondrous curiosity about where the adventure is going to take you. This is not only possible; it is your birthright.

The House of Your Being

This place of being okay with yourself and okay with your life, no matter what is happening, has always been with you. It may be just a tiny rivulet that you are hardly even aware of, but it is there nonetheless. The clouds in your mind do not eradicate this place; they just keep it buried deep inside.

If you are like most people, you live almost exclusively in a story in your head, cut off from the nourishment of being connected to yourself. You are hardly ever aware that just below the thousands of thoughts you pay atten-tion to everyday lies another world, one of trust in yourself, trust in Life, and the joy that is your own true nature.

How can it be that we knew such a deep connection with Life when we were young and yet most of the time as adults we find ourselves, on some level, struggling with Life and feeling just half-alive? The best way to understand this is to imagine a glorious house, airy and full of light, with the music of laughter flowing from room to room. This was the house of your *being* and when you were little, you lived here, fully open to Life.

You lived *in* your body, grounded in the basement of your belly, and the energy of Life flowed freely through you. The floors above were the realm of your heart and all the windows and doors were open to Life. Your heart was so alive that with every beat the joy of loving yourself and of loving Life was pumped through all the nooks and crannies of your *being*. And the attic of your mind was a wonderful place of imagination and curiosity, open to the whole house of your being. You were able to simply show up for the amazing adventure that is Life rather than always trying to make it into what you thought it should be.

Being so open to Life, everything touched you to your core. Remember tasting every single bite of your ice cream cone? Remember lying on your back and watching in wonder as the clouds danced for you? Remember the ballet of dust particles, highlighted in the beam of sunlight from your bedroom window?

> *It is possible to wake up in the morning with an abiding love for yourself, a deep appreciation for the gift of Life and a wondrous curiosity about where the adventure is going to take you. This is not only possible; it is your birthright.*

Basking from the glow of living fully in your body and being in contact with your own true nature, when you said, *"I am!"*— that was enough. In fact, it was more than enough, for you were simply and purely yourself! You hadn't yet bought into the belief that you had to be somebody other than who you were in order to be okay. And all of the feelings that are a part of human life moved through you. You hadn't learned how to tighten down around them nor run away into the attic of the mind. So sadness, madness and gladness danced through you like the clouds dance across the sky.

You were open to the whole house of your being, and you hadn't yet gone to school so it was fun to learn how to name things and even count them. During that precious time, there was no part of the house of 'you' that wasn't okay and you knew the joy of loving yourself from the inside out. You hadn't yet come to believe that you needed to be anything other than what you were in order to receive the nourishment, attention, and connection that you required in order to survive.

This wouldn't last.

In the openness of your youth, you were not only available to the pure joy of *being alive*; you were also vulnerable to the actions and expectations of the people around you. The giants in your world (called parents, siblings, aunts and uncles, teachers, neighbors, nuns, and a host of others, all of whom had mostly forgotten their connection with Life) began to influence your experience of yourself. Life had wounded them and they passed their wounds to you. Even if you had parents who loved you, along with what looked like a picture-perfect childhood, this wounding still occurred.

Nobody was there meeting you in the place of your wounding, showing you how to stay open to Life in the presence of pain. For survival you learned how to close off parts of yourself, holding your breath and tightening your

> *If you look at pictures taken of you as a child, you will be able to see when, after closing off enough of your feelings and hiding them in your body, you became cut off from the joy of being you.*

body. Every time you contracted your body and tried to deny a feeling you were experiencing, you put another part of yourself in a box and hid it in one of the rooms of the house of your body. On the door of each room you put a sign that said, "Do not open." In little letters underneath those words was the statement, "This room is filled with bad feelings." But this didn't get rid of them! Behind closed doors, they still influenced your life and eventually fueled your compulsion.

As you grew up and the circumstances of your life disappointed, overwhelmed and threatened you, more and more rooms of your house became locked. Rather than being airy and filled with light, your house became so dark that it was hard to really see anything. You were no longer dancing from room to room and the music of laughter was rarely heard. If you go and look at pictures taken of you as a child that are hanging in the hallway of this house, you will be able to see when, after closing off enough of your feelings and hiding them in your body, you became cut off from the joy of *being you*. That cutoff was when the light went out of your eyes and it is evident in these photographs.

Soon all the rooms of your body were filled with your boxed up feelings, so you had to move some of them down into the basement of your *being*, hoping that they would never torment you again. These were the ones that you were most afraid of—your rage, your terror, and your despair. It was very, very important to keep your belly tight and never to breathe a full breath for that is how the door to the basement opens again and you definitely didn't want that to happen.

But all was not lost.

As you were boxing up all of your feelings, you were also learning more about the world of thought. You were discovering what a magical tool thought is, but you were also learning that thought was a place where you could hide from Life. One day, while exploring the attic of your mind, you discovered a big screen TV along with a VCR and boxes of videotapes. You found out that you could sit up there and watch pictures in your mind *about* Life which, by this time, felt a lot safer than being open to Life as it was.

Eventually you found yourself spending more and more time in the attic, especially when strong and confusing feelings were present. You left the now curtained and closed off floors of your body for the tightly enclosed attic of the mind. Because the images of the mind were so compelling, you hardly even noticed that you had lost the true and abiding connection with yourself and with Life that was the hallmark of your early childhood.

The more you lived in your mind, the more you began to truly believe one of its core ideas: "In order to be safe, you must be in control." Becoming lost in control, you found yourself cut off from the deep wisdom of your own authenticity. Trained to distrust your feelings and distrust your life, you became absolutely certain that you must never go back into the lower floors of the house, and most especially the basement. Instead you must control, control, control! Gone is the willingness to be open to Life. Gone is spontaneous creativity. Gone is the pure joy of *being alive*.

Even though there was a faint memory of living in the entire house of yourself with all of the light and laughter that went with it, the movies in your mind were enough to compensate and things stayed fairly balanced for a while. And when they weren't, you discovered your first experience of trying to recreate the joy you knew when you were fully connected to yourself and to Life. Maybe it was the glass of wine that turned your body into liquid warmth, or the deep relaxation after that first bite of a forbidden food, or the joy that comes from a buying spree, or even the thrill of winning at gambling. They were faint shadows of the wonderful feelings that you had when you inhabited the whole house of your *being*. But because the house was not available to you anymore, those actions seemed to be adequate substitutes for joy.

Unable to be naturally who you *were*, you began to try to figure out who you *should be* and there were plenty of video tapes lying around the attic that would tell you how to be a *successful you*. You were so intent on making yourself different than what you were that you didn't even notice the voices coming over a loudspeaker in the attic of your head that were critiquing how you were doing in your endless quest for perfection. You also didn't notice that you had left the wonderful world of *I am!* that you knew so well when you were young, for the world of *I am not/I should be*.

As the wonderful movies you first watched when you crawled up into the attic of the mind gave way to movies full of *have tos*, *shoulds*

> *...you discovered your first experience of trying to recreate the joy you knew when you were fully connected to yourself and to Life...the glass of wine...that bite of a forbidden food...a buying spree... winning at gambling.*

15

> *The deep peace of enoughness will only come when you move back into your body and inhabit all the floors of the house of your being.*

and *ought-tos*, there arose an undercurrent of discontentment, boredom, and a quiet despair that you tried very hard not to notice.

Cut off from the nourishment and perspective of the floors of your heart and disconnected from the wellspring of wisdom and support that comes from being grounded in the basement of your *being*, your whole existence in the attic became a constant search for the peace that you knew when you lived in the full house of your whole *being*. You looked for it in the next relationship, in more money, in a better body, in a more positive outlook, in a fancier car, in a better-educated mind. This search took you into classes, therapy, and religion, with the hope that if you just got yourself in order, then everything would be okay.

These actions are all fine. But even if you accomplish them—if you win the lottery, get your Ph.D., understand where your pain came from, or learn how to affirm 20 times a day that you are a radiant and peaceful person—*it is never enough!* There is an essential emptiness that will never be filled by all of the doing, accomplishing, and acquiring that is the hallmark of the attic.

The deep peace of *enoughness* will only come when you move back into your body and inhabit all the floors of the house of your being. The mind, however, will have absolutely nothing to do with moving back into your body, for it remembers how scared it was right before you retreated to the so-called *safety* of the attic. So in the attic you stayed.

Even though things were not all that happy in the world of the attic, you carried on. There was one thing more than any other, however, which upset the careful equilibrium you were trying to establish through control. *Feelings do not like to be boxed up* because they come from the river of aliveness and they love to move and dance through your *being*. Every once in a while, you could hear them crying from the floors below, demanding attention, but you would just put in another movie and distract yourself again.

You were so busy distracting yourself, you didn't notice that feelings are very crafty and extremely skillful at getting out of the most enclosed spaces. As they learned how to escape from their boxes, they would come pattering up the stairs to the attic, knock on the door and ask to be let in. But there was a sign on the inside of the door that said, "Never, ever open this door! The only safety is in staying in control." And you knew that if you let those feelings in again you would definitely be out of control. So you turned up the volume of the VCR to drown out the feelings that were asking for your recognition.

But feelings don't give up easily, and over time, no matter how far you turned up the volume, you couldn't drown out their persistent knocking on the door. That was when compulsions came into full bloom. It was a sip of wine that turned into glass after glass. It was a cookie that turned into a dozen. Maybe it was a fun night of gambling that turned into a nightmare. It could also be the to-do list that kept on getting longer as you frantically ran around trying to gain control over your life. The deep urge within you that just wanted to be out of pain discovered that if you gambled, overate, drank enough, or got overly busy, you could pretend there was no such thing as any feelings knocking at your door.

Very quickly the painful urge for *more, more, more* turned into *not enough, not enough, not enough.* Over and over again, after the wave of compulsion moved through, you would be left in self-hatred and despair. No matter how passionately compulsions promised you they would bring you the peace that you longed for, it was never true. But you didn't know how to get out of the attic and back into what you were truly hungry for – a deep and satisfying connection with yourself and with Life. No wonder you had moments – and maybe even weeks, months, and years – where you were depressed and overwhelmed, consumed by a loneliness that nothing could fill.

The more you ran away from the feelings, the madder they got and the harder you had to try to keep them at bay, never knowing that the safest thing to do was to open the door, invite them in, and get to know them again. So on you went for years and years, lost in your head, while your feelings knocked at the door and compulsions kept them at bay.

You became even more cut off from yourself as you were taught that compulsions were bad and must be controlled, and if you couldn't control them, then you were bad. Lost in an ever-increasing battle in the attic of your mind, every once in a while you would hear the sound of the wind outside the attic of your mind and you would get a funny feeling in the core of your *being* that there was something more to Life than the endless struggle that is the hallmark of the attic of the mind.

One day, however, you find a dusty videotape that had fallen behind the TV. When you put it in the VCR, you realize it is a tape of what it was like when you lived in the whole

> *You became even more cut off from yourself as you were taught that compulsions were bad and must be controlled, and if you couldn't control them, then you were bad.*

> *You finally understand that in order to live in the whole house of your being, you need to meet the feelings that are standing in the way.*

house. How light and airy it was! As you watch yourself in this video, you notice there was such exuberance in your body! There was such a light shining out of your eyes!

The longing to be connected to yourself and to Life again gives you courage. You finally understand that in order to live in the whole house of your *being*, you need to *meet* the feelings that are standing in the way. The next time a feeling is knocking at the door, you decide to listen rather than turning up the volume of your VCR. What you hear your feelings saying as these voices come through the locked door is, "Please don't ignore me. I am a part of you. If you meet me, you can move back into the house of your *being* and I will be your friend." It becomes clear that the safest thing you could do is open the door and invite them in for a heart-to-heart talk.

So you open the door just a crack. There are your feelings all standing in a row, waiting to be heard. Immediately you get scared and slam the door again. But a wise voice within says this is not about feeling these feelings and getting lost in them again. This is about *meeting* them, giving them your undivided attention so they can transform back into the free flowing energy that is Life.

Remembering the video of what it was like to live in the whole house, you discover the courage to open the door and invite the first feeling in. You are astounded that the feeling is more afraid of you than you are of it! You ask the feeling to sit down and tell you its story. You listen with rapt attention as the feeling describes how it was born and what it was like all of these years to be boxed up in the dark and empty rooms of your body.

You realize in a flash that what you have been running from your whole life are very young feelings that you boxed up long ago. And instead of being flawed or defective parts of yourself, they are just very vulnerable parts that are hurt and afraid and need your help. It finally comes clear to you that as long as you run away from them, you will be confined to the attic, cut off from the joy of living in the full house of yourself.

As the feeling finishes speaking of its heartache, it then goes on to tell you what a joy it was to be a part of you when you were young and how much it would like to be a respected part of you again. You can really hear this and you realize with stunning clarity that it is okay to have this feeling be a part of the wholeness that you are. With an eagerness you have not experienced in years, you then invite another feeling in for a chat, and then another, listening as they tell you their story.

Soon they are inviting you down into the closed rooms of your body, and with joy you begin to unpack all of the other boxed parts of your self. Even though the feelings that you find there may be a little grinchy, or even quite scared from being boxed up for so long, you know they are just very young parts of you that need your undivided attention.

> *You realize that whenever you were compulsive, this is what you were truly hungry for – a deep and abiding connection with yourself that brings forth the joy of being comfortable in your own skin!*

As you wander through the rooms, opening windows and doors, you begin to remember how wonderful it was when you lived fully in your body. You see everything through new eyes and discover that when you were locked in the attic of your mind, you had forgotten how vibrant colors can be.

As you become fully present for your life, everything calms down and loosens up, and the joy of *being* alive begins to flow throughout your whole body again. Your shoulders relax and a smile fills your entire *being*. The tight band of sadness across your chest begins to lessen and your breath becomes fuller and easier. The tense fist of endless trying in your stomach starts to let go and the fear of not being enough begins to melt away. Even the empty hole that your compulsion has ever been able to fill becomes a warm glow deep in your belly.

This is the first time since your childhood that you have felt safe enough to open to Life, safe enough to be yourself. You realize that whenever you were compulsive, *this is what you were truly hungry for* – a deep and abiding connection with yourself that brings forth the joy of being comfortable in your own skin!

Compulsions look less and less interesting to you, for you are being nourished by the joy that comes from living in your body and becoming yourself again – *not an idea of what you should be, but the* Real Thing.

> *Your compulsions look less and less interesting to you, for you are being nourished by the joy that comes from living in your body and becoming yourself again – not an idea of what you should be, but the Real Thing.*

As wonderful as it is, you find you can't stay here very long. It is all so new and sometimes very scary to be this open. So you find yourself retreating back up into the mind and closing the door, especially when strong feelings are moving through you. Sometimes you turn up the volume of your VCR so you don't have to hear

> *Rather than becoming lost in your compulsions, you listen to them and allow them to remind you to be present for these parts of yourself that are asking for the healing of your understanding attention.*

the knocking at the door and sometimes you even find yourself being compulsive again.

But compulsions are now your ally for you know that whenever you are compulsive, there is another part of you standing right outside of the locked room of your mind asking for your undivided attention. Rather than becoming lost in your compulsion, you listen to it and allow it to remind you to be present for these parts of yourself that are asking for the healing of your understanding attention.

But there is still one place you have not had the courage to explore. That place is the basement of your belly. This is where you hid the BIG feelings – the monsters of rage, terror, and despair. Everything you heard about that dark and foreboding place makes you feel that if you ever got the courage to even open the door of the basement, you would be instantly devoured by the monsters from the deep.

You are not only afraid to go down there into the basement of your *being*, you don't even know how to find these elusive deep feelings that only seem to come to the surface when your life is in chaos. So you watch and wait for the next wave of compulsion with the awareness that it only comes now when these parts of yourself are close to the surface. And so with flashlight in hand and heart pounding furiously, you bring your attention down into the basement – into the deepest and most tightly held parts of your body - wanting to meet whatever is there.

Much to your amazement, rather than monsters you find the youngest parts of yourself cowering in the corner. They look almost like little wild animals with deep fear in their eyes. Your fear evaporates as you realize how scared they are. You sit down in order to reassure them and say quietly to them, "I'm here. I understand."

It takes them a moment to get over the shock that you were even willing to come down into the basement (you haven't been there for decades) and the even greater shock that you are willing to talk to them. But hope springs eternal and in a flash, tears of gratitude begin to roll down their cheeks. With a little coaxing, they come out of the dark corner where they were cowering and with deep relief crawl into your arms. You find yourself saying to them over and over again, "I'm here now. It's okay; I'm here."

You realize they have been waiting your whole life for you to grow beyond your fear of them so you could give them exactly what they needed when they had to be boxed up all those years ago—non-judgmental, loving attention. As you carry them up the stairs, they are a little overcome by the rooms filled with light. But as with all young ones, they adapt very quickly. They can be this free for they know that they are now a valued and accepted part of your *being*. The last of the curtains that held back the light are whisked away and the joy of laughter fills your light-filled rooms again.

> *Your painful feelings have been waiting your whole life for you to grow beyond your fear of them so you could give them exactly what they need – non-judgmental, loving attention.*

Every once in a while you feel a wave of compulsion now, but rather than retreating to the reaction of your head, you are able to sit down wherever you are, close your eyes and breathe all the way into your belly. You can then listen to what you are experiencing there. *You have finally awakened enough to take responsibility for your feelings, which is, after all, simply the ability to respond to them.* And just a few moments of being with the feelings releases them back into the flow of aliveness that is your birthright and the wave of compulsion moves through, leaving hardly a trace.

Looking back over this amazing journey—beginning with the joy of living so fully in your body when you were young, only to lose this connection with yourself and now finally to rediscover it again—you feel gratitude for what you now know. But something inside of you knows that this journey back to yourself is not yet complete. Sitting quietly one day on your favorite window seat, gazing out on the beauty of nature, you feel compelled to go down to the basement. No longer cluttered with all of the scary feelings you so desperately tried to hide here, there is a vast openness in the basement that you now experience as joy.

This joy draws you to the very center of the basement where you notice a circular room. When you come close, you realize it is radiating a wonderful warmth that was previously hidden by all of the boxes of feelings you had stored here. When you were unpacking them, you were certainly aware of this circle of warmth, but you were more concerned with being present for your feelings. Now you are drawn to be with the warmth.

You know from the deepest part of your *being* that you are supposed to sit down close to this circular room, basking in its warmth as you breathe long and slow breaths. As your belly softens and you settle into your body, you become aware of the same kind of warmth glowing inside of you. As you open to it, this glow radiates throughout your whole body as waves of Light and Love fill you from head to toe. When you open your eyes, much to your amazement, the walls of this circular room have dissolved and there before you is a beautiful spring of burbling water, lush with vibrant green foliage and beautiful flowers.

With a deep recognition, you see that this is the wellspring of your true essence that has always been with you. Its source is the Creative Forces at the heart of Life, the forces that show up as the radiance of the sun, the unfolding of the seasons, and the beating of your heart. All of the Wisdom, all of the Love, all of the Light that are a part of this Source permeate the healing waters of your wellspring. And it is inside of you!

You feel an indescribable joy as you kneel beside it and dip your hands in to drink from its essence. As this water flows through your body, you realize that this wellspring is what fills the house of your *being* with so much love, light, and the pure joy of being alive. It contains all of the elements that truly fulfill your life: the fire of passion for living, the strength of the Earth for endurance and perseverance, the lightness of air for play and exuberance, the healing quality of water that allows all things to flow and the Love that unites everything.

With deep clarity, you understand that this wellspring has always been within you even when you forgot that it was there. You can also understand that even though you have never left it, your whole life has been a journey to reconnecting with this wellspring within. On this journey, you were *supposed* to know the wellspring and play with it when you were young, and then leave its healing presence for the long journey into your unique experience of separation. Now it is time to return.

You also realize that every single part of that journey was necessary. Even though you made many *wrong* turns, every single one of them was a perfect part of the journey away from and then back to yourself. Now, no matter where you are and no matter what is happening, with just one deep breath you can return to this wellspring within and drink your fill.

Finally you understand that you have been given the gift of Life because you have arisen out of the Creativity at the heart of Life. *You are one of a kind.* In the vastness of all time, the great and wondrous unfolding of Life has never ever shown up exactly as you. Life is expressing itself as you because it *needs* to express itself as you. You carry a piece of the creativity of Life that nobody else *ever has* and *nobody else ever can be a better you than you.*

You don't have to figure out what your piece is or how to get to it, or even what to do with it. All you need do is drink from this wellspring of Wisdom and Support that resides in the core of your *being*. What you are here to do and be will unfold in its own time and its own way. As the last vestiges of tension leave your belly, your whole *being* feels a sense of deep relief. The old, familiar sense of discontentment gives way to an ease that nourishes you to your core.

You realize that you aren't just one of the lucky few that can know and live from the healing waters of the wellspring within. Everybody has one and you see that more and more people will be discovering and then living from the integrity, courage, wisdom, and compassion that come from being connected to their own wellspring.

Drinking deeply from its healing waters one more time, you see that you will never again feel alone, for the creative powers at the heart of Life are with you and within you. Life will ebb and flow, and you will still live the cycles of remembering and forgetting. But there is no sorrow in this, for you now know the deep peace that is beyond the opposites of Life, the peace of *being*. In this knowing, you are willing to show up with a keen, curious mind and a spacious, open heart for whatever Life gives to you.

As you stand up again, you realize that finally you are truly yourself. You walk up the stairs and into the unfolding of your life, overflowing with exuberance, curiosity, and the joy of *being* alive.

Core Ideas in Reconnecting with Yourself:

❖ Early on, the river of Life flowed through you, sometimes in torrents, sometimes in stillness, full of the peace of being connected to Life and of being comfortable in your own skin.

❖ When you were very little, the house of your *being* was a wondrous place to explore. There was no part of the house of you that wasn't okay, and you knew the joy of loving yourself from the inside out.

❖ When Life threatened you, confused you, and disappointed you, you learned how to close off parts of yourself and began to live in the *I am not/I should be* story in your head.

❖ The more you live in your mind rather than your heart, the more you believe that in order to be safe, you have to be in control. This hides deep within you the spontaneous creativity and pure joy of being alive.

❖ The deep peace of *enoughness* will only come when you move back into your body and inhabit all of the floors of the house of your *being*.

❖ It is possible to wake up everyday with an abiding love for yourself, a deep appreciation for the gift of Life, and a wondrous curiosity about where the adventure is taking you.

Transforming Our Relationship
with Compulsions

✦ COMPULSION BEGAN AS A FRIEND ✦

Whenever we are compulsive, what we are really longing for is to reconnect with ourselves. We are hungry for the experience of being grounded in our own bodies again so we can live from the wellspring within that connects us to Wisdom, to our hearts, and to our lives. This is the connection with ourselves and with Life that we knew so well when we were little, and that has, since then, been waiting for us to grow up enough so that we can know and live it again on an even deeper level.

Compulsions are our guides back into a connection with ourselves that relaxes our mind, opens our heart and brings a twinkle to our eyes! In order to take this journey back to ourselves and into our full potentiality, we need to transform our relationship to compulsions.

If we follow compulsions back to their roots, it is easy to see that they emerged in order to help us manage feelings that were too much for us. As infants, we were completely available to our feelings, both the joyful ones and the painful ones. The joyful ones kept us connected to our essence. The painful ones caused us to pull back from Life. No matter what they were, feelings danced through us like a river dancing through a narrow channel.

Imagine yourself as a little child when you read the following experiences. To some of us, these may be very familiar. To others, they may not. But they are designed to hint at the multitude of experiences we all had when we were young, and which caused us to pull back from Life.

❖ *Imagine the exuberance cascading through your body as you yell loud enough in the grocery store to hear your own echo, only to have an angry clerk grab you from behind and shake you unmercifully.*

❖ *Imagine an older sibling stealing your favorite toy and then taunting you with it. The powerless rage is almost too much to bear, even as a memory!*

❖ *Imagine the pleasure of playing with your body only to have a horrified adult face loom above you saying, "Bad, bad, bad!"*

❖ *Imagine being two years old and having a huge dog run toward you while barking fiercely. As you wail in fear, imagine your parent berating you for being such a ninny.*

❖ *Imagine flinging yourself into your father's lap, full of love, only to be told, "Stop being such a bother."*

❖ *Imagine the time you experienced the death of a favorite pet and felt the despair of recognizing that everything dies.*

❖ *Imagine the pain of being left out that came from being the last one chosen for a team at recess or not having anybody to sit with in the lunch room.*

Even if you don't remember any of these types of experiences from your childhood that caused you to close off to Life, you had them in some form. And they were very intense, for you felt these expectations, disappointments, and wounds more deeply and for longer periods of time when you were young. Time is different for a child. A day felt as long as a week does to an adult. A week was a lifetime. And you, like most children, probably didn't have people in your life that could help you meet and channel these feelings. So you experienced these sometimes scary and often overwhelming visitors all by yourself.

On top of being afraid of the powerful feelings that moved through you, you also got the message that most of those feelings were not okay. Verbally and non-verbally, you were talked out of your own feelings. From the powers to be in your life you were taught:

"Big girls and boys don't cry."

"Sit still."

"Don't make such a big deal out of it."

"That is nothing to be afraid of."

"Don't be so exuberant."

"I'll give you something to cry about."

"I am not angry!" (while screaming at the top of their lungs.)

You were not only being trained to hide your feelings; you were also being trained to distrust and dislike them.

No little body could survive the onslaught of feelings you experienced. Something had to be done to cope. Every time Life confused, threatened, or disappointed you, you learned to pull back, hold your breath, and tighten your body in hopes that this would keep the painful feelings at bay.

Your exuberance was confined in shallow breathing. Sadness and a deep sense of longing became hidden in your chest. Self-judgment became buried in your neck and shoulders. Both fear and anger were tightly locked in your stomach. Despair, especially the despair of loosing sight of your natural, free flowing joy, was concealed deep within your belly. And under that

> *To understand that our compulsions are created in order to try and take care of us is an essential point in transforming our relationship to our compulsions.*

despair was a hole of emptiness that nothing could fill.

When you were young, you could control a lot of your feelings by just holding your breath, tightening your body, or getting distracted by something else. You also learned how to use your mind to try and make yourself and your life into what you thought it should be. But as we have seen, these feelings that you have buried underneath a thin layer of control are huge. When your veneer of control was stretched thin, you created other stronger and more elaborate systems called *compulsions* in order to keep those unmeetable feelings at bay.

Compulsions can be recognized as any recurring activity you use to manage your feelings which ends up controlling you. This can be an external activity, such as eating, drinking, over-working, spending, or gambling. Or it may be an internal activity, one in which you repeatedly think or feel in a certain way – i.e., self-judgment, worry, or struggle.

One of the most important things I can say, after having listened to my compulsions for many years, is that whenever a compulsion began in your life, *it came as a friend.* Compulsions are intricate survival systems that are created because we don't know how to be there for ourselves. They build upon themselves over the years like castles with mazes of hallways, tunnels, hidden rooms, and secret dungeons.

To understand that our compulsions are created in order to try and take care of us is an essential point in transforming our relationship to our compulsions. They originally had two main intents. The first was to keep us far away from the unacceptable feelings buried deep within so we could be numb enough to survive, and the second was to bring comfort.

Let us look more closely at these two intents.

Hiding Our Painful Feelings

When we were young, we didn't have the capacity (without skillful adult help) to meet the storms of rage, the dragons of fear, the rivers of sadness, and the terror of inadequacy that moved through us. What better way to stop these feelings than eating a whole bag of donuts, becoming a *perfect* student, or getting lost in the mind-numbing world of alcohol and drugs?

I can vividly remember a time when I was 11 years old, lying in my bed late one night. After dinner I had read *Ask Andy*, a favorite column in our newspaper where you could get answers to the most obscure questions. Even though I loved it, I always felt I was too stupid to send in a question. Looking out my bedroom window, I saw Venus resting almost within the crescent of the moon.

The next morning, with great pleasure that I was finally smart enough to send in a question, I announced at breakfast that I was going to ask Andy why Venus and the Moon were always so close together.

My family let me know very derisively that this was a rare occurrence. I left the table like a dog slinks away after it has been beaten. I can still remember that feeling in my body—the bottomless pit of self-rejection. In order to numb that depth of revulsion, I snuck into the kitchen after breakfast and stole some of my Dad's candy. Hiding under the table in my room, I ate the whole bag. Even though I have memories of comforting myself with food before that time, this was the first memory I have of stuffing myself in an attempt to stop painful feelings.

There was a time we needed to bury our feelings in order to survive, and the feelings we buried weren't always painful; we have also tried to hide from our joy. Have your ever noticed that when your life is opening up again and you are feeling really good, you find yourself drawn to your compulsion? We have been cut off from our feelings for so long that the aliveness and openness that joy brings can feel scary. And so we find ourselves wanting to hide in the familiar world of our compulsions.

Whether it is fear, anxiety, irritation, anger, joy, exuberance, sadness or despair, if we stay disconnected from our bodies and all of the feelings that our bodies hold, these feelings will fuel our compulsive cycles from underneath our everyday consciousness where we have no choices around them.

Comforting

Besides trying to numb our feelings, each act of compulsion is an attempt to reconnect with the deep comfort we knew when it was okay to be *ourselves.* This feeling that everything is all right with ourselves and with our world is a necessary component for survival. In the *1950*'s, Dr. Harry Harlow of the University of Wisconsin took a group of baby monkeys from their mothers at birth. They were then given a choice of two surrogate mothers. The first was a wire monkey that could feed them from a bottle suspended at its center. The second was a cloth monkey that, while it did not

> *The belief that we should be different or better than what we are in order to be okay is based upon the voices in our minds that tell us we are not okay right now.*

feed them, could be held close for comfort. Over and over again the baby monkeys chose the surrogate monkey of comfort over the surrogate monkey that would feed them! *The nourishment of comfort was more important than the nourishment of food!*

As an adult, the primary source for this level of connection is within ourselves. We also need it from other human beings in our lives, but if we haven't learned how to be connected within ourselves, the love and support from the outside won't penetrate our armor. Reconnecting with ourselves means living in our bodies, trusting our essences, and being okay with ourselves no matter what is happening in our lives.

The belief that we should be different or better than what we are in order to be okay is based upon the voices in our minds that tell us we are not okay right now. And no amount of becoming better will ever quiet these insidious voices! Just like a drop of dye in a glass of clear water, this belief can eventually permeate our entire relationship with ourselves, removing us from the essential comfort of being at ease with ourselves exactly as we are.

When we live on the endless treadmill of *I will be okay when I make myself/ my life better*, we find ourselves starving for the comfort of being comfortable with ourselves. We have closed the door to the deep connection with ourselves that we knew when we were young, and we look for the source of our comfort and meaning *out there* – in some beautiful body we haven't yet attained, in some task we haven't yet accomplished, or in some person that hasn't yet loved us *right*. And finding our idea of comfort missing - and even more painful, discovering it, only to watch it slip through the fingers of our control - we have to, for survival, replace it with something else.

This is where compulsions enter the picture. A fresh baked cookie, the purchase of a new dress, the warm glow from a glass of wine, all of these relax the inner world of struggle and open the gates to the pleasure of comfort. But these can only give us short-term comfort. If the intent in partaking of them is to relieve the pressure of not being okay with who we are, one cookie is not enough. It is like trying to scratch an itch by waving the air a few inches above our skin. So we try two cookies and then four and then more and more. *The desperate need for comfort is so great that we will keep on eating with the hope that it will bring us again the peace of being comfortable within our own skins, even though it is doing the opposite!*

30

I can remember another pivotal compulsive moment when I was 12 years-old, right after my parents announced they were divorcing. I was sitting in a big chair at a friend's house, eating handful after handful of chocolate chips. I don't remember who the friend was and, even though I can remember other friends, I don't remember their houses, let alone their furniture, but I vividly remember that chair and the bag of chocolate chips. It was a pivotal moment in my life, for I had finally found someone to love me like I loved me when I was little. It wasn't a person; it was a bag of chocolate chips! This flood of eating eased my agony for a few moments and then threw me into the raging cauldron of being sick in mind, body, and heart.

For most of us, the wave of longing to find comfort *out there* has crashed against the rocky beach of despair so many times that we are finally beginning to realize that *this endless craving for comfort from the outside will never satisfy us if we are not comfortable in our own skins.* We are ready to see that there is a richer, deeper more healing comfort that we long for—the comfort of loving ourselves from the inside out, connected to ourselves, to our lives, and to our wellspring within.

Both of these ways that our compulsions have taken care of us – comfort and numbing – were at one time necessary. But now the price we pay for taking care of ourselves through our compulsions is not worth it.

Life is now saying that it is time to take care of ourselves in more skillful ways. In this shift, compulsions can be our guide back into a deep and abiding connection with ourselves and with Life. For whenever we are compulsive, all of the feelings that stand in the way of this connection are close to the surface where they can be healed. The truest gift from our compulsions is that they won't let go until they teach us how to become conscious and compassionate with ourselves.

Core Ideas in Compulsions Began As a Friend:

❖ Compulsions are any recurring activity that you use to manage your feelings, around which you have little or no choice.

❖ Our compulsions are not the enemy, they are our great teachers, and they will not go away until they have taught us to be curious about what we're experiencing and compassionate with everything that we discover.

❖ Compulsions are a survival system that was created in order to manage all of the overwhelming, disappointing, and unmeetable experiences of your life.

❖ Compulsions bring you the temporary comfort you knew when you were fully connected to yourself. This endless craving for comfort from the outside will never satisfy you if you are not comfortable in your own skin.

❖ Compulsions are not evidence that you are weak-willed or defective. They are powerful forces that have come here to heal you to your core.

❖ You are never really hungry for your compulsion. What you are really longing for is a deep and loving connection with yourself that relaxes your mind, opens your heart, and brings a twinkle to your eyes!

✦ OUR COMPULSIONS ARE HERE ✦ TO HEAL US

Even though all compulsions begin as a friend, and even though at times we are happy to have a visit from them, the longer compulsions are a part of our lives, the more they become like visitors who have overstayed their welcome. This type of visitor leaves dirty laundry on the floor, makes expensive calls, and eats you out of house and home. For many of us, compulsions are not just unpleasant visitors. Compulsions become mean and nasty monsters, taking over our lives and breaking our hearts.

So of course we want to get rid of the monster. We try everything we can think of, only to have the monster come roaring back again. It may be in a different form, but it is still compulsive behavior. Why is this?

There is something about compulsions that is so important to understand. These aren't just random events that well up from some infinite abyss to make a mess of our lives. Compulsions are also not evidence of our lack of discipline, nor are they proof that *they* screwed up (usually our parents), you screwed up, or God fell asleep on the job. Instead, compulsions are calls to awaken and will, if we learn how to listen, guide us into our *true selves*.

Compulsions, along with all of the fear, self-judgment and despair that they bring, are here to empower and heal us to our core. They come from the deepest and wisest parts of ourselves and bring all the experiences we need in order to move out of the prisons of our minds so we can make contact again with Life. *Compulsions come from the longing at the heart of Life for us to trust ourselves and trust Life again so we can become partners with the creative force that flows through everything.*

From *Reaction* to *Response*

There is practically nothing that is a better teacher of how to be truly alive than our compulsions. *The key to gathering all the wisdom that compulsions bring is to transform our relationship to them.* We usually live in reaction to them, fighting them, giving in and then fighting again. There is a huge difference between living in *reaction* and living in *response*. We have been trained to react. We think in terms of what *should be* and what *shouldn't be*, of what *was* and what *will be*. We push and pull, grab and resist instead of *being interested in responding – in listening to the experience of compulsions, learning from it and bringing the light of our atten-*

33

tion to what is happening right now in order to tap into the awesome power of pure curiosity.

We live in reaction to our compulsions because we hate them and we fear them. We try to dominate them only to be dominated in return. But this urge to dominate our compulsions will never bring the healing we long for. In fact, attempted domination only fans the flame.

I have a very strong will. Many times I went without eating for long periods of time, only to binge uncontrollably afterwards. Many times I thought I finally had this urge to overeat under control. Thank God, I was never quite able to do it! These are very powerful forces. These are forces that cannot and should not be tamed. If you try to break a horse, you may be able to ride it, but the horse will have lost its spirit. If you discover how to be in true relationship with a horse, it will give you the gift of its wildness and its speed. An example of this truth is shown in the movie *Horse Whisperer* which was based on Monty Robert's work with gentling rather than breaking horses.

What works with horses works also with our compulsions. If we try to break them, they have a tendency to 'bite us in the butt!' But if we learn how to *be in relationship with them*, we can not only heal our compulsions, but we can be healed by them! It was when I learned how to let go of my hatred and fear of my compulsion and became curious about what was happening inside of me that I began to heal and be healed by my compulsions. Each and every wave of compulsion that I was able to be present for dissolved a little more of the prison of my mind and opened the doorways to my heart. In the beginning I was only able to be there for a moment or two, but each moment made a difference. Rather than leaving me in deep despair, my compulsions began to leave mercy and joy in their wake.

Even though it felt like I paid a high price for my compulsions, in the long run they have brought me much more than they have ever taken away. They didn't allow me to *manage and control* my way to a temporary healing that kept me separate from the lasting healing that I longed for. Crashing over and over against the bulkhead of my own impotence, they narrowed down my options until the only one left was to open and engage with my compulsions. I had to allow them to bring me back to myself—not an idea of what I should be, but a true and loving connection with myself *exactly as I am.*

> *If we learn how to be in relationship with them, we can not only heal our compulsions, but we can be healed by them!*

As I was finally able to tell myself the truth of my experience and accept it –

rather than being ashamed or afraid – the clouds of struggle began to part. I slowly moved from *I am not/I should be* to the wonderful and nourishing experience of *I am!* This has melted so many of the *I am not knots* in my body, mind and heart. In this melting and opening to Life, deep joy has again made itself known allowing me to live from the wellspring of knowing within myself that is connected to the unrestricted flow of Creativity that is Life.

The Gifts of Our Compulsions

Learning how to *respond* to our compulsions rather than *reacting* to them is a radically different experience from what we have been taught. In order to make this shift, it helps to look at the many gifts that we will receive as we learn how to listen to our compulsions rather than living on the pendulum of reaction.

Compulsions can show us how caught we are in our heads and can reveal to us the futility of domination. It is amazing how much we all believe muscling our compulsions into submission will bring us the healing that we long for, even though the evidence is there that it doesn't. Remember that the Surgeon General of the United States reports that 98% of all the weight that is lost is gained back plus some within a year and a half! And yet diet books are perennial best sellers. It is also true that the recidivism rate at drug rehabs and eating disorder programs is very high. And it seems that if we do control one compulsion, often another takes its place.

Our compulsions are trying to teach us how to be curious. They will only let go of their grip as we learn how to respond *to what is happening rather than* reacting. This is a much more effective way to use our minds. Rather than constantly trying to change *what is*, a person who has learned how to be curious about what is happening, even for just a moment, can move through the thickest of mind states and the most closed of hearts to bring the healing of spaciousness and mercy.

As we learn how to listen to our compulsions, they will bring us back into the safety of living *in* our bodies, along with the pure *aliveness* and *joy* that is there. The experience of being fully in our bodies is one of the things we are truly hungry for when we compulsively reach for a cigarette, a drink, a bite, or a credit card. There is also deep wisdom that is waiting for us there. Even just a little bit of dropping out of our heads and back into our bodies will put us in contact with the many gifts our bodies have to give, dramatically lessening the power of compulsions.

> *As we become more curious about our compulsions, opening our hearts in the process, we make contact with an inner radar that knows the most kind and skillful thing to do in any given situation, especially around our compulsions.*

Compulsions open the doorways back into our hearts, revealing the understanding and mercy that we are so starved for. This is one of the most important gifts that compulsions bring, for it is in the heart that all true healing happens. Compulsions do this by revealing how closed our hearts are to ourselves! In recognizing how deep our self-judgments are, there is the possibility of meeting every single part of ourselves with mercy. This is the healing we long for, the healing of a loving relationship with ourselves.

Compulsions will reconnect us to the joy of making kind and wise choices. In the past, we have often made choices that were against ourselves, causing such heartaches in our lives. As we become more curious about our compulsions, opening our hearts in the process, we make contact with an *inner radar* that knows the most kind and skillful thing to do in any given situation, especially around our compulsions. This radar contains what I call our *Empowered No*. This *No* is not against anything – it is for the good of the whole. It knows when to say "yes" and when to say "no" so that we can again trust ourselves and our lives.

When we over-eat, over-spend, over-work, or just *over-over* in our lives, *what we are truly craving is ourselves.* We long for the joy of seeing the beauty of our own eyes and to feel the thrill of our own heartbeats. We long for the sensuous pleasure of chocolate melting in our mouths and of having that one bite be enough. We long for the freedom of a full breath rather than a puff of a cigarette. All of these examples come from that wondrous relationship where, *no matter what is happening, it feels okay to be in our own skins*. That doesn't mean that Life is always pleasant, it just means that we have learned how to meet ourselves in our hearts in the midst of whatever is showing up in the moment. Compulsions won't let us go until we know this kind of connection again.

Compulsions also reveal and bring clarity to all of the blocks that stand in the way of knowing and living from this kind of connection with ourselves. *What fuels every wave of compulsion is all of the painful feelings and thoughts that we have boxed up inside of ourselves. Compulsions bring them close to the surface where they can finally be seen and then healed through understanding and mercy.*

This trust of ourselves and of our lives brings us back to the truth. As Jesus once said, "You will know the truth and the truth will set you free." Most of us imagine him to be speaking about lofty ideas and concepts. Truth with a capital 'T' has nothing to do with ideas *about* Life. Truth is *what is* – right now. Truth is that you are sitting here and reading. Truth is that you are thinking and feeling exactly what you are thinking and feeling. To let go of focusing on what you *should* or *shouldn't be*, and for just a moment, to connect with the truth of *what is*, taps you into the *authority of your own authenticity*, and brings clarity, freedom, and peace.

Ultimately compulsions are here to show us that we are not alone. There is a power that is greater than we are. There is a power that is so awesome that it keeps the planets spinning as they do with a precision that is mind-boggling. That power also orchestrates the seasons with a rhythm that is astonishing and even permeates every single cell of our bodies.

When we try to heal our compulsions solely with our minds, we are relying upon a limited power. But when we learn how to use our minds to be curious, cultivating an alert appreciation for what is really going on inside of us, a wiser part of us that is connected to the Wisdom of Life begins to have a voice in the process. As we learn how to listen, answers come flowing up from deep inside of us with a clarity that is a joy to behold. As the wellspring of wisdom within us has a voice in this process, it will take us experience by experience into the wholeness that we long for.

A Glimpse of the Possibility

Because we are so used to seeing our compulsions as the enemy, it may be difficult to let in the possibility that not only can compulsions be a guide back to ourselves, but that also, hidden in their depths, are the treasures that we have longed for our whole lives. In order to get over the hump of disbelief, I want to give you a glimpse of the place compulsions are trying to open you to in the following exercise:

> *Taking the hand that is not holding this book, begin to shake it. Get it going as fast as you can for a few moments. Go for the gusto with this so you can get your energy moving. Now close your eyes, stop shaking your hand, and bring your attention to it. Can you feel the free-flowing energy?*

Now let us get a glimpse of how it feels to have energy moving throughout our whole body.

After you read the following section, put the book down and start shaking your hand again. Let that shaking move up through your entire arm and then over to the other arm. When both of your arms are involved, see where the shaking wants to go from there.

Watch for the voices in your head that want you to stay contained. This may be the predominate voice in the beginning. That voice comes from the I am not/I should be *training you got when you were young that says you always have to do it 'right' and look cool. Give yourself permission to move beyond that voice for these few moments and let your exuberance and your natural inclination to play come on board again. Have fun with this! Shake, rattle, and roll! (My hips love to get involved!)*

Now close your eyes and stop shaking. Bring your attention into your body and enjoy the experience of free flowing energy. Let that bliss bring you fully back into your body and into yourself – not an idea *of you, but the* real thing!

You and I were this alive and joyous when we were little. As adults, most of the time we are off someplace in our minds – in the *should*s, *ought to*s, wants, and fears that make up most of our inner conversations. Leaving ourselves for the attic of the intellect, we learned to become contained, holding our breath, tightening our bodies. This not only cuts us off from the nourishment of free flowing energy, it also cuts us off from the wellspring of wisdom within us that is filled with clarity, joy and love.

We don't need to go around shaking our bodies in order to know the joy of true connection with ourselves and with Life. *All we need do is learn how to open to Life again.* This opening comes through a fascinated curiosity about what is happening right now and a deep willingness to meet it all with an understanding heart.

I want to share with you the first time I became open enough as an adult that the free flowing energy coming from the wellspring within me could fill me with its presence. It happened early one morning right after I woke up and my mind was still very quiet. Rather than getting out of bed, I began to breathe slow and deep breaths while still snuggled under the safety of the covers. Using my mind to connect with *what is* rather than *what was* or *what will be*, I became passionately curious about what I was experiencing right then. Immediately I noticed a tingle of *aliveness* throughout my whole body. By paying attention to it, it began to expand from the very core of myself into every nook and cranny of my being as the energy of my wellspring revealed itself in me.

The more present I became, the more my body radiated the joy of being alive. Every once in a while the thoughts in my head would try to capture my attention, but I could easily let them go and return to being fully present for myself, for Life, and for the joy of being alive. After a while the insistent mind began to take over. When I noticed that I was again paying attention to only my thoughts, I would gently bring my attention back into my body. Every time I returned, I discovered the free flowing joy had dimmed as I had held my breath and slightly tensed my body when I was again caught in my head (the training from our childhood).

I began to see that my thoughts truly believed that this openness would be as bruising and as wounding as it had been when I was a child. But I am not a child anymore, and even though I had to pull back from Life in order to survive when I was young, I knew as an adult that in opening to Life I would thrive. With a few deep breaths and a sense of relaxing into my body, I returned over and over again to myself. I did this by pulling my attention away from the thoughts in my head and placing it back into my body and the immediacy of Life. There to meet me was the free flowing energy of being completely alive.

Oh, the thrill of that! There was no war inside of me. All expectations that I be any particular way fell away. I was back in the land of *I am!* and that was enough. In fact, it was more than enough. It was allowing myself to again be animated from my core. The joy that flooded me while I was this connected to myself and to the wellspring within nourished me deeply.

This joy stayed with me as I got out of bed and headed to the bathroom, but I began to lose contact with it before my shower was done. I had had a glimpse, however, of what was waiting for me when I learned how to open to Life and live from the wellspring of energy, wisdom, and support that was within me.

There were still many things I had to let go of and many things I needed to relearn in order to know and live from my essence. I had to learn how to use my mind to *engage with* Life rather than constantly trying to *manage* it. I also needed to learn how to recognize the thoughts and feelings that caused me to pull back from Life. And finally I needed to meet those thoughts and feelings with compassion and understanding.

Every step of the way my compulsions were my guide, showing me the futility of my attempts at control and

> *Every step of the way my compulsions were my guide, showing me the futility of my attempts at control and inviting me into being curious about what was going on.*

39

inviting me into being curious about what was going on. My compulsions pointed out to me the feelings I had boxed-up and hidden deep in my body so that I could now work with them, touching them with my compassionate heart.

Little by little, with moments of curiosity and even more wonderful moments of mercy for all of my inadequacies and my fears, the wellspring within me has become more real until I can now return to it even in the middle of a busy day. I still have some boxes of feelings scattered around the house of my being that I haven't yet opened. When I become aware of those feelings, my automatic reaction is to tighten down and distract myself. But not for long! After having lived in the joy and aliveness that comes from being open to Life, the loss of this kind of connection is very evident when I close again. When I notice this, I immediately become curious and then very compassionate. As my heart opens, my body softens and my mind lets go. I can then meet these feelings and transform them back into the free flowing energy of Life.

You are reading this book because you are ready to know and live from the wellspring within you with all of the joy, nourishment, wisdom, and creativity that it holds. You are ready to meet your boxed-up feelings with understanding and mercy so that you can love yourself from the inside out. And you are ready to be healed by your compulsion which will be your guide on this journey back to yourself.

We will now explore a new kind of relationship with compulsions.

Core Ideas in Our Compulsions Are Here to Heal Us:

❖ Compulsions are not random events. They come from the deepest, wisest part of yourself, bringing all the experiences you need in order to unravel the web of struggle that you find yourself caught in.

❖ If you listen to compulsions, they will guide you back into a deep and abiding relationship with yourself and with Life.

❖ Compulsions are here to open your heart so you can meet every part of yourself with mercy.

❖ Compulsions won't let go until they reveal to you the inner radar of your wellspring that knows when to say "yes" and when to say "no" in every experience of your life.

❖ Healing is about becoming yourself again – not an idea of what you *should be*, but the Real Thing. You then can live from the *I am!* again, passionately present for your life.

❖ Compulsions come from the longing at the heart of Life for us to trust ourselves and trust Life again so we can become partners with the creative force that flows through everything.

✦ THE JOURNEY BACK TO OURSELVES ✦

Managing Our Compulsions

If we look closely at our relationship with our compulsions, we can see that we truly believe they are bad and must be fought. Because of this archaic belief, the only type of relationship we have learned is *management*. From the rooftops of fitness clubs, from the slick advertising of diet centers, and from the pages of fashion magazines, we have become brainwashed with the idea that our power lies in *controlling* our unwanted urges.

We try to deny, dominate, annihilate, or run from our compulsions and the feelings that fuel them, only to have both roar back with a force that astounds us. We have lived with this dynamic long enough now to see that *what we try to control controls us.* Our very resistance to our compulsions, along with our hatred and fear of all of the feelings they are trying to take care of, fuel that which we are trying to resist!

The tricky thing is that management does appear to work initially, but eventually it gives diminishing returns. Remember the feeling of *absolute power* when you lost all the weight the first time? But the next time you couldn't stay on the diet as long or lose as much. And you stayed caught in the web of management because you believed that the only reason you failed was because you were doing something wrong!

Even when management did seem to work, if you look closely you will see that you just switched to another compulsion. That is why so many people gain weight after they quit smoking or smoke more after they quit drinking.

This idea that our power will come from dominating what we don't like actually causes us to lose our power in the long run. This was true in my own life, and I have seen it over and over again in the people who come to me for counseling. Frustrated because they see themselves as failures for having failed to control their compulsions, many of them express a heart-breaking sense of inadequacy along with the deep despair that comes from the belief that there is no way out.

> *This idea that our power will come from dominating what we don't like actually causes us to lose our power in the long run.*

Trying to manage our compulsions puts us into a downward spiral where the more we fail, the more our self-judgment turns into shame, fear turns into terror, and sadness turns into despair. Believing that our only option when these feelings are present is to eat, drink, shop, over- work, or television and computer ourselves into numbness, we find ourselves in a vicious cycle of controlling and being controlled.

One of the most harmful downsides to the idea that management will bring us the healing that we long for is that it keeps us caught in our

> *The wisdom that we each carry and that can take us step by step out of the maze of struggle is always speaking to us—especially in a wave of compulsion—and is waiting for us to pay attention!*

heads with a penchant for endless struggle. This cuts us off from the very information we need in order to heal! It is like walking down a path with signs on either side that point the way. We don't notice the signs because there is a perpetual cloud of struggle enveloping our heads.

Mumbling to ourselves words of *have to*s and *ought to*s, along with *I can't*s and *I won't*ts, the cloud gets thicker through confusion, self-judgment, and despair. And yet the signs never leave. The wisdom that we each carry and that can take us step by step out of the maze of struggle is always speaking to us—especially in a wave of compulsion—and is waiting for us to pay attention!

On top of that, all of our mumblings come from the idea that some outer authority has the answer for us – some diet will tell us what to eat; some book will tell us how to think, some *expert in living* will tell us how to behave. And yet there is no better expert for our lives than ourselves!

If we believe that something or somebody else knows what is best for us, we stop trusting ourselves. This cuts us off from our own inner radar, the authority of our authenticity that is an essential part of the wellspring within.

This inner radar knows what is appropriate for us in any given situation. It knows when to say "yes" and when to say "no." It knows when to act and when to be still, how to eat and when to sleep. It knows how to make wise and kind choices that are for the benefit of our whole being. And even though we have been educated out of it, it has never left us and is waiting for our return. Once you rediscover your inner wellspring of wisdom, you will wonder how you ever functioned without it.

We will never know this wellspring within as long as we stay caught in our heads, trying to manage our way to the Love and freedom that we long for. So let us now look at a new way of being with our compulsions that will take us back to a deep and abiding relationship with our own inner knowing.

Engaging With Our Compulsions

This new relationship with our compulsions is one of *engagement,* which is the ability to be present, in a curious and open way, for whatever is happening. Rather than struggling with compulsions, engagement is about listening and learning from them, for engagement trusts that hidden within every single wave of compulsion are the keys to our healing.

Engagement is not permission to indulge in compulsions. That would just be more unconsciousness. *It is the willingness to stop fighting compulsions so we can see what is going on.* As we are curious rather than controlling and merciful rather than judgmental, the pieces of the puzzle of our compulsions will reveal themselves so we can be free.

> *The clues to the healing that we long for lie in whatever experience we are having right now.*

Remember those picture puzzles from your childhood that showed a drawing with objects hidden within it that you had to find? It may have been a knife drawn into the trunk of a tree or a cat in a cloud. You had to shift your perspective to see what was there. As we shift our perspective around our compulsions, becoming curious rather than controlling, we discover that all of the clues to the healing that we long for lie in whatever experience we are having right now. Our compulsions amplify those clues so we can see them more clearly.

Engagement is neither for nor against the compulsion. *Engagement is simply a passionate interest in what is happening and a compassionate meeting of what is there.* In learning how to listen curiously to what is happening either before, during, or after a wave of compulsion, the clouds engulfing our heads are removed, and we become able to see the signs that are pointing the way along the path. Our very attention not only fleshes out the clues, but also highlights the hidden parts of ourselves that are fueling the compulsion. And in adding compassion to attention, they are transformed in the vast region of our hearts.

The Foundations of Engagement

Engagement comes out of a foundation of respect and forgiveness. Let us look now in greater depth at these two qualities inherent in this new way of relating to our compulsions.

◆ **Respect**

Respecting our compulsions is something most of us have never even considered. We have never been taught to respect these vast forces that come roaring up from the depth of our being. The dictionary defines respect as follows:

> *"...relating to; referring to for information; take into account; to have in view."*

Those phrases succinctly describe the type of relationship that we are cultivating. It is a type of relationship that will not only heal our compulsions, but will also allow us to be healed by them.

Rumi, a thirteenth century Sufi poet, speaks about the power of this kind of respect in the following poem:

The Guest House

This human being is a guest house.

Every morning is a new arrival – a joy, a depression, a meanness

– some momentary awareness comes as an unexpected visitor.

Welcome and entertain them all.

Even if they're a crowd of sorrows who violently sweep your house empty of its furniture,

still, treat each guest honorably.

He may be clearing you out for some new delight.

The dark thought, the shame, the malice, meet them at the door laughing and invite them in.

Be grateful for whoever comes because each has been sent as a guide from beyond.

Be grateful for whoever comes because each has been sent as a guide from beyond!

In the adolescence of our species, we thought that if something unpleasant was happening, it was because we or somebody else (maybe even God) had done something wrong. In the *right and wrong* of duality thinking, the typical reaction to the unpleasant in our lives is to try to get rid of our unwanted guest, but this has never brought us the peace we long for.

What Rumi is alluding to is one of the great secrets of transformation. *We are not given difficulties in our lives because we have screwed up or because God has it in for us. The challenges of our lives are like weights on a weight machine. These kinds of 'weights' strengthen within us the*

> *We are not given difficulties in our lives because we have screwed up or because God has it in for us.*

capacity to become conscious human beings. We are given them –especially our compulsions – because Life longs for us to mature enough so that we can know the wellspring within us and live from its wisdom, support and love.

It takes a keen ability to pay attention, a spacious and embracing heart, and a deep humility in order to consciously know and live our full potential. Just as the knights of old knew that they needed a *noble adversary* in order to develop their skills, we too need the great teacher of our challenges in order to develop these talents so we can recognize and live as ourselves.

Imagine a master, a sometimes fierce but very benevolent master, standing in front of you holding the keys to lasting freedom. Would you not bow to her in deep respect? The wondrous thing is that you do have a great master within you in the guise of your compulsions. These forces have come from the heart of Life itself to burn out the dross of your forgetting so you can become a conscious human being.

Cultivating respect allows us to recognize that the urge to be compulsive is a very strong force, often much stronger than our attempts to control it. How many times have you tried to wrestle your compulsion to the ground, only to fail? The key is that *in the face of respect, compulsions lose their strength.*

In J. Allen Boone's book *Kinship With All Life,* he speaks about a woman named Grace Wiley who was a well-known snake expert. One of the passions in her life was to transform people's relationship with snakes. She felt that "deep within the heart of every snake is not a troublemaker but a fine gentleman who strikes only because someone has invaded his domain and cornered, frightened, or hurt him."

She also loved to *gentle* snakes that were considered notorious troublemakers. In a bare room with a heavily built oblong table in the center, she would place herself at the far end of the table and become as motionless as possible. When the snake was first let out of the box, it would immediately go into defense or attack position. But to its obvious astonishment and bewilderment, there was no moving target to attack.

From the moment she entered the room, she silently talked across to the snake— not down to it as if it were an inferior being, but across to it with the knowing

> *In the face of respect, our compulsions lose their strength.*

46

that they were each an out-picturing of the vast intelligence that orchestrates all of Life. She used her favorite rule of action in all relationship contacts: that all living things – regardless of their form, classification, or reputation – will respond to genuine interest, respect, appreciation, admiration, affection, gentleness, and courtesy.

Moving from silently communicating with the snake to actually talking to it, Grace praised it for its many excellent qualities, assuring it that it had nothing to fear. The big snake would slowly uncoil and cautiously stretch itself the full length of the table, finally resting its head within inches of where Grace was standing. Then she would reach out and touch its back, beginning with a soft padded stick and, when there was no resistance, with both of her hands! The snake would then arch its long back in catlike undulations in order better to feel the care and respect of her hands.

This is true for your compulsion too. You have a relationship with it just as you do with friends, pets, plants, and loved ones. And it longs for Grace's rule of action—interest, respect, appreciation, admiration, affection, gentleness, and courtesy. I know that at times you feel like it is a deadly snake, coiled in your belly and ready to strike without a moment's notice. But it only strikes because you have cornered, frightened or hurt it

> *Giving our compulsions respect is not giving them free reign.*

through your fear and your disrespect. Your compulsion can also be *tamed,* just as Grace *tamed* her snakes – not through force, but through a relationship of respect and all that that means.

Your compulsion is longing for your respect. At first you offer it from a distance. And just as Grace's respect moved the snake from attack mode to calm and ease, your respect has the same effect on your compulsion. Know however that, just like with the snake, as you begin to extend respect to these forces within you, at the beginning they may coil in anticipation of attack because that is what you have always done in the past. Slowly, as the compulsion begins to trust your respect, it too will uncoil and undulate under your respectful gaze, sharing with you the gifts it has been carrying.

Giving respect is not giving our compulsions free reign. It is the art of becoming a skillful host to these temporary visitors from the depths of our being. A good hostess welcomes her visitors, making them comfortable in her home. She gifts them with the most important gift a good hostess can give – *her undivided attention.* She may even extend tenderness and mercy by letting the visitor know that they are understood. But a good hostess does not let a guest run amok through her house. And when it is time for the visit to come to an end, the guests are graciously bid farewell.

47

Not only is it possible, it is wise to cultivate respect. The first time I ever heard of the power of respect was from my mentor. She had been a long time smoker and came to a time in her life where it was clear that it was no longer appropriate. She didn't try to wrestle this compulsion to the ground. Instead she gave herself six months. Every time she lit a cigarette she would acknowledge the part of her that smoked, thanking it for all that it had done for her. She then let it know that at the end of the six months she would be saying good-bye. Two weeks before the end of the six months, she got bronchitis and was unable to smoke. She never picked up a cigarette again!

It can be difficult at times to remember to treat these visitors with respect for they can be very demanding and manipulative. But all we have to do is recognize that when we fight them, we not only lose our power, we also amplify their power! Remembering that they are just messengers bringing us gifts from the depths of our being helps us to stay centered in our power.

This kind of respect is not only about respecting our compulsions. *It is also about respecting ourselves for having taken on compulsions in the first place.* What would it be like if, instead of judging yourself for being compulsive, you honored the courage of your soul to use compulsions in order to grow you into the fullness of your potential? Feel the shift in your energy as you move from *disempowerment* to *empowerment.* Now feel the difference in your body when you shift back to the old idea that you are a failure for having failed to conquer compulsions.

Rather than seeing compulsions as proof of how weak-willed you are, comprehend that the more your soul longs for you to become fully yourself, the stronger will be its push to awaken you. In order to do this, it is always looking for ways in which to show you where you are caught in struggle so you can open again to the ease and peace that is right beyond the struggling mind. There is practically no better place to do this than with compulsions.

> *True forgiveness is about letting go of struggling with what has happened in our lives. It is about allowing things to be as they have been so we can let ourselves off the hook and move on.*

You are nothing less than a soul that is on a journey back to itself. As you develop a relationship of respect for both your compulsion and yourself, managing your compulsion will become less and less interesting. As you learn how to engage with it instead, you will turn a former enemy into an ally, forming a partnership that will open the door again to the joy and aliveness that is your birthright.

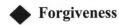 **Forgiveness**

Before we take a look at the skills that will allow you to heal and be healed by your compulsion, I invite you to write a letter to your compulsion. This letter is about extending and receiving the healing power of forgiveness.

There has been much misunderstanding about forgiveness. It is not saying that what you are forgiving was wrong and now you are *letting it off the hook* by giving it absolution. True forgiveness is something far different than that. It is about letting go of struggling with what has happened in our lives. It is about allowing things to be as they have been so we can *let ourselves off the hook* and move on.

If we stay in resentment or fear about something that has happened in the past, we stay stuck to it like glue. One of the core wounds I experienced from being raped in my early twenties was my hatred of the rapist. For years, I stayed attached to the rape by getting caught in rage and bitterness. It was only when I could forgive him—*not the action but the person behind the action,* understanding that he would have to have been deeply wounded himself in order to violate another person in that way – that I became free from the rape and all of its ensuing trauma.

Forgiveness works in the same way with our compulsions. Our compulsions are asking for forgiveness from us. They are asking that we meet them in the vast regions of our hearts, understanding that they were created in order to help us cope. Our compulsions also long for us to ask that they forgive us. All they have gotten from us is our enmity and they need to hear us acknowledge how nasty we have been in relationship to them. Extending forgiveness and asking for it in return removes the veil of distrust so that the door to a respectful and healing partnership can open.

As we learn how to give forgiveness to our compulsions and receive forgiveness from them in return, we can become truly free. Let us look at how we can extend forgiveness to our compulsions, receive forgiveness from our compulsions, and then forgive ourselves to the core.

❖ **Extending Forgiveness**

I began the process of forgiving my compulsion in the middle of an eating binge. Sitting on my couch with a container of ice cream in my lap and a whole row of cookies set up along the back of the couch I began speaking to this part of me, the one that was desperately shoving food into my face. While I don't remember exactly what I said, the following words that I wrote in my book *Belonging To Life* convey the feeling that I experienced in these first moments of opening the door to communication:

> *I want to get to know you. I am learning how to not hate you. In fact, I am learning how to respect you. I can see that you were birthed out of a desire to take care of me. In numbing me out, you intended that I wouldn't feel the maze of terror, self-hatred and despair. But this never brought us the cessation of pain that we yearn for, and now you are out of control. I want to heal beyond this war that we have with each other. I want to listen to what you have to say. I want to invite you back into my heart. We have both paid a heavy price for our lack of communication.*

This little bit of connection changed my whole experience. I realized I wasn't hungry for the food. *I was hungry for the feeling of curiosity and compassion that was moving through me in that moment.* Because it was hard in the beginning to hold on to this level of compassionate attention while in the middle of an eating storm, I began to write letters to my compulsion, both to forgive it and to ask for forgiveness.

> *Writing a letter to your compulsions is a great way to open the doors to forgiveness.*

These letters kept my intent to heal and be healed in the forefront of my mind. They also became a place where I could look back and see the transformation from hatred and fear to a partnership based on respect and trust. In the beginning, my letters were filled with rage and despair, with only a little of the space that comes from engagement and understanding. At the end they were filled with gratitude, understanding, and compassion.

Writing a letter to your compulsion is a great way to open the doors to forgiveness. A skillful way to begin a letter to your compulsion is to write at the top of the page:

> *I am writing this letter to invite you back into my heart.*

It is a perfect opening line for it will either bring up your longing to heal and words will flow from this longing or it will bring up all of your rage for the abuse you have suffered at it hands. Whatever it brings up, tell your compulsion exactly how you feel. The key to writing this kind of letter is to trust exactly where you are.

A paragraph from one of my letters said:

> *I am here to invite you back into my heart. I may fear you and even hate you, but even bigger than that is my desire to heal my heart. You have caused me much pain in my life. I am beginning to*

realize that you are an essential part of the community of my being, and I forgive you. I forgive you for all of the embarrassment, for all of the agony, for all of the upsets you have caused. I now want to allow you back into the healing of my heart. I have grown immensely from your presence and rather than seeing you as an enemy - as a defect in my being – I realize you come from the depths of my being to awaken my heart. I forgive you."

When I was forgiving my compulsion, I would always end this part by reminding it that my intention was to create a healing relationship with it. I also would remind it that there would be times that I would forget this and act out of my conditioning that says I must hate and fear it. I would tell it that when I got lost again, I would make every effort to remember this commitment to partnership.

❖ Receiving Forgiveness

For a long time, I didn't realize that forgiveness was a two-way street. I was communicating with my compulsion, but I hadn't yet opened the door to my compulsion communicating with me. With startling clarity, I realized one day that I was on the path of forgiving it for beating me up all of those years, but I had not even contemplated opening the doors to being *forgiven by my compulsion!* I saw that every time I had put it out of my heart, it received another load of hatred and fear from me, instead of the wisdom and compassion that was necessary for it to heal. It needed for me to acknowledge that. Because I had never contemplated asking for its forgiveness, it couldn't trust my overtures of forgiveness. A paragraph from another letter shows the power of asking for forgiveness from our compulsions.

I ask you to forgive me for how much I have hated you. Rather than including you as a part of me, knowingly and unknowingly I have sent hatred and violence your way. I ask now that you forgive me for my ignorance, forgetfulness, confusion and rage. I did not see that you were sent from my soul to awaken me. I did not see that it is in letting you back into my heart that we are both healed. I ask that you forgive me for constantly warring with you.

As I allowed myself to open to the possibility of being forgiven by my compulsion, it began to write letters to me! At the beginning I was a bit dismayed by the rage and hurt that it expressed, but all I had to remember was the great violence I had sent into these wounded parts of myself. Like all beings, it just wants to be heard. I could then make space again for it to speak its truth. I could finally hear the grief, rage, and terror that fueled my bouts of overeating. I listened to them in the way they needed someone to be with them when they were created in my youth.

The more I listened, the more I understood that underneath all the rage and bitterness, my compulsion carried great wisdom and had been waiting for the opportunity to share it with me. My heart began to melt and the Compulsive Eater and I became friends. Because it was recognized, respected, and heard, we became partners in our healing and it didn't need to scream so loudly in order to get my attention.

It can be more challenging to allow your compulsion to write to you than it is to write to them. They may not be at all sure about trusting your new intention to heal. Because of this, you may not get any response at the beginning. After all, they have never had a voice in your life. But if you are willing to keep this dialogue open, they will eventually make themselves known. Compulsions, just like people, respond to apologies and a willingness to listen.

A way to get things flowing is to imagine what you would feel like if you were in a relationship where someone constantly ignored you or put down everything you said. Then realize that this is how you have been with your compulsion and it probably has some things to say about that! Or, if you are beginning to listen to your compulsion, imagine what it feels like to finally be respected and heard. Then put your pen on the paper and allow yourself to write down whatever thoughts and feelings come to you.

❖ Forgiving Ourselves

If forgiving your compulsion doesn't call to you right now, explore forgiving yourself. Say,

> *"I forgive you _____,"*

adding your name at the end of the phrase. Just chanting this phrase is very powerful. It will either open your heart or reveal to you the places where your heart is still closed to you. You can amplify it by saying,

> *"For all of the mistakes in your life, for all of the reactions of a closed heart, I forgive you _____. I see now that you are an awakening being and every single experience of your life was necessary on the journey. I forgive you."*

Forgive the unlikable, the contracted, and even the unacceptable part of you. Allow yourself back into your own heart. You are worthy of this kind of mercy. If the mind throws up all of the reasons why you can't be forgiven, watch how unkind the mind can be, and permit this hard edge to be forgiven. Repeat these words numerous times, making them your own and allowing them to open you to a tender, caring, relationship with yourself.

In the willingness to explore forgiveness, we need to know that the roots of reaction and resentment are buried deep in all of our hearts. At times, a forgiveness practice will help us to see how closed our hearts still are and we can then explore this

> *The power of forgiveness is not in having any particular thing happen. It is in the intention to forgive.*

armoring. At other times, it will reawaken us to the spaciousness of an open heart, allowing our ancient pains to float in the healing of mercy.

While practicing forgiveness with your compulsion, there will be times when you say, "I forgive you," and your heart will slam closed in rage at how much agony this part of you has brought into your life. And there will be times when you will be able to thank your compulsion for all they have given to you.

The power of forgiveness is not in having any particular thing happen. *It is in the intention, the willingness to at least explore forgiveness.* And in those times when this brings up your inability to forgive, you can use it to explore the ancient armoring around your heart. Rather than trying to force your way through, you can then shift into forgiving the part of yourself that doesn't want to forgive!

Just as in all relationships that are healing, there will be ups and downs in this process. Writing letters to your compulsion is a great way to begin. It claims your willingness to forgive and be forgiven, to heal and be healed. If it doesn't call to you to do this, trust that. The ideas that we explored in this section are powerful seeds that will grow within you in their own time and in their own way. If it does call to you, keep writing. For it is a very effective way to keep the lines of communication open between you and your compulsion.

As you write your forgiveness, allow not only your rage and grief to have a voice, but also your deep longing to heal. Speak about the hope you have discovered as we have explored a whole new way of working with compulsions and about the awakening of your desire to discover the gifts that compulsions carry. This hope may at times turn back into distrust and the despair that nothing will ever change. Allow these feelings to have a voice too for they are there as the next step in your healing. And when you are ready, share your gratitude for all that your compulsion has been trying to awaken within you. Everything responds to appreciation.

Listening to the Monster

After having been so thoroughly trained into believing that controlling and managing is the only way to freedom, it feels to most people that if they become curious about their compulsions rather than always trying to control them, they will be helpless in the face of them. Nothing could be further from the truth. Our ability to listen to our compulsions exerts an influence that is a million times more effective than any attempt at control. It allows us to see what is truly going on without the resistance that keeps compulsions going – the resistance that comes from the old style of management.

There is a story from my book *Belonging To Life* that I have adapted for this work with compulsions about the monster of compulsion living in your house. It begins with you living in reaction to this unwanted guest and gradually moves to the healing of engagement. It honors management, but shows us that it only takes us so far into the healing that we long for.

This story also shows that the shift from management into engagement is a gradual one. What we are exploring isn't about getting rid of all of our managing tools. *It is about adding curiosity to the process.* Over time managing your compulsion will become less and less interesting as engagement brings you the freedom you long for.

> *Imagine that you once had a wonderful friend. This friend promised you the sun, the moon, and the stars, along with their undying love. But, as we have all discovered, relationships can be challenging, and as this one deteriorated, this former friend turns into a monster and you order him out of your house.*
>
> *You come home one evening after a long day at work and discover this monster sitting in your living room.*
>
> *"What are you doing here?" you ask with great indignation.*
>
> *Getting no response, irritation takes over, and again you order him out of the house. He doesn't move. Racing into the kitchen, you ask the other family members why they let him in and they say he just appeared! Returning to the living room, you announce that you are going to call the police, and he still does not respond.*
>
> *Calling 911 you say, "There is an emergency. A monster has moved into my house, and I want you to take him away."*
>
> *Kindly but firmly they tell you that this is not their job. You call social services, moving companies and even the zoo, hoping to get rid of this unwanted guest. Nothing works. In desperation, you*

even toy for a while with the idea of calling in a hit man (your Uncle Joey could probably arrange it), but that is too abhorrent for your tastes.

Believing that you are solely responsible for your own reality, you decide that the monster is here because you are not doing something right. So off to counseling you go. You describe this monster in your living room and the counselor takes you back into childhood, discovering a trauma there. This understanding brings deeper layers of mercy and you let go of a big chunk of self-judgment. You drive home with a lilt in your heart and a smile on your face. With great hope you enter the living room, fully expecting that the monster will be gone. He isn't.

In your frustration, you begin to listen to what the monster seems to be saying. You become convinced that you would feel a lot better if you got lost in your compulsion, and without a second thought, you go in search of its promise of peace and comfort.

The relief you get from indulging in your compulsion is temporary, leaving discomfort, judgment, and maybe even despair in its wake. So you decide you will never do that again and claim that you will now be on top of these urges from the deep. You read books that show you how to be in control and with great perseverance you add these skills to your life. And for a while it seems that the monster of compulsions is gone, for when you go into the living room you don't see him there.

One evening, while watching television, the pile of blankets in the corner begins to move and there, much to your dismay, is the monster again. In a flash you realized that the whole time you thought you were in control again, he was taking a nap. Deep self-judgment and despair roar through you.

"I will never be free of this monster," you rage and you immediately get lost in a wave of compulsion.

After the wave moves through, you pick yourself up and say, with great determination, "This monster isn't going to get the best of me!"

When you go into the living room you sit on the couch, close your eyes and say powerful affirmations, repeating to yourself over and over again "I am in control of myself and this irritant is gone from my life." You feel more empowered as you say these words and you know that he is evaporating right now as you speak.

In a very confident move, you take a peek through your closed eyes, only to discover that he is still there! And you fall into your compulsion again.

The more you go to your compulsion for relief, the deeper your self-judgment and despair. For you know that you are supposed to be in control of this monster. You are certain that everybody else can do this and you have failed only because you are weak-willed, stubborn, and rebellious. So you try program after program, each one promising that they will eliminate compulsions, thus getting rid of the monster.

The sense that he would be gone if only you could figure it all out and understand how to 'do' Life right begins to eat at your heart. The edges of despair flood your being, but with great strength you affirm that you will just try harder and then it will work.

One morning, after a particularly rigorous week of controlling your compulsion, along with all of the counseling, affirming and visualizing that promised to get rid of it, feelings of deep grief and rage begin to overwhelm you.

"Nobody else has a monster in their living room." (They all do, of course, but they hardly ever speak about it.) "And if I can't get rid of mine, there must be something terribly wrong with me." You collapse on the floor in a flood of tears, self-judgment, and hopelessness.

In the middle of this storm you hear a very faint, melodious voice. "Ask me why I am here."

In shock you look up at the monster. In this whole time he had never before spoken!

"What did you say?" you ask in amazement.

"Ask me why I am here," he repeats.

"Well, I don't want to talk to you. You are the enemy. I didn't invite you into my home. You came unbidden and are deeply unwelcome," you respond. In a huff you turn your back to him.

"What have you got to lose?" he asks. "Nothing else has worked. I haven't gone away."

In your desperation you realize that this is true. Picking yourself up out of the heap of self-failure, you slowly approach him. (This whole time you've never come any closer than 10 feet.) Your heart is racing wildly. "This is the enemy," you chant to yourself. "What am I doing? I must be crazy. I will be overwhelmed and lost if I get any closer." But your desperation urges you on.

As you sit down on the chair across from him, the first thing you notice is that the monster has kind eyes! "Why, you have beautiful eyes," you say. "And they are even twinkling with joy and laughter. Why have I never noticed before?"

"Because you made me the enemy," he says in his melodious and healing voice. "I am not your enemy. In fact, from the depths of your being you invited me into your life in order to awaken you. I am not here to disturb you, even though I do evoke that in your mind. I am not here to harm you, even though I do bring up your fear. I am your ally, highlighting the old beliefs you have taken on about yourself that keep you separate from all that you yearn for. If you listen to that which is upsetting in your life, it will show you the way back to yourself."

In some corner of your being you know that what he is saying is true. Rather than wanting to run away, you begin to listen to this monster that had formerly bothered you, and your heart begins to melt. A surge of joy races through your body, and you become curious about the monster rather than living in reaction.

"You truly are my friend," you say. His laughing eyes answer yes. "And you have been waiting a long time for me to pay attention and listen to what you have to say."

With a big sigh, he affirms this truth.

You realize that every time he is present, he is revealing another piece of your healing. Even with this connection, at moments your fear and confusion take over. But you notice the kindness in his eyes and again you find yourself present for this former enemy. Something he said finally becomes clear to you.

Life is for you! *Who you really are includes both the dark and the light, and it uses the dark as a tool of awakening. When you understand this, it becomes evident that your life – all of it – is trustable. And the deep safety you long for comes when you learn how to be present for yourself in a curious and compassionate way."*

Engagement In Action

Everything we have explored so far has been about transforming our relationship with our compulsions so we can move beyond constant struggle into the ease and peace that is our birthright. I had an experience that reveals what it looks like as we transform our relationship from management to engagement. I share it with you to give you a glimpse of what can happen as you transform your relation to compulsions. This won't happen overnight, but it is the pathway to freedom. As I share it with you, if overeating isn't your compulsion, replace that in your mind with whatever your primary compulsion is.

> *It was late and I was tired. It had been a long day with even a longer day coming tomorrow. After leading a group, I had an hour's drive to my home. Into this space, like a monster from the deep, came the desire to EAT. This wasn't hunger. This was a desperate craving to EAT AND EAT AND EAT AND EAT.*
>
> *I hadn't had a visit from this old teacher in a long time. After a long hibernation, the Compulsive Eater had returned on this dark and rainy night in a powerful way.*
>
> *"I want a chicken sandwich at Burger King and I want it now," it said! "In fact, if I don't get one, I am going to die!"*
>
> *I am highly allergic to wheat and to eat this sandwich would have devastating results. For a few moments my unconscious mind reacted, "Oh, my God, it's back!" Right on its heels came a wave of self-hatred. "What have I done wrong to have my compulsion show up again?"*
>
> *But this ancient reaction lasted only a few moments and then curiosity took over. "It feels like there is something inside of me that is very vulnerable and very young and desperately needs my attention."*
>
> *Knowing I needed help to meet this, I asked the wellspring of wisdom inside of me to show me what I should do. Immediately what came to mind was the Serenity Prayer, but in an entirely new way. Rather than asking to change anything, what came were the words, "God grant me the serenity of staying curious, the courage to be present for what is asking to be met, and the wisdom to keep my heart open."*
>
> *Driving down the road, breathing long and slow breaths, and with*

each breath repeating these healing words, my mind calmed down. Moving out of reaction, I asked the question, "In this moment, what am I experiencing right now?"

I didn't ask this of my emotions, I asked it of my body. My attention settled in my body, exploring the sensations that were there.

As I made it through the feeling of deep weariness, I found the empty hole in the pit of my stomach that fueled this rage for food. I had been so busy the previous week that I had lost a sense of my own center and this feeling of emptiness was raging for my attention. Instead of meeting it in the last few days and giving it the loving attention it needed, I had ignored it and now its only option was to go back to the old pattern of trying to be filled by food.

Knowing that these feelings needed to be received, I stayed with the physical sensations, asking questions of these angry, terrified, and overwhelmed parts of me. Just in the act of responding rather than reacting, the urge to eat began to calm down, even though there was a part of me that still felt I would die if I didn't get the sandwich.

Not demanding that this be different, I spent the drive to the restaurant in openhearted, responsive communication. I knew that if I forced the Compulsive Eater at all, it would take the power and run. These feelings that fuel an eating binge are so primitive and so scared that they usually can override the best of intentions.

Close to the freeway exit where the restaurant was, I felt we had progressed far enough that I reminded the Eater how ill I would feel if I ate wheat. Making space and truly respecting and listening to these feelings created the possibility of compromise. Rather than a sandwich, which would make me sick, I suggested a big bowl of quinoa (a grain that my body loves) along with lots of extra toasted sesame oil—all to come when I got home. The desperate desire for the sandwich faded away and I drove by the exit. I then had a few moments of panic as the Eater raged. "You fool!" it said. "You missed the chance to eat what you really wanted." I felt a surge of anger at myself for not having followed my compulsion! But then curiosity kicked in again and rather than following this thought, I could see what the Eater was doing.

This ancient and lumbering beast truly felt that the only avenue of comfort was something that would bring devastation in its wake! I reminded it of the joy that comes from making a kind choice and how much better I would feel tomorrow after eating something healthy.

When I got home, I crawled into bed with my bowl of quinoa (with extra oil!) and turned my heating pad onto 'Mother.' I knew that in responding to what was going on rather than reacting, I had taken another step beyond struggle, another step back into myself and all of the joy, aliveness, wisdom, and support that resides there.

Step by step and experience by experience, through curiosity and compassion, I untangled the web of compulsions. As clarity began to dispel confusion and compassion replaced self-judgment, it became easier and easier to simply *be* myself.

It is safe to be curious about what we are experiencing when we are compulsive. It is not only safe – it is the doorway to our healing. We start this process of engaging with our compulsions gradually. We don't let go of all of our old methods of control in the beginning. That would be like throwing someone in the middle of the ocean in order to teach them how to swim! What we do instead is just go sit by the ocean and contemplate the possibility of being curious about our compulsions rather than always reacting, opening to the possibility that maybe we don't need to keep fighting and struggling forever. Then we put one toe in the water, feeling for a moment the truth that our compulsions comes from the depth of our being to heal us, not to destroy us. As we become more curious, we learn how to *respond* to ourselves rather than constantly *reacting*, and one day we find ourselves floating in the warm ocean of our own true nature. With deep gratitude we thank our compulsions for taking us there.

You can know this type of healing relationship with yourself too. Let us now explore the five skills that will allow you to heal and be healed by your compulsion.

Core Ideas in The Journey Back to Ourselves:

Management:

❖ Compulsions are not here because you are doing something wrong.

❖ Controlling compulsions never brings you the lasting healing that you long for.

❖ The tricky thing is that management does appear to work initially, but eventually it gives diminishing returns. If you do manage to control one compulsion, another one usually pops up to take its place.

❖ Managing a compulsion is only a stopgap measure, temporarily keeping these powerful forces from overtaking your life.

❖ Trying to control compulsions actually fuels the compulsive cycle. What you fight controls you. What you resist persists!

Engagement:

❖ The key to gathering all the wisdom that compulsions bring is to transform your relationship to them.

❖ Compulsions thrive in reaction. They heal in response. They won't let go until they teach you how to respond to what is happening inside of you rather than reacting.

❖ Managing compulsions is about trying to control them. Engaging with compulsions is about becoming interested in what is going on. It is a passionate interest in what is happening and a compassionate meeting of what is there, for it knows that hidden within every single wave of compulsion are the keys to your healing.

❖ *What* you are experiencing isn't as important as *what your relationship is* to what you are experiencing!

❖ Engagement isn't about *getting rid of* all of our management tools. It is about *adding* curiosity and compassion to the process.

❖ Engagement comes out of a foundation of respect and forgiveness. In the face of respect, compulsions lose their power over you and, instead they become allies, forming a partnership that will open the door again to the joy and aliveness that is your birthright.

❖ You can respect yourself for taking on the great teacher of compulsions.

❖ True forgiveness is about letting go of struggling with what is. To extend forgiveness to a compulsion and to receive forgiveness from it in return is healing.

❖ Over time, managing compulsions will become less and less interesting as engagement brings you the freedom you long for.

❖ It is safe to be curious about what we are experiencing when we are compulsive. It is not only safe – it is the doorway to our healing.

From Management
to Engagement

✦ BASIC SKILLS FOR WORKING ✦ WITH COMPULSIONS

As we realize that our customary ways of working with the challenges in our lives – challenges that range all the way from compulsions to international conflicts – do not bring the healing we long for, we become open to exploring new ways of working with, learning from, and eventually being healed by the very things we formerly resisted and tried to control.

In this book, we are using our compulsions to explore a very different and very healing way to work with the challenges of our lives. Even contemplating changing our relationship to the great teacher of compulsions, from one of trying to dominate them to becoming empowered through engagement with them, is a significant step. It opens the possibility of listening and learning from the experiences that Life is giving us rather than always trying to fight or flee.

In order to learn how to listen and gather all of the wisdom that compulsions are trying to bring to us, there are some basic skills we can cultivate. These skills will come naturally when we understand that our compulsions are taking us step by step back into a conscious and loving relationship with ourselves and with our lives.

The first four skills – Curiosity, Loving Ourselves from the Inside Out, Open Breathing and Coming Home to Ourselves – are all woven into the fifth skill – Living in Questions. In the fifth skill, the essence of everything we are exploring together will be encapsulated in three basic questions that you can use in any situation to heal and be healed by your compulsion.

These skills may be different than anything you have tried before. They are not about *doing something* to stop our compulsions. They are about cultivating the *ability to be present* for ourselves and for our compulsions. Each of them helps us to bring our attention to what is happening right now in a spacious and curious way, for the doorway back to ourselves lies in whatever experience we are having right now. This is the art of engagement. And its power is beyond anything that we have ever tried before.

The Five Concepts

Before we explore the skills there are five important concepts to cultivate on this journey back to ourselves. These concepts will allow us to make the best use of these skills.

① Letting go of managing our compulsions is not permission to be compulsive. It is permission to be conscious.

② Patience is a necessary ingredient on the journey back to yourself.

③ Know that you don't have to do anything with what is being offered in this book. Reading it will awaken your own truth and you will be able to live this truth in your own time and your own way.

④ Trusting resistance is essential.

⑤ Rebellion *is a part of the process and is workable.*

As these are core concepts, let us take a close look at each of them now.

① Permission to Be Conscious

You may, at first glance, think that letting go of managing our compulsions is permission to be compulsive. Nothing could be further from the truth. *It is permission to be conscious.* It is the art of letting go of our grip on control so that we can bring curiosity to the process. It also is about not fanning the flame of compulsions through control, so that our lives can come back into balance.

In the very beginning when you let go of the tight grip on control, your compulsion may go a little crazy for a while. But this wave of reaction will calm down as you explore the art of engagement. For underneath this rebellion, your compulsion has a deep longing to be included in the healing consciousness of a curious mind and an understanding heart. It also is a little tired and overwhelmed, having carried the full responsibility for taking care of your feelings for all of these years.

② Patience

We won't change our old relationship of managing our compulsions over night. We have all deeply bought into the belief that compulsions are here because we are doing something wrong and the only way to get rid of them is to stop the behavior. On the road back to ourselves, we will get lost in these old beliefs over and over again. But as we cultivate these new skills, we will not only be able to work with the power of curiosity, we will be able to see that in trying to control our compulsions we end up being controlled.

> *Letting go of managing our compulsions is not permission to be compulsive... It is permission to be conscious.*

We have also been trained to expect immediate results. "Lose 10 pounds in 10 days," says the tabloid headline, and we buy into it hook line and sinker. *What we are exploring here is not a quick fix but it is the pathway to freedom.* One of the greatest gifts you can give to yourself is patience. It has taken you a long time to get thoroughly lost in the maze of struggle, trying to fight your way to freedom. It will take some time to find your way out again. You can try the quick fixes again (and you probably will), only to find yourself more deeply caught in the maze of disempowerment, self-judgment, and despair. Or you can walk, step by step, out of the maze.

In cultivating patience, it is important to understand that compulsions come in waves. I didn't understand this for a long time. That is probably because from the age of 11 until the age of 33, I was caught in one continuous wave of compulsion. I was either lost in one of my many compulsions – eating, drinking, taking pills, and getting very, very busy – or I was trying to dominate them, or was lost in deep self-judgment and despair for my failure to control them.

Slowly, as I let go of my addiction of trying to control my compulsions, it began to dawn on me that I wasn't hungry for all of those cookies, candies, cheese, chips, and ice cream that I would gorge on. What I was hungry for was my own attention! As I learned how to be present for myself, eating unskillfully became less and less interesting. Rather than continuous waves of compulsion – where I was either trying to control them or being controlled by them – there began to be long periods of time between the waves.

In those years of slowly, step by step coming back to myself, a pattern began to develop. It was a pattern where the times between the waves of compulsions became longer and the times of being caught in compulsions became shorter. This wasn't always true, especially when I became too tired and stressed by my life (I was raising two children all by myself), but over time this new pattern became evident. Not only that, compulsions taught me to be passionately curious about what was going on in my inner world. So I started to learn from the waves of compulsion when they came. The more curious I became, the shorter the waves were.

I now have very long times between waves of compulsion, and they are more like little ripples when they do come. I am connected enough to myself that I have become very savvy! I can recognize the times where I could

> *Be willing to give yourself time. You don't have to do this all at once. You just have to deal with what is going on right now.*

become vulnerable to compulsions again, and most of the time I can make kind and skillful choices. There are still times where the little ripples of compulsion in my life become a small wave. If I can't negotiate or compromise with these urges from the depth of my being, I then give myself permission to be compulsive. *But this isn't permission just to indulge. It is permission coupled with curiosity.* Every time I do this, I learn another piece of wisdom from my compulsions. In fact, the waves of compulsion are so far apart now that I actually trust them when they come.

So be willing to give yourself time. You don't have to do this all at once. You just have to deal with what is going on right now. For the next step in your healing is always whatever experience you are having right now! Know that there may be a phase in the beginning where it doesn't seem like much is happening and you may feel discouraged. Because you cannot yet see the benevolence of this journey back to yourself, it is easy to mistrust it. But I have seen it over and over again where people, measuring their progress by the old standard, don't feel like they are making very much headway. And then, just like the sun breaking through the clouds on a winter's day, they turn a corner, and their whole relationship with their compulsions and with themselves changes. It is wonderful to share in their joy during these times of inner transformation.

⟨3⟩ Seed Thoughts

It is also important to understand that ultimately you don't have to *do* anything with what is being offered in this book. The most important thing is just to read it. Each chapter will contain ideas and techniques that you can add into your daily life, but this is not a *have to* book. The core nuggets of each chapter are more like precious seeds that will be planted within you as you read them and *they will grow in their own time and their own way. What they grow into will be your truth* – not somebody else's idea of how you should heal, but your own, unique pathway back to yourself. For nobody knows how to heal you better than you.

As you read this book, take out what is true for you and leave the rest. From these pieces of your own truth you will find your way back to yourself and back to Life. This is the new way of healing – healing from the inside out.

The old way was from the top down: Your head takes on somebody else's idea of how you should be and then you try to legislate it into your life. We have all done this enough to see that it has never brought us the healing that we long for. *When you heal from the inside out, you listen deeply to yourself, trusting your own unique timetable for healing.*

Letting go of the struggle mode, you can now partner with the wellspring of wisdom and insight within you that not only trusts your journey (all of it) but also knows exactly what is needed for the next step. For that is where all lasting healing comes from. This wellspring is so much smarter than anything you can figure out on your own. As you make contact with it, it will take you step by step into the healing that you long for.

So the invitation is to listen carefully as you read each chapter. There will be some skills that will call to you more than others. Those skills will bring a feeling of hope into your heart and an open breath to your body. Play with those skills. Don't make any of them into a *have to* as that only brings up the resistant and rebellious parts of yourself that will try to convince you that you will never know the freedom that you long for.

◇4◇ Trusting Resistance

Trying to heal compulsions through management is like standing knee-deep in a mountain stream, desperately trying to catch a fish with your hands! All it does is get you wet and frustrated. Now that you are reading this book, you are finally realizing that you don't need to dominate your compulsion. You can engage with it instead.

Healing and being healed by compulsions is a little like fly-fishing. As you stand by the stream of your life, casting your line of curiosity into the river of your experience, your compulsion will begin to nibble at your line of communication and will eventually catch hold. A very important concept that you need to understand in order to land the fish of your compulsion is *to honor resistance.* If you have ever been fishing, or even seen somebody else fishing, you will see that as the fisherman reels the fish in, there are times when the fish is fighting so hard that it could slip away. What the fisher-man does in that moment is let the line out to give the fish room to move.

The same principle is true in healing our compulsions. There are times in this journey back to ourselves when the last thing we want

To trust resistance is to trust your own process, remembering that there is a ripening going on.

to do is pay attention and any attempt to be curious and merciful is met with resistance. These are the times where our attention is too scattered and our heart too closed. It is okay to honor the resistance and to turn away. I have made it so deeply into my healing because I trust resistance.

In those times when I could feel that my resistance was stronger than my ability to stay curious, I learned how to trust it. It was telling me that I hadn't yet built the capacity to open to whatever I was experiencing. I would then back off either into the mercy of my heart or into the wonderful world of distraction. If you have ever been around a young child, you know the amazing power of distraction. A child might throw a temper tantrum because he can't have a third Popsicle in a row. You hand him a magnifying glass, showing him the amazing world of a magnified rock, and the tantrum transforms into curiosity!

As adults, we need to cultivate the skill of constructive distraction also, because the feelings we will uncover as we unravel our compulsions are very young, very vulnerable, and very scared. There are times to meet the feelings and there are times not to. Distraction is the art of doing something just to have fun, forgetting for a while all of this growing stuff. It is also the art of numbing out in the kindest way we can discover – renting three videos, turning off the phone and reading an entire novel in a day, or going to visit an entertaining friend.

To trust resistance is to trust your own process, remembering that there is a ripening going on. In our ripening, there are times to be curious about what is going on, there are times to turn away, and there are times when it is important to distract ourselves. To trust resistance allows us to stay in the game for the long haul.

⟨5⟩ Working With Rebellion

The biggest downside to not honoring our resistance is that it will inevitably turn into rebellion! Through fighting rather than listening, we find ourselves creating a monster within us that says "*No!*" when we say "*Yes!*" and "*Yes!*" when we say "*No!*" We all know this place. Every good intention flies out the window and we find our compulsions vehemently defending their right to be compulsive.

We also know how seductive this rebellion can be. I can remember a time that I was white-knuckling myself into submission shortly after I was told that I couldn't eat wheat any more. I could feel a volcano building inside of me, but at that point in my process, the only skill I had was trying to dominate my urge to eat wheat. In the middle of this, I woke up one day with the absolutely very logical idea that I may not be able to eat wheat, but of course that didn't mean whole wheat! That meant only white wheat. Well, anybody in his or her right mind knows that wheat is wheat, but I was so deep into the rebellion mode that I could convince myself that whole wheat wasn't wheat!

> *In trying to annihilate our compulsions, we create an opposing, and usually very rebellious, force.*

This rebellion doesn't just show up around compulsions. Think about how many times you have committed to a kind and skillful choice in your life only to find yourself doing the opposite. Why is this? It is because we have been taught to be soldiers. A soldier is a person who is trained to annihilate his enemy and that is exactly what we do with our compulsions. In trying to annihilate our compulsions, we create an opposing, and usually very rebellious, force that can eventually take over our lives.

To recognize the way in which conquering something only creates resistance, all we have to do is to look at the ebb and flow of war across the span of time. In country after country, when a stronger force comes in and tries to take over, there is a natural urge to resist. And that resistance can be very, very tenacious. Even if a country is seemingly conquered, the urge to rebel usually goes underground and can continue to foster revolution right under the conqueror's nose. Bosnia and Northern Ireland are good examples of the way in which resistance is handed down through generations.

As I look back on my journey, I can see how I lost the ability to make kind and skillful choices. Forgetting how to listen to myself, I read every book, I tried every program, and I followed every idea I could find *out there* that promised me relief from my compulsion. I approached every one like a great soldier. I could muscle my compulsion underground and sometimes even control my urge to overeat, losing as much as 10 pounds in a week. But it never lasted, and over time I had less and less success.

The rebellious one inside of me gained more and more power with every attempt to annihilate my compulsion. My Overeater would hear the voice of the soldier, "You can't do this. You have to do this. You should have done that," and in rebellion would dig in its heals with a vengeance that none of my efforts at control could equal.

Because I was bullying and belittling rather than listening, my rebellious part became shrewd, devious, and all-encompassing. It eventually became stronger than any of my attempts to control it. I thought it was because I was just an undisciplined human being! I didn't recognize that my rebellion

> *Warriors realize that to reach their true potential, they need noble adversaries. Their intent isn't to destroy. Their intent is to engage with their adversary so that they come away with more of themselves.*

was being created and fed by my resistance to my compulsions.

Having not been taught any other way, I got lost in an endless cycle of conquering only to be conquered again. The part of me that knew what was the right thing for me at any given time was continually being overridden by this intractably rebellious "NO!"

The dentist told me to floss my teeth, and even though my gums were bleeding and there was floss by my bed, in my car, in my purse, and in the bathroom, I resisted flossing my teeth! I was also a sporadic meditator for years, even though I had seen the tremendous benefits of a regular meditation practice. And though I had a back that at times hurt so much I could hardly sit, I would begin an exercise program only to give up after the first few days. I now enjoy doing all of these things on a daily basis. On top of that, I eat wisely and experience the joy of bringing vitality and health to my whole body.

How have I come to know this healing place after living in endless war for decades? I discovered it by learning how to be a warrior rather than a soldier. A warrior operates from his or her own sense of integrity and honor. Rather than seeing enemies, warriors realize that to reach their true potential, they need noble adversaries. Their intent isn't to destroy. Their intent is to engage with their adversary so that they come away with more of themselves. In this engagement, they are very observant, knowing that their true power comes from respecting and getting to know their adversary – watching and learning how they operate. Fighting is one of the last options for a warrior. The warrior understands that fighting is a crude and messy way to triumph and that such triumphs will be only temporary.

Compulsions won't let us go until they teach us how to be a warrior. This is why they are a call from the depths of our being to awaken. Compulsions are showing us that it is in *responding* to ourselves rather than in *reacting* that we will be healed. *They are highlighting that it is in mercy and compassion rather than judgment and fear that we will again know and live from the wellspring within us.*

As we prepare to cultivate the skills of engagement, it is important for you to know that you can't make this journey back to yourself go any faster than it needs to go. Nor can you slow it down. You are part of a process that is much wiser than you are. Know also that you will try to use these skills to stop your compulsion. But every single time you let go of the addiction to trying to be somewhere other than where you are and are present for yourself instead – whether it is a wave of compulsion, a busy day, or just taking a shower – you take another step into your healing. Those moments where you are curious about what is happening rather than living in reaction are powerful beyond your wildest imaginations. Even though they may feel like just a drop in a bucket, one day you will discover that your bucket is filled to the brim and your life is spilling over with the joy of being fully connected to yourself.

Now that you have an inkling about the power of *responding* rather than *reacting*; and now that you can comprehend that it is possible to trust yourself and trust your life again, let us explore each of the five skills for healing and being healed by compulsions.

Core Ideas in Basic Skills for Working with Compulsions:

❖ The basic skills for working with compulsions are not about *doing* something to stop them. That only fuels more compulsions. Instead, they help you cultivate the ability to be present for yourself and listen to your own inner wisdom that will guide you into the healing that you long for.

❖ Letting go of controlling compulsions is not permission to be compulsive. It is an invitation to be conscious.

❖ Patience is an important ingredient on the journey back to yourself. It took a long time to weave the web of compulsion. It will take a while to unravel it.

❖ You don't have to do this all at once. The next step in your healing is in what is happening right now.

❖ The core nuggets in each chapter of this book are like precious seeds that will grow in their own time, allowing you to heal from the inside out.

❖ You don't have to do anything with what is being offered in this book. Discover within its pages the seeds of your own truth and let them grow inside of you.

❖ To trust resistance is to trust your own process, remembering that there is a ripening going on.

❖ Our compulsions highlight that it is in mercy and compassion rather than judgment and fear that we will again know and live from the wellspring within us.

✦ SKILL 1: CURIOSITY ✦

If you watch young children, you will see that they are passionately present for their lives. Rather than living in ideas *about* Life, they are truly *here*! Let us glimpse again what that is like through the following:

> *After you read this paragraph, lift your eyes from the book and without changing anything, notice* what is. *See where you are. Don't just look,* see*! Be present for Life. Now shift your focus to just one thing that is close to you – your hand, a lamp, or a pet – and see it as if you have just arrived from another planet. Be fascinated! And finally, shift your focus to the rising and falling of your breath. For just a few moments, recognize it and feel it. You are alive! You are not only alive; because you are present for Life, you are ALIVE!*

If you are like most people, you were probably only able to be present for a moment or two before ideas *about* Life took over again. But a moment or two can show that there is a big difference between being lost in ideas and being fully present for Life. Curiosity is one of the main tools you can use to cut through the clouds in your mind in order to really experience your life.

Curiosity is the zoom lens of your mind that can let go of the wide focus that includes past and future in order to be present for what is *right now.* The healing power of curiosity is beyond your wildest imaginations. If you discover the willingness, the insight, and the courage to really look at what is happening *right now* in your life, not only to look but to *see*, you will be healed.

Most of us have left curiosity far behind in our childhoods. Rather than being present for Life, our curiosity is captured by a constant stream of thought. From the moment we open our eyes in the morning until after we close them at night, attention attaches itself to all of the thoughts in our heads and then goes wherever they go – with hardly a thought about thinking. It is said that we can have as many as 65,000 thoughts a day, and 95% of them are repeats from the day before! You'd think we'd get bored, but we don't. All of these thoughts build a fascinating story in our heads that is full of all sorts of themes, the core one being, "How to get it all together." None of this story is new. It is all based on the past projected onto the future, having very little to do with what is happening right here and right now.

Within this story is hardly a drop of curiosity. Instead, there are habitual patterns of thought chasing themselves through our heads and our attention follows them like a dog chases its tail. If you had a little window on your

> *Our biggest compulsion is to struggle with Life, always trying to make ourselves and our lives different than what they are!*

forehead and could watch the stream of thought that passes through your mind all day, you would see what I am talking about. You would see your constant search for peace, believing that if you make yourself into the *right* kind of person and then make your life into the *right* kind of life that you will know the peace that you long for.

This endless maze of trying is often so subtle we hardly notice it except as a faint undercurrent of unease with the periodic flare ups of everyday struggles. When it does explode into the *big* struggles of our lives – and this happens to all of us – we can begin to see how desperately this story in our heads tries to control Life. We can also see how much it loves to judge how we are doing and how easily it makes problems out of the smallest of things.

We could say that our biggest compulsion is to struggle with Life, always trying to make ourselves and our lives different than what they are! It could also be said that all of the other compulsions we engage in during our lives are an attempt to numb ourselves out from the endless wanting, fearing, judging and trying that happens in our heads all day long. And yet right underneath our busy, busy minds is a world of ease, connection, wisdom, and love. It is our birthright to know and live from this wellspring within us.

Becoming Free

If your mind is like most people's minds, you are asking now, "Yes, but how do I get rid of this struggling mind so I can know the peace that is waiting for me?" The answer we usually get is that we must do away with struggle. But that would just be more struggle!

One of the core skills for moving out of the attic of the struggling mind and back into the peace and joy of the house of our *being* is *curiosity.* Why curiosity? It is a neutral force, one that has nothing to do with struggle. It doesn't want nor need to change anything. Curiosity simply wants to see *what is,* for it comes from the wisest part of ourselves that knows that no matter what is happening in our lives, it is all workable.

Curiosity is focused attention. *It is neither for nor against whatever it focuses on.* It is simply interested in what is happening right now, whether it is a feeling inside of ourselves, the beauty of a sunset, or the tears of a loved one. *Because it doesn't want to change anything, it takes us out of the struggling mind and taps us into our wellspring of deep knowing.* Its beauty is that it is so simple, and yet it is powerful beyond our ordinary comprehension.

> *Curiosity is neither for nor against whatever it focuses on. It is simply interested in what is happening right now.*

As young children, we were naturally curious and were engaged with whatever was happening right here and right now. But as we grew up, we were taught that our power came from fixing, changing, dominating, and controlling our lives, and especially our compulsions. This has kept us on an endless pendulum of controlling only to be controlled. The power of our attention has become like weak, winter sunlight. When we relearn how to be curious about what is happening, it is like putting the weak, winter sunlight through a magnifying glass. That light can literally start a fire!

I put this skill first, because of all the skills we will explore, it is one of the most important ones to have on the journey back to the house of our *being*. *The quickest way to the healing that we long for is to stop striving for results and start meeting things as they are.* There is a direct relationship between the quality of our curiosity and the depth of our healing. Curiosity cuts through the war in which we have been engaging with our compulsions – a war that we will never win – and gives us the nourishment and the information we need in order to heal.

The Gifts of Curiosity

Curiosity is the cornerstone of the ability to engage with our compulsions rather than being lost in endlessly trying to manage them. There are four ways that curiosity can help us to heal and be healed by our compulsions:

1. It brings us into immediate contact with Life, nourishing us with the ease and contentment that is always there.

2. It gives us information that is necessary in dismantling the web of compulsions.

3. Pure attention is the great transformer. When it makes contact with the thoughts and feelings that are fueling our compulsions, it transforms these formerly unwanted guests back into the free-flowing energy of aliveness and joy.

75

It awakens the wellspring within us that is our source of wisdom, peace and love.

If we are willing to look – to be curious about our compulsions rather than reactive – we can know freedom. Let us explore each of these aspects of curiosity in depth.

⟨1⟩ Contact With Life

We all long to be fully connected to Life again. Rather than always trying to *do* Life, we want to relearn how to *be* Life. Because most of us have forgotten how to *be*, we carry an unspoken longing for a deep and nourishing connection with ourselves and with our lives.

In this homesickness for ourselves we become vulnerable to compulsions. They promise us the sun, the moon and the stars and leave frustration, self judgment and despair in their wake.

The reason our compulsions never truly satisfy us is that they cannot give us what we want them to give – the contentment, ease, and joy that comes from being fully connected to Life. I invite you to explore the present moment again, taking this experience a bit deeper so that you can know what I am talking about.

> *When you finish reading this italicized section, put down the book and explore with deep curiosity exactly where you are.*
>
> *All of the millions of moments of your life have led you to this day, to this place you are sitting in, and to this moment. Everything, absolutely everything, about this moment is completely brand new. You will never, ever again experience Life as it is right now.*
>
> *Open to it!*
>
> *See the quality of the light. Hear the symphony of sounds as they cascade all around you. Feel the river of sensations that is your body. This is it. This is the only moment of your life that is totally brand new, the only moment where you are truly alive. In this doorway between past and future, what is here to meet you is ease, contentment, and, even though you may not recognize it yet, joy. Whenever your mind takes over, for these few moments, let it go and open. Explore Life as it is right now as deeply as you can, and when you are ready, pick up the book and begin reading again.*

You have just experienced moments of pure curiosity. It probably wasn't continuous. You had moments where you were using your attention to be fully present for Life. You also had moments where your attention crawled back into the attic of your mind with ideas such as, "This is boring." or "I am not doing this right." or "I need to take a painting class in order to paint the light." Off you go into ideas *about* Life, leaving the present behind. Every time you go back into the attic of your mind, the living moment of your life goes by untouched and unused. But the house of your *being* is always here, waiting for you, right below the endless stories in your head.

Cultivating curiosity moves us beyond *ideas about Life* into fully engaging with the present moment and all of the wonder, joy, and support that reside there. *It gives us what we have been looking for through our compulsions.* When we try to get to the end of our To Do list or reach for another cigarette or sneak another piece of food, that is not what we are truly wanting. *What we are longing for is Life.* We long for those moments when we move beyond thinking *about* Life and use our minds instead to truly connect. These are moments where our minds, bodies, and hearts are in the same place at the same time. While our minds frantically search for this experience through our compulsions, what they are seeking is right here, right now, in this moment *no matter where we are, no matter what is happening.*

Joseph Campbell, author of *The Power of Myth*, understood this truth when he said,

> *People say what we're all seeking is a meaning for life. I don't think that's what we're really seeking. I think that what we're seeking is an experience of being alive so that our life experiences on the purely physical plane will have resonance within our innermost being and reality, so that we actually feel the rapture of being alive.*

To be purely present for something, whether it is the beauty of a flower or the feeling of grief welling up inside of us, taps us into the rapture of being alive. The alertness of curiosity transforms the smallest things and the most ordinary moments into the bright and vibrant *aliveness* that they truly are. At the same time, it takes the sense of overwhelm out of the deepest of pains, allowing these pains the space to flow through us like they did when we were young. Because curiosity allows things to be, we can finally see the absolute perfection of this moment, no matter what is happening.

Just a little bit of paying pure attention to whatever is happening right here and right now – the smell of a newly mown lawn, the taste of a ripe and succulent strawberry, the sound of a symphony of song birds – will tell us in no uncertain terms that most of us are starving for pure experience. We

> *Our starvation for the nourishment of pure connection with Life makes us vulnerable to the cravings of our compulsion and their chant of "more, more, more."*

knew pure connection with Life when we were young. Both in the womb and while growing up, our whole body made immediate contact with Life – mouth, hands, skin, toes, and even our nose. As children, we loved to touch and be touched by Life. We rolled on the ground, we had fun with water, and we definitely knew that our tongue loved to play with our food.

As an adult, our contact with Life is very limited and we have lost sight of the wonders of our senses. When was the last time you went barefoot in soft, velvety grass, or lay on the Earth and listened to the sounds of the birds, or swung on a swing in pure joy? When was the last time you really tasted your food or truly saw your loved one's face?

As adults, we don't *see* things as much as we *think* about what we see. We don't *taste* things as much as we *shovel* and *swallow*. And we usually are so lost in our minds that we rarely hear the astounding symphony of Life. This puts us in the middle of a life of isolation, starving for pure experience – much as a person imprisoned in a dungeon hungers for the light.

This starvation mode makes us vulnerable to the cravings of our compulsions and their chant of "more, more, more." What we are starving for is the nourishment of pure connection with Life! No wonder we get compulsive! One bite of a delicious piece of cake is not enough, so we take bite after bite, hoping to make immediate contact with the wonders of taste, only to have the compulsion take us over as we shove more and more into our emptiness. This is not just true for over-eating. All compulsions are an attempt to fill our inner emptiness so that we may know a few moments of peace. But it never lasts because the peace we long for comes from a deep and abiding connection with ourselves and with Life.

The aliveness in us that comes from pure experience has never been lost. It has only been covered over by all the shoulds, ought tos, have tos, can'ts, and won'ts that are the hallmark of the attic.

There is a story from my book *Belonging to Life* about the first time I truly understood the difference between being caught in my mind and being truly present for Life. I was attending my first meditation retreat which involved ten days of silence in the wilds of Canada, and it felt like I was being asked to do the Iron Man Triathlon without having trained! It also rained for nine of the ten days, and the only heat was in the meditation hall. Boy, did my mind struggle! If I hadn't ridden with another woman, I would have left.

On the eighth day, I was doing walking meditation in the Provincial State Park next door to the retreat center. In pouring down rain, with a garbage bag tied around my waist so I could keep a semblance of dryness, I was

> *Every step of the way, curiosity gave me the nourishment I had formerly been trying to get through my compulsions.*

walking back and forth while my mind was having a meltdown. "I don't know how to do this. I can't do it right. I never do anything right. There is no way out of the endless struggle of my life." I was crying, and it felt like more tears were pouring out of me than raindrops from the sky.

Then, as I walked under a tree, a huge drop of water was dislodged from the limb above my head. It fell into a puddle beside my foot, making a sound that was different than the sound of the pouring rain, and it captured my attention. As I watched the beauty of the ripples dancing across the puddle, I was moved by wonder. One moment I was lost in my struggling mind and the next moment I was fully *here*. My heart and my senses opened in delight. The rain, rather than being the enemy, became some of the most beautiful music I had ever heard. The formerly dark and brooding forest became a land bursting with Life.

Just a little bit of curiosity about what was happening *right now* brought me out of the narrow confines of my struggling mind, allowing me to make immediate contact with Life. I rested in that deep peace for at least an hour before my struggles took over. I now knew that there was something more than the endless struggle I had been lost in for decades!

Through this experience, I recognized the deep hunger that resides inside of me and inside of every single human being. This is the hunger to again be available to my own life; not an idea about it, but the real thing. The magic and the mystery of those moments in the cul-de-sac were a *keyhole* glimpse into the world of aliveness and joy that is our birthright. It was enough to keep me going for years, as I slowly was able to see and then weave back into my wholeness all the parts of my ancient belief systems, which fueled my compulsions and kept me almost completely cut off from Life.

Every step of the way, curiosity gave me the nourishment I had formerly been trying to get through my compulsions. Each moment that I was curious transformed my life from a B-grade black-and-white movie into a Panavision®, Dolby® surround-sound, Technicolor® wonder. The more present I was for Life, the less interesting my compulsions became.

⟨2⟩ Information

Life is not a random series of events, disconnected from one another. It is a highly intelligent and intentional process, one where every experience is speaking to us, giving us the clues to our healing. This is especially true with our compulsions. They are not just uncontrollable urges that are out to get us. They are messages from the depths of our being and they are loaded with information. Rather than being lost in them, if we learn how to be curious about what is going on before, during, or after a wave of compulsion, we can gain valuable insights that will allow us to heal and be healed by our compulsions.

Krishnamurti, the author of many books about what happens when we are able to be with *what is* rather than always trying to make it different, wrote about the power of observation (his name for *curiosity*). In this quote, he is writing about fear, but we could easily replace that word with *compulsions* and it would speak directly to what we are exploring here.

> *It is not that you must be free from fear. The moment you try to free yourself from fear, you create resistance against fear. Resistance in any form does not end fear. What is needed, rather than running away or controlling or suppressing or any other resistance, is understanding fear; that means watch it, learn about it, come directly into contact with it. We are to learn* about *fear, not how to escape from it, not how to resist it.*

Becoming free of compulsions means being *present* for them, rather than trying to *escape* them. We have tried to escape from our compulsions many, many times, only to strengthen them. Healing comes about through learning how to be curiously present for our compulsions, watching them in action, discovering the clues to our healing that are hidden in their depth.

This kind of watching is amazingly powerful. Imagine being lost in one of those complex mazes that are sometimes created in cornfields. See yourself turning corner after corner, going around in endless loops, only to discover numerous dead ends. Feel the overwhelming frustration and eventual despair that comes from 'no way out.' This has been our usual experience around compulsions, controlling them only to be controlled. Now imagine someone arriving with a

> *Healing comes about through learning how to be curiously present for our compulsions, watching them in action, discovering the clues to our healing that are hidden in their depths.*

hot air balloon and sending down a ladder. Up you go! From this vantage point, it becomes easy to see the pathway out of the maze.

That is what curiosity can do for us with our compulsions. As we learn how to be curious, we can begin to find our way out of the maze of compulsions – for the clues are always there. As we look, they will reveal to us the step-by-step process that will take us back into a nourishing connection with ourselves and with Life.

What We Can Discover

As you begin to watch, the first thing to notice is that *compulsions happen in waves. You are not always compulsive*! It is easy to miss this fact because you are so thrilled when a compulsion is gone that you try to tell yourself that it will never, ever return again. When you do this, there is no part of you that is alert to the onset of a new wave.

As you recognize this, you can then see that compulsions come in waves and that each wave has three distinct phases: the build up, the middle where we become lost in the wave, and then the aftermath. For reasons that will become clear later, we will look at them in reverse.

❖ If you watch as a wave is building up, it promises to take you away from whatever pain you are experiencing and deposit you right at the feet of bliss. We follow this belief just like the children in the fairy tale followed the pied piper.

❖ After a few moments of bliss – the first puff of a cigarette, the soft glow of an alcoholic buzz – the *more, more, more* kicks in and the wave gets out of control becoming *not enough, not enough, not enough.*

❖ After the wave moves through, you find yourself beached and be-draggled upon the shore of your consequences.

Rather than being helplessly caught up in each phase of the wave, as you learn how to pay attention, you will gain information that will allow you to make clear and kind choices, even in the face of a strong wave of compulsion. And even if your compulsion doesn't seem to come in waves, you can use the skills that are suggested for each part of the wave any time you become aware of being caught in your compulsion.

Later in the book, we will explore how to stay curious no matter where we are in a wave of compulsion. For now, I want to give you a glimpse of the healing that curiosity can bring during each of these phases. We'll start with the third one, because it is usually after the third phase that we notice we have gotten caught in our compulsion and so it is the easiest place for us to begin paying attention.

❖ As the wave begins to build

When we have learned to respect and listen to our compulsion, we become attuned to its rhythms and can feel a wave just as it is beginning. This is the time where we have the greatest influence and the greatest possibility of making wise and kind choices. At times, we will be able to access our *Empowered No* and the wave of compulsions will evaporate. At other times, the urge to be compulsive will be stronger, but it will be amenable to negotiation. Then there will be times when our compulsion will be absolutely adamant about its need to be compulsive. We can then choose to be compulsive, entering the wave with curiosity and gaining many valuable pieces of information all the way through.

❖ During the wave

As we begin to trust and listen to the great teacher of compulsion, this opens the possibility of remembering curiosity in the middle of a wave of compulsion and recognizing what we are doing. "Here I am," our awareness says, "in the middle of a wave of compulsion trying to deaden my feelings again, and this always makes me feel worse in the long run."

Recognizing that getting lost in our compulsion has never brought us the peace we long for gives us the courage to meet the feelings that are causing us to be compulsive in the first place. For it is guaranteed that if we are trying to distract ourselves through compulsion, the feelings that fuel it are very close to the surface.

If we can be present for these feelings rather than becoming lost in them, even for a moment or two, they begin their transformation back into the free flowing energy they came from and no longer fuel our compulsions.

❖ After the wave has passed through

After a wave of compulsion has passed through is when most of us can begin to learn how to be curious about what is happening within us. As a wave passes through and the cravings have subsided enough for us to feel ourselves again, instead of paying attention to what is going on, however, we usually get caught in self-judgment, "I did it again!" and despair, "I will never stop!"

Being sidetracked in this way, we don't allow ourselves to experience the truth that compulsions take away much more than they give. We may know it intellectually, but to feel with great clarity what happens after a wave of compulsion moves through allows us to face the truth that this behavior brings only devastation in its wake. This is true whether it be the rages of a food hangover, the guilt of unskillful sexuality, the cloud of fear after a buying spree, or the imbalance in our body from drinking too much.

There are compulsions that don't seem to come in clear and concise waves – you may feel that you overwork all the time or perceive yourself to be a constant worrier. You can still have moments where you recognize that you are paying a heavy price for being compulsive in this way.

To really *experience* the price we pay is invaluable information. For when compulsions cast their spell again, promising that if we follow them they will give us all the comfort and peace we long for, we can remind ourselves of the price we will pay for believing what they are promising.

⟨3⟩ Transformation

Imagine what it would be like if you found a tool that could clear up your most challenging feelings just like the morning sun dispels the fog. Imagine what you would feel if you could transform your anxiety, anger and despair into the free-flowing aliveness of joy. That tool is curiosity.

The pure attention of curiosity is an amazing alchemical process. It turns the *base metals* of all that we don't like about our lives into clarity and joy. It can transform the darkest of emotional states and even the cruelest of thoughts. This happens when we learn how to bring the light of compassionate attention first to the act of compulsion and then to the deep feelings that fuel it.

I call this *Treasure Hunting*, for when we can be present for what is happening with our compulsions, we discover the treasures that have always been hidden in their depths. We will explore this in greater detail in the *Treasure Hunting* chapter. Right now, let me share with you a story that will give you a glimpse into how the light of curiosity can transform not only our relationship to our compulsions, but also the feelings that are fueling it.

I was working with a client who had seen the futility of trying to control her eating, but hadn't yet learned how to bring the healing light of attention into whatever she was experiencing. Having had a falling-out with her father, she hadn't talked to him in quite a while. It was through a friend of the family that she discovered the health challenges he was experiencing. Her first thought was, "I don't want to deal with this. I have done all the healing that I want to do with him and I will forget I even heard that he was ill."

As much as the mind believes that it can compartmentalize experiences, it can't. It is like telling a jury to disregard the supposedly inadmissible fact that the defendant has killed other people in the past!

Two days after hearing about her father, she noticed a very heavy feeling in her chest. Not yet having the skills of paying attention, she ignored it, hoping it would go away. That night she found herself lost in a huge wave of compulsion, and by the time she arrived at my office, the flavor of her sharing was, "When am I going to stop this bad behavior?" As she looked at her experiences leading up to this binge, the information about her father came out.

In the safety of our relationship, the heaviness in her chest revealed itself again, along with deep resistance to experiencing whatever feelings were there. Rather than running away this time, I invited her to close her eyes and bring her attention to her body, describing what was there. Immediately her body took a deep breath and the whole experience lightened as she met the sensations of a tight chest and a band of tension in her throat. With the safety of pure attention, healing tears flowed as she experienced a lifetime of grief from having an unavailable father.

Not only did her attention free up these boxed up feelings, it also brought her important information straight from the heart of her experience. She could see the validity of her grief and understand that it was one of the core feelings that fueled her waves of compulsion. When she met the depth of sadness that resided in her chest, her relationship with her binge had changed. Rather than judging it, staying caught in a cycle of self-hatred and despair, she understood why she had binged in the first place. This aware-ness left her spacious and merciful with herself and much more willing to be curious when she was compulsive. Eventually this curiosity will take her to the place where she can be attentive to these feelings without needing to numb herself with a binge.

◇4◇ Awaken the Wellspring

Imagine what it would be like to know with absolute certainty that you are not alone. And imagine what it would be like to be in contact with a source of Wisdom within you that is guiding you every step of the way. This is the healing that compulsions are bringing you – nothing less than a partnership with the Wisdom at the heart of Life!

Remember what it was like in the story of *The House of Your Being* where, in the dark and fertile basement of your *being*, you came across the circular room? As its walls dissolved, revealing a place of such lush beauty and flowing water, you probably felt pure joy. Well, that is not just a wonderful fantasy. That is what you discover on the journey back to yourself.

There is a wellspring of wisdom within each one of us that is the source of our deepest knowing. When we are in contact with its healing presence, we can accept ourselves as we are –

> *When we are in contact with our inner wellspring's healing presence, we can accept ourselves as we are – both our strengths and our weaknesses.*

both our strengths and our weaknesses. We can also trust ourselves and we can trust Life, for inherent in our wellspring is an inner radar that can guide us skillfully through our lives. People call it a gut knowing but it is much more than that. It is a grounding in ourselves and a grounding in Life.

The seat of this wellspring is our belly. Most of us are lost in our heads, lost in ideas about how our lives should be. Because our center of gravity is in our heads, we are not grounded in our bodies and thus are unable to listen to the wisest parts of ourselves.

How we awaken our wellspring again is through curiosity. Every time we bring our attention out of what was and what will be, and instead become curious about exactly what we are experiencing right now, we energize our wellspring. Every time we feel our body rather than think about it, we also awaken this wellspring.

No matter how confusing our lives are or how lost we feel, our wellspring is waiting for us in the basement (belly) of our being. It may be blocked from view by all the boxes of hidden feelings we have stashed down there. But it is still there. Through our ability to be curious, along with Three Questions we will be exploring in Skill #5, we can clear the boxes and awaken our wellspring again. We can then know a deep and abiding relationship with the Wisdom at the heart of Life.

The beauty of curiosity is that it is so simple. You don't need to do anything with it except pay attention. Once you have made contact with what is happening inside of yourself, you don't need to change what you discover there. You don't need to figure out where it came from or even try to get rid of it. Your focused attention is enough. In fact, it is more than enough. It is nothing less than the healing you have longed for.

This drives the mind crazy for a while because it is so used to doing *some-*

thing to stop the behavior! Healing doesn't come from changing anything! It comes from the relationship itself – from the ability to be present for exactly what is happening.

Can you remember a time when you were upset about something in your life and somebody just listened to you? They hardly needed to say a word and yet something lifted inside of you after being heard. *That lifting comes from the power of focused attention.*

Cultivating Curiosity

Instead of being curious about what is happening right now, our attention is usually lost somewhere inside of our heads, moving from past to future and back again at lightning speeds. Even though we watch TV or read a book and say we are paying attention, mostly what we do is mindlessly fall into the experience. And even when we are listening to another person, believing we are paying attention to them, we are usually paying attention to our reactions to what they are saying. This is one of the main reasons we can stay so vulnerable to compulsions. We don't see what is going on, both inside and outside of ourselves.

Curiosity offers a completely different experience. *Curiosity is acceptance coupled with a passionate interest about whatever is happening right now.* Curiosity is the willingness to be as present as you possibly can, intimately exploring whatever is going on right now. Under the light of pure attention, healing begins to automatically happen.

As we explore ways to cultivate curiosity, notice what is being offered and work with what interests you. There will be some practices that will call to you and others that won't. Trust your own instinct. As you do, your own unique way back into curiosity will reveal itself.

A Returning Practice

In order to gather the gifts of curiosity, we need to strengthen the muscle of our attention. This is what I call a *returning practice*, and it is very simple. It is about choosing a focus and then returning to it whenever your attention is captured by the thoughts in your head. Anything can be a focus – sounds, a pain in your knee, the taste of your food, or the rising and falling of your breath.

Let us explore what this is like in the following exercise:

After you read the following paragraph, put down the book and close your eyes for a few minutes, listening as if you have just arrived on planet Earth. Every single sound is completely brand new, coming straight out of the heart of mystery. Be fascinated. This is the music of your life. Hear loud sounds and soft sounds. Hear the ones that are close and the ones that are far away. Whenever you notice that you are not listening to the sounds, without judgment return your attention to the sounds. If your attention wanders a lot, count how many different sounds you hear. When you are ready, open your eyes.

You will notice as you do this that at times you will be purely present for the sounds of your life. Then, without noticing, your attention will slip back into the thoughts in your head. No judgment. You have only been lost in thought most of your life. Every time you bring your attention back to the sounds, you strengthen the muscle of your attention. The more you do this, the stronger it will become, increasing your ability to be curious about *what is*. It also becomes easier to see that there is a very big difference between being caught in ideas about Life and being with the living experience of it. People are often amazed when they first begin a returning practice to not only see how busy their mind is about essentially nothing, but also to recognize that an unattended mind has a tendency to stay caught in struggle.

The key to a returning practice is to know that your attention will drift off into your thoughts over and over again. Big surprise! You have only been lost in thought for most of your life. The mind loves to think about life's dramas rather than experiencing what is happening right now. *The healing of a returning practice isn't in staying on the focus. It comes from the willingness to return.* And it is important to return gently. There is no need to judge how lost you get in your mind or to jerk yourself back.

Just as you go to a gym in order to strengthen your muscles, it is helpful to set aside time everyday where you strengthen the muscle of your attention. For most of you, what will work best is just a few minutes every morning before your day and your mind begin to pick up speed. Find a quiet spot in your house, one where you won't be interrupted. Sit comfortably with both feet on the ground and with your spine as straight as possible. Then close your eyes and chose one focus. It could be the listening to the sounds around you, paying attention

> *The healing of a returning practice isn't in staying on the focus. It comes from the willingness to return.*

to the rising and falling of your breath, or watching a candle flame. Be willing to return to your focus over and over again whenever you find your attention drifting off. Start with five minutes, and as the muscle of your attention becomes stronger, try extending the time.

Know that you won't do this perfectly. Some days it will be easier to stay with your focus than other days. As one of my teachers once said, "If you sit for an hour and only return to your breath once in that hour, it is time well spent." Of course that is an exaggeration, but it invites you not to judge how you are doing or even how you are progressing. Just be willing to return. Know that a few moments of returning your attention to exactly *what is* will transform your life in ways that your heart deeply longs for.

Returning Throughout the Day

If you aren't inclined to sit with your eyes closed, choose one thing to do everyday and do it with curiosity. It could be your morning shower, bringing your attention back to the sensations of the water cascading down your back, the tingle of your skin under the roughness of the washcloth, and the sweet smell of the soap. Ask yourself over and over again, "In this moment, what am I experiencing?" Every time the mind goes off into the past or the future, bring it back into curiosity about the sensations of the shower.

We can make a returning practice out of most anything in our lives. You could take a deep breath at every stop light, experiencing it as fully as you can. Or you could choose your morning walk or run, coming back to the experience of your feet making contact with the Earth. Every time I use the bathroom, my gift to myself is to wash my hands with full attention. All the bathrooms of the world are now my portable monasteries, places where I return fully to Life!

Moments of returning throughout the day are like drops of water that eventually become a trickle, then a stream, and finally a whole river of awakening that brings you to the healing you long for.

At moments it may seem like returning to the water on your back while taking a shower or the rising and falling of your breath won't help to transform anything in your life. Don't discount the power of even a few moments of *returning* during the day. Those moments are like drops of water that eventually become a trickle, then a stream, and finally a whole river of awakening that brings you to the healing you long for.

Moments of pure attention teach you how to make contact with Life, a contact that you are deeply hungry for. Attention and returning will teach you how to listen, discovering that all of the clues to your healing are in the experience you are having right now. Attention and returning also show you how to relax into the present without trying to fill it up with endless details, discovering that what you were truly longing for is the present anyway! Finally, attention and returning reveal to you how to let go of the reactive mind that keeps you caught on the pendulum of control, moving you to the responsive mind that knows how to make kind and skillful choices.

◇ Deepening Your Curiosity Practice

We need to be gentle as we invite ourselves to be curious for we have been caught in the struggling mind for a long time. But remember, *the power is in the returning, not in the staying on the focus.* The more you return, the more fascinated you become by *what is* rather than *what was* or *what will be.* You then become interested in discovering what it is that keeps you from an alive and joyous engagement with Life. What is it in your mind that is so fascinating and compelling that it feels like it is more important than being present for Life? It is possible to cultivate enough curiosity that you can see all the familiar struggles in your head rather than being lost in them.

In the beginning, this can be a little bit like trying to see your own face without the benefit of a mirror. You have been so close to your thoughts that it is hard to see what they are doing. In order to create space, there is a wonderful technique you can add to your Returning Practice. This technique will begin to develop the part of yourself that can see your thoughts rather than always being lost in them. Let's explore it now.

> *After you read this exercise, close your eyes and choose a focus. When you notice that your attention has left your focus and is again lost in thought, take a moment before you return to your focus to notice whether your thoughts are about the past or the future. Squeeze your left hand and say "past" silently to yourself whenever you notice yourself thinking about the past and then return to your focus. Squeeze your right hand and say "future" whenever you notice you are paying attention to the future and then return to your focus. If it takes more than a split second to recognize past or future or if you find yourself just spacing out, squeeze both hands and say "thinking, thinking" and then return to your focus.*

This practice teaches you how to be curious about what your mind is doing.

> *What passes through our heads all day long is a story about Life rather than the full and immediate experience of Life.*

Where there is awareness, there is choice about what you are going to pay attention to. Where there is choice, there is freedom.

As your curiosity deepens, whenever you find yourself off your focus, you can take this ability to watch your thoughts to a deeper level. This happens by naming exactly what *thought* is doing. The things that you are most likely to see going in your head are *planning, remembering, fearing, wanting, struggling, judging,* and just *spacing out*. There are myriad other things the mind does, but these labels will give you a start. When you see what the mind is doing, note that action silently to yourself by saying it twice (like "planning, planning") and then return to your focus. Again, if it takes more than just a split second to see what is going on, simply say "thinking, thinking," and return to your breath.

The more you watch what your thoughts are doing, the more you come to realize that what passes through your head all day long is a *story about Life* rather than the full and immediate *experience of* Life. This story has been built through experiences in your life, with the experiences when you were young creating the core themes of this story.

The more you watch the story, the more your heart opens to how much wanting and fearing you have lived in your whole life. And the more your heart opens, the more you realize this truth: *Who you are is that which can see the story, not the story itself.*

This is the freedom that compulsions are bringing to us. Whenever they are strong, the core girders of our story are close to the surface, available for the light of our compassionate and curious attention. And in that attention, they are dispelled like fog is dispelled by the warmth of the sun. And as the fog of our story lifts, we find ourselves connected to ourselves and to Life in a way that touches us to our core.

◇ Weather Reporting

What we are doing here is returning to ourselves – not an idea of who we are, but the truth of our experience in any given moment. This is the doorway to freedom. We have been gone for a long time and there are a lot of boxed-up feelings and habitual thought patterns that need to be met in the light of our curiosity. As we meet them, we can know the freedom and ease that comes from living in the house of ***being***.

We have spent our lives running away from our boxed feelings and habitual thought patterns, so there will be times when we won't have the curiosity or the insight that are needed in order to not fall into them. As we are turning the light of curiosity onto our immediate experience, it is helpful to check in, both with ourselves and with another person, in order to claim the truth of our experience. I call this kind of check-in *weather reporting,* for our experience is as variable and as uncontrollable as the weather. Just as a weather person doesn't try to change the weather, our check-in with ourselves is about reporting on what is happening, not trying to make it be different than what it is.

The first and most available way to weather report is to speak the truth of our experience to ourselves. We can do this silently or out loud. It is very powerful to be lost in a reactive state of mind and to simply acknowledge where you are. You can even do this when you are confused about what your experience is, for the truth is you can't see what your experience is!

If you can understand that weather reporting isn't about changing anything, you will begin to get a glimpse of how powerful it is to claim what is going on without the need to judge it, fear it or change it. I find I do this a lot while driving. If something is blocking my peace, I start by asking the question, "In this moment, what am I experiencing?" I then bring my attention back to my immediate experience and, because I have been doing this for a number of years, it is fairly easy to see exactly what is going on. Since I don't need to struggle with it, everything calms down quite quickly and I am again in contact with my inner wellspring of wisdom.

We can also weather report by writing down our experiences. The most powerful way I have discovered is to weather report by keeping an *Awareness Diary*. In this diary we make three columns on a piece of paper. We put on top of the first column *What is happening right now*? On top of the second column, we put *What is happening with my compulsion*? On the third column we write *What am I experiencing inside*?

> *It is very powerful to be lost in a reactive state of mind and to simply acknowledge where you are.*

I saw the full benefit of an *Awareness Diary* when a woman in one of my groups began to keep track of her food intake. At first it was very difficult for her to write down what she was eating because every time she had done this before, it was to try to control her input of food. This time she was writing it down simply to become aware of what was going on. When she began noting what was

> *Healing lies not in what is going to happen, but in what is happening right now.*

going on in her external and internal life when she was eating, she could see very clearly some ancient patterns that were running her. The *Awareness Diary* also moved her out of judging what she was doing into a much more compassionate relationship with herself.

We can also write our experiences in the manner that Julia Cameron suggests in her book, *The Artist's Way.* The core intent of this kind of writing is to allow the pen to move across the page continuously so that the censor in your head doesn't stop the flow. The more you do it the more you become connected to yourself. You discover parts of yourself that have never had a voice. They not only get heard, you get to hear the wisdom that they have been trying to share with you for years.

Weather reporting with another person can be done with either a friend or a counselor. This person is your listening partner. They are not there to fix you, change you, or help you to understand anything. They are there to simply and profoundly listen. As you speak the truth of your experience, you are not only being heard, but also the space is being created so you can hear yourself. The benefit of choosing a counselor is that a counselor is more likely to be trained in the art of listening. The benefit of choosing a friend is that a friend is usually more available when challenges come up.

It is very important to wisely choose the person to whom you weather report. This person needs to understand the power of pure listening. Just as we don't listen to weather reports in order to change the weather, this person shouldn't try to make you be any different than you are. If you don't have someone in your life that knows how to do this, you may need to educate your listener. Before you speak, tell this person that all you want is deep listening and acknowledgment of what is being heard. Ask the person to refrain from giving advice, offering pity, or expressing judgment in any way.

This person also needs to be someone you can trust. You need to check this out with them before sharing. This trust includes that person's commitment to never speak to another person about any of what you share unless you give your permission. It also includes their commitment to not judge you for what you will be revealing. These commitments create the safety you need in order to discover that you have practically every possible thought and emotion available to a human being. If you can speak the truth of what you are experiencing without fear of judgment or tattle tailing, not only will you be heard, but you will also be returned to the place of true healing, which is the compassionate recognition of your own experience.

Whether you choose a friend, a counselor, or both (Why not? You deserve it!), the key to speaking your truth and discovering the space to listen to yourself is to let go of beginning a sentence with the words *I am*. When you say "I am sad," or "I am mad," or "I am hurting,," you narrow your perception of yourself to just those experiences and lose perspective in the process.

A better way to say it is: "My body is," "my emotions are," or "my mind is." This slight linguistic shift creates space where you can relate to what is happening rather than being lost in it. This shift from *I am* to *it is* allows you to discover a jewel of freedom. You are so much more than your experiences. The core of you is awareness itself – the ability to see *what is.*

It is also skillful, when you are talking or writing about another person with whom you are having difficulty, to speak or write about the *feeling* you are experiencing, rather than speaking or writing about that other *person*. This is the difference between saying, "George makes me so angry. I don't know why I ever married him." and saying, "When I think about George, I feel judgment and frustration inside of me." Rather than speaking about George, *you are speaking about what was brought up inside of you through relationship with him.*

I also invite you to weather report as you read this book. What I am offering to you is not about arriving at a place where you are cured. That is the old style of thinking where your healing happens sometime in the future. This process is about inviting you into relationship with *what is right now,* for *healing lies not in what is going to happen, but in what is happening right now.* This book will empower you and confuse you. It will bring waves of joy and sometimes fear. It may reveal distrust and self-judgment along with hope and mercy. In fact, it is designed to do so. Every single experience you have in reading this book is a part of your healing, and it can be skillful to name to yourself over and over again what is happening inside of you as you read.

Learning how to be curious so that we can be intimately and passionately present for Life is an unfolding process, the work of a lifetime. Along the way we gather patience, compassion, trust, and the willingness to show up for the lives we have been given. The payoff is nothing less than the rediscovery of the rapture of being fully alive. So I invite you to cultivate moments of pure attention throughout your day. Be curious about what is happening inside of you *and* what is happening outside of you, knowing that in each moment of curiosity, you are healing not only your own life, but also the world.

Core Ideas in Skill #1 – Curiosity:

❖ Becoming free of compulsion happens through being present for it rather than trying to escape it.

❖ If you discover the willingness, the insight, and the courage to really look at what is happening right now in your life, not only to look but to see, you will be healed; for all the clues to your healing are in the experience you are having right now!

❖ Curiosity is an alert acceptance coupled with a passionate interest about whatever is happening right now.

❖ Moments of pure curiosity are powerful beyond your wildest imaginations. Curiosity is neither for nor against whatever it focuses on. It is simply interested in what is happening right now.

❖ The quickest way to the healing that you long for is to stop striving for results and start meeting things as they are.

❖ Lasting healing comes from being curious rather than controlling.

❖ Through curiosity you can learn to bring the light of compassionate attention first to the act of compulsion and then to the deep feelings that fuel it.

❖ The beauty of curiosity is that it is so simple; you don't need to do anything with it except pay attention.

❖ It is easy to get lost in a story in your head, a story *about Life* rather than *Life itself.* You then don't see that right beneath your busy, busy mind is a world of ease, aliveness, wisdom, and love.

❖ A Returning Practice will help you to cultivate pure attention. The key is to know that your attention will drift off and that the healing power in a returning practice is from the gentle willingness to return to your focus.

❖ The healing of "weather reporting" and asking "In this moment, what am I experiencing?" lies not in what is going to happen, but in what is happening right now.

✦ SKILL 2: LOVING OURSELVES ✦ FROM THE INSIDE OUT

I am in love. I am joyfully and deeply in love. Her name is Emily and she is six years old. Before I got up to speak at a four-day conference in the beauty of the Cascade Mountains, I looked across the aisle and there, nestled in her mother's arms, was Emily. This image of a child totally safe in the world and completely loved touched me deeply. As the program began on stage, I kept turning my head and drinking in this nourishing image. Soon, Emily noticed my gaze and we began a love affair with our eyes that quickly developed into dancing and laughter, hugs, and a shared love of horses.

Matthew Fox was the keynote speaker, and the next day I felt compelled to attend his talk. This was a bit unusual because usually when I am teaching at a conference, I treasure my quiet time. But compelled I was and off I went! He spoke from his heart, moving us into a passionate willingness to hold vision for the world. He then had us dance this vision, and there was Emily beside me, so alive and so free. She reminded me of my own aliveness before I became withdrawn and frozen as a child.

After dancing our remembering, Matthew had us get down on our knees with our foreheads on the floor and wail for all of the forgetting that is happening in the world – our collective rage, bigotry, arrogance, self-judgment and on and on and on. About a minute into it, I had the urge to sit up and there was Emily, with tears streaming down her face, weaving through all of the kneeling people, desperately looking for her mother.

As she headed toward me, I put my arms out, but at the last moment she veered off to the left in search of mama. I felt a wave of grief that almost knocked me over. It only lasted for a few moments as wave after wave of relief came when I saw Emily's mom lift her right arm as if it were a wing and scoop Emily underneath her in an act of true mothering. Tears came roaring up from my heart and poured down my checks, tears for both the grief of not being able to comfort her and the joy of seeing her comforted.

I realized with stunning clarity that this was a metaphor for my own life. For most of it, I had wandered in disconnection, desperately looking for some place where I could rest in Love. The waves of grief were not only for all the times I felt so isolated and alone. They were also for all the times that I was unable to be present for myself. The wave of relief was because I now knew how to *lift my wing* and enfold *myself* in my own heart no matter what was happening in my life.

> *Love is accepting and honoring. It is allowing and understanding. It sees what is without any need to change it and its power to heal is phenomenal.*

On that floor with the voices of hundreds of people crashing all around me, my heart opened. I let in all the love that my struggling, judging, fearing mind had separated me from for so long. Waves of Love moved throughout my whole body as tears of joy cascaded down my face. Ahh, the healing of the heart, the healing of acceptance, the healing of Love.

For those few moments, I let in the Love that is at the heart of Life. I was opened beyond my struggling mind and Love flooded me with its presence. For thousands of years people from all parts of the globe, from all types of religion and from all walks of life, have spoken and written about what it is like when the truth of Love unfolds from the deepest part of themselves, filling them with its radiance. They *all* say that it is like coming home. By Love, I don't mean what most people mean when they use that word. That is why I capitalize it. By Love, I am pointing to the essence of our *being*, the Source of the wellspring within us, the Truth at the heart of Life.

It is not just some chosen few who can know and be loved by this Love. It is the birthright of every human being. To know the Love that is the essence of Life is why we have been given birth. We are here to know the truth of Love, to live the truth of Love, and to be loved by the truth of Love.

But if you are like me, for most of my life I didn't have a clue about the truth of Love. Even when I began to get an inkling of what was there, right beyond the struggling mind, I was like an infant without the ability to focus on Love and without the capacity to reach out and touch it.

What Takes Us Away

Why, when Love is our birthright, do most of us live our lives separate from its healing presence? One of the main reasons is that we have been trained in the exact opposite of Love. Love is accepting and honoring. It is allowing and understanding. *It sees what is without any need to change it* and its power to heal is phenomenal. Rather than dividing things, it unites, bringing them together in harmony, whether it is our families, the world, or parts of ourselves.

Instead of being taught how to be in a loving relationship with ourselves, we have been trained to struggle, dominate, judge, and compare. We believe that when we get it together we will know the Love that we long for – both inside of ourselves and on the outside. This is the *I am not/I should be* style of relating to ourselves that causes such pain. Remember the red pencil from grade school that was all over your schoolwork, saying excellent, good, fair, or poor? The power of that red pencil to determine how we perceived ourselves was so great!

In childhood we are taught to read and write, ride a bicycle and do our chores, but *we are not taught how to be okay with ourselves as we are.* So we become ongoing projects to ourselves, focusing on what needs to be different, rather than meeting ourselves as we are in the vast regions of our hearts. There is nothing wrong with wanting to better ourselves. In fact, wanting to better ourselves is a part of Life. But for most of us it becomes our primary mode of existence, causing us to miss the *enoughness* that we are right now! It also makes our lives so very challenging. There are many difficulties we all have to face. Without knowing how to meet ourselves with understanding and mercy, we wound ourselves instead. Eventually the wounds weave a layer of scar tissue around our hearts.

If you doubt that, go back to a time where you made a big *mis-take*. It may have been on the job or in your relationship. Choose a mistake for which you believe that you were the one to blame. Then reconstruct in your mind how you related to yourself after that experience. If you are like most people and if you are honest, you would have to say that you beat up on yourself unmercifully. This doesn't just happen around the big 'mistakes' of our lives. Imagine you are on a job interview, one where it is very important to you that you get the job. Can you feel the knot in your stomach? That is the endless knot of *trying* that comes from never having been trained how to value and accept yourself as you are.

Often this urge to want ourselves to be *better* than what we are isn't always so evident. It is there, nonetheless, as a subtle, quiet unease deep within, keeping us caught in a vicious circle of trying and failing. The more we expect ourselves to be better or different than what we are, the more we judge how we are doing. The more we judge, the thicker the scar tissue becomes around our hearts. The more disconnected we become from understanding and mercy, the more we expect ourselves to be different from what we are.

If self-judgment is allowed to run rampant through our minds and hearts it can solidify into shame. Self judgment says "I did it wrong." Shame says, "I am wrong." To live a shame-based life is an agonizing way to live, for it is

> *Self judgment says "I did it wrong." Shame says, "I am wrong."*

> *Mercy knows that there is not one part of ourselves that is not deserving of being met in a compassionate and merciful way.*

one of the most corrosive experiences a human being can have. It is a rejection of ourselves by ourselves.

To be filled with shame is to wake up every morning to a person we don't like and that person is ourselves! Imagine what it would be like to be locked in one room 24 hours a day, 365 days a year with someone you didn't respect and weren't keen to be with. That is what it is like to live a shame-based life.

Even if we don't feel we live a shame-based life, we all know it. It is a primary human experience whether you are aware of it or not. Every single one of the hidden parts of ourselves is wrapped in shame. This shame can be so thick around our hidden feelings that we can't even see what is going on This shame can be so strong that it can engulf us like a tidal wave leaving us gasping for air, and the painful truth is that we feel if we look at what is going on inside ourselves, we would *die in shame*.

The key to healing the core of our shame is mercy. Mercy is such a wonderful word and it is such a powerful healer. It means "to refrain from harming; to relieve suffering." *Mercy understands that the most unacceptable parts of ourselves are the most wounded. It also knows that there is not one part of ourselves that is not deserving of being met in a compassionate and merciful way.*

One of the core roadblocks to discovering mercy is the belief that, if we were merciful with ourselves, we would never be enough. So we flail at ourselves hoping this will make us acceptable enough to get the love that we long for. Round and round this vicious circle we go, often hurting ourselves when we are hurt, rejecting ourselves when we need mercy, and abandoning ourselves when we most need to be met.

This was dramatically illustrated in a sequence of the television program *20/20 Downtown* in which a heroin addict and prostitute named Duran was interviewed. In a gravelly voice deepened and scarred by years of living on the streets, she eloquently spoke about her self-rejection. Her story gives us a glimpse into the feeling of self-rejection we all carry. When asked if she would ever give up drugs, she said, "I will never give up drugs. Giving up dope is confessing pain, and I am not going there because I have had too much goddamn pain in my life. *I will never give up drugs as long as it means that I have to experience who I am in private.* I am a hundred miles an hour on top of three or four hundred dollars of heroin a day, and *that buffers me down just enough to the level I can deal with who I am."*

Can you feel her self-rejection? "I will never give up drugs as long as it means I have to experience who I am in private." My heart ached for her as I heard these words. My heart aches for all of us. Even though we may not be prostitutes or heroin addicts, on some level we all have difficulty accepting ourselves as we are, especially our pain.

Cut off from our own mercy, each of us carries, in the deep regions of our being, a desperate longing for the warmth of a tender heart. Into this longing for understanding, exacerbated by self-judgment, come compulsions to numb and comfort our hurting hearts. We either use our compulsions to lessen the tension that is building inside of us or we use them to grab hold of a sense of ease that seems so far away. All of this keeps us very far from a kind and loving relationship with ourselves.

Schoolroom of the Heart

It is possible to open our hearts again, learning how to meet ourselves in understanding and mercy. It is possible to relearn how to love ourselves from the inside out so we can know again the Love at the heart of Life. It is not only possible; it is what healing is all about. This is one of the core treasures that our compulsions are bringing to us. They won't let us go until we see that it is *acceptance* that heals. They will show us over and over again that all of the fixing, judging, and rearranging of ourselves has never brought us the peace that we long for.

The enoughness *that we seek isn't about changing anything. It is about discovering the* enoughness *that already is!* The doorway back into an abiding and ease-filled connection with ourselves and with Life is through *accepting ourselves as we are.* As Joseph Chilton Pierce, author of *The Magical Child*, once said, "The mind creates the abyss; the heart crosses it." Acceptance is so powerful that it can heal bodies, heal relationships, and even heal nations.

- ❖ *Do you want to heal yourself? For just this moment accept yourself as you are.*

- ❖ *Do you want to help heal your family? For just this moment accept yourself as you are.*

- ❖ *Do you want to help heal the world? For just this moment accept yourself as you are.*

To *be* just as we are rather than constantly trying to be *better* is not lazy nor is it weak. In fact, it is the most courageous thing a human being can do. To

> *If you can accept yourself as you are, you can accept others as they are. You then become a healing presence in the world.*

accept ourselves as we are is also not unproductive. In fact it allows us to be more productive, because we are living from our truth. To fall in love with ourselves is not a selfish thing to do. It is one of the most selfless gifts a human being can give to the world! *If you can accept yourself as you are, you can accept others as they are. You then become a healing presence in the world.*

As far as I can see, learning how to love ourselves and then live from our inner wellspring is what Life is all about. In order to understand this, I invite you to take a trip up to the moon with me. There is a cozy armchair up there that will allow you to sit down and reflect on Life from a broad perspective. I ask you to suspend all judgment until the end of this section and *feel* what I am saying here.

As you settle in, there before you is the Earth in all of its beauty. See the blues of the rivers and oceans; the whites of the snowy peaks and fluffy clouds; the gold of the rolling hills and the green blankets that pour across them. All of this is framed against the black, velvety backdrop of space. Take a moment and be stunned. And if your heart hasn't yet gotten how miraculous your home is, look over at Mars, beautiful in its own right, but basically just red rock. Now look back at the Earth and be stunned by the creativity of Life.

Our planet wasn't always this way. At its inception, it was nothing more than a roiling, boiling cauldron of gas and dust. But from the very beginning, a river of creativity has cascaded down through time and has learned how to weave itself into waterfalls and iridescent wildflowers, dolphins and jaguars, wildly colored parrots dancing through orchid covered trees, and a two legged creature called a human being that populates every nook and cranny of the globe.

What is all of this about? Why has Life brought forth such creativity on this planet? None of us can ever really know the purpose of Life. It is too big for our minds to comprehend. But we can make a guess; and I believe that if a guess is close to the truth, it invigorates and inspires us.

Of all of the ideas I have tried over the years, none has resonated so deeply as the one that sees the Earth as a schoolroom of the heart. It is a place to learn about Love, to recognize Love, and to live from Love. In other words, we are Love waking up to the truth of Love.

The best way to comprehend what we are exploring is to recognize that every step of the way – from the gas and dust of the universe's beginning, to the stupendous creativity that is the oceans and the rivers, to the air we breathe, to the land that we walk upon, and even you and me – was about a coming together into greater communities. This happened all the way from atoms to molecules, from molecules to cells and from single cells to multi cell beings. *Every step of the way the parts of Life were being drawn together into a greater whole.*

The best word I have ever heard to describe this drawing together is *allurement*. The definition of allurement is the power to attract. Another word for it is Love. Love is the activity at the heart of Life that draws molecules together to make rocks, cells together to make animals, and all forms of Life together to procreate so this great river of creativity can continue.

Deepak Chopra, a physician and author who, when describing this force-field of Love that is at the heart of Life, quoted one of Rumi's poems that speaks straight to the heart of what we are talking about here:

> *I have discovered Love!*
>
> *How marvelous, how good, how beautiful it is!*
>
> *I offer my salutation to the spirit of passion*
>
> *that aroused and excited this whole universe*
>
> *and all it contains.*

The Love that he discovered is the *allurement* at the heart of Life that holds it all together. This spirit of passion is bringing us to the next great coming together in the unfolding of Life. It isn't a physical coming together this time. It is a coming together in consciousness. *It is a coming together of the community of Life in the minds and hearts of human beings!*

Why human beings?

You and I have arisen out of the Life of this planet. Each of us *is the Earth*. We may not have roots like a tree or fins like a fish, but we have been woven out of her mighty mountains, her cascading rivers, and her dancing wind. We have the oceans of the Earth coursing through our veins. Our bones are particles of mighty mountains that have dissolved into us. We are each an animated piece of the Earth that has learned how to walk, talk, write, and sing.

One of the core gifts we have been given by Life is that we can explore it all. The dolphins can explore only the seas; worms only the ground; gorillas only the forests. But we can travel from the highest of mountains to the deepest of seas and be awed by what we discover. From all of our exploring, we can begin to see that we have very special gifts to give back to Life:

- ❖ We can be moved in wonder by the vast creativity that was necessary in order to make this planet and everything on it, including us. We can see, dance, laugh, think, and love because of all that has gone before us.

- ❖ We can recognize the beauty of absolutely everything. Nothing is ordinary! Even a straggly plant is an amazing creation.

- ❖ We can recognize that everything is necessary, working together in the great tapestry of Life.

- ❖ We can celebrate that each and every particle of this planet is a unique expression of the creativity of Life, never having been seen before and never to be seen again.

- ❖ We can also begin to see that we are all in this existence together, living on a tiny, fragile jewel that is floating through vast oceans of space.

Can you feel what I am saying? You and I are nothing less than the part of Life that can now recognize and celebrate its stupendous creativity and its dazzling beauty.

Let it in. Allow this vision of Life to inspire your mind and open your heart. Love is calling to you, asking that you wake up to the wonder of Life, to the miracle of you. You are enough. In fact you are more than enough. You are a unique and necessary expression of Life. And Life is asking that you see the entirety of yourself – all of your strengths and your weaknesses, your joys and your miseries – through the eyes of your heart. *For it is within your heart that you can weave all the parts of yourself back into the whole that you are.*

If you truly understand that you are a part of the Earth, then it becomes evident that as you heal, so too does the Earth. In a multitude of human hearts, all of Life will be woven back into the whole that it is, so that Love can flourish on this planet.

As Teilhard de Chardin, the beloved Jesuit priest once said, "Someday, after we have mastered the winds, the waves, the tides and gravity…we shall harness the energies of Love. Then, for the second time in the history of the world, mankind will have discovered fire."

Let us now explore how compulsions can become our guides into loving ourselves, loving Life, and allowing ourselves to be loved by Life.

Compulsions As Our Teachers

This awakening to the essence of Love that permeates all of Life is happening in the minds and hearts of individuals all over the world. That includes you. You are a part of it, and everything in your life is tailor-made to open you again so that you can do the most courageous, most challenging, but also most healing thing a human being can do – that is to fall in love with yourself. The particular body you have been given, the type of personality you have, the exact family you were raised in, your work and your community are all a part of the your schoolroom of the heart. And your compulsion is your graduate course.

There is practically no better place to learn about self-acceptance than around compulsions. They teach us how deeply we are disconnected from ourselves. Think about what happens right before a wave of compulsion. There is usually a high degree of tension coming from the pressure of not being *okay* with our selves and our lives. Compulsions also bring to light how much we believe that self-judgment will whip us into shape.

Think about what happens after a wave has moved through. Usually your heart is closed tighter than a drum and you are berating and belittling yourself for 'screwing up again.' Our compulsions trip us up over and over again, revealing the places where our hearts are closed to ourselves.

> *There is practically no better place to learn about self-acceptance than around compulsions.*

Compulsions also reveal to us the power of mercy and how deep our hunger for it is. *Compulsions will bash us against the wall of control, judgment, and despair until we discover the tiny flicker of light that is a merciful heart.* We go to that light like a traveler lost in the night. The closer we get, the brighter it becomes until we crawl into its warm embrace and discover that it had always been waiting for us right outside the prison of our closed hearts.

My compulsion was the only thing painful enough to crack open the illusion that I could *purchase* the Love I longed for by making myself into an *acceptable* person. Caught in the endless maze of fixing, changing, managing, and controlling, I would numb myself when failure and self-rejection came again, hoping I could get away from the pain of my closed heart. Compulsion was also an attempt to alter my experience in hopes I could know a little of the joy that is naturally there when my heart is open. But

103

> *All of the desperate wanting of your compulsion is really a longing for a tender acceptance of yourself.*

usually this running away from what I was afraid of and this running toward the oblivion of compulsion brought only short relief before the self-cruelty began again.

It took me a long time to realize that this numbing would never work and that it wasn't food that I was hungry for. Instead, I was hungry for the tender understanding of an awakened heart. It wasn't somebody else's heart. Even if a friend or loved one met me with understanding and mercy, it was never enough. *It was my own heart that I was hungry for!* I finally had to face the fact that the person I really wanted to hear "I love you" from was me! My compulsions narrowed down my options until the only thing that was left was to meet myself *as I was*. Dropping out of my mind and back into my heart, I finally discovered the healing that I longed for!

This view of compulsions may be a stretch for you, but just think about it for a moment. Has it ever really worked for you to deal with your compulsion as the enemy and as proof that you are a screw-up or are defective? Soften your stance for a moment and contemplate the idea that *all of the desperate wanting of your compulsion is really a longing for a tender acceptance of yourself.* You've just never known how to meet yourself in that way.

A number of years ago I had an experience at a doctor's office that reveals what we are talking about. I have a very sensitive body, and there are times it is so easy to become scared and confused. I was going through a time when my body was unbalanced and I was very uncomfortable. I was with an HMO at that time, so the doctor I went to for help was not one I would have chosen. While she was very learned, empathy was not one of her strong suits. As the appointment progressed, her coldness, along with the reality that there really was no answer for my beleaguered body, threw me back into that desperation of my childhood, and there to meet it was the old sadistic urge to reject myself.

"You are a wimp," the bully inside of me said. "It doesn't matter that you can't raise your arms to comb your hair. It doesn't matter that you are running unexplained fevers. You always make a big thing out of nothing. Here you are doing it again and being such a bother." It was relentless, cunning, and almost engulfing. In the face of this self cruelty, I wanted to run out of there, straight to a grocery store, and inhale the first thing I came across. But because my compulsion had shown me that judging myself for being vulnerable and then falling into overeating only made it worse, I turned to acceptance, understanding, and mercy instead.

104

"These are old voices from the past," my awareness said. "I need to get out of here and meet them with my heart." I went to my car and took long, deep breaths. Even though I had been slowly removing the scar tissue from around my heart, this was still a place where the old bullying and belittling voices could get a temporary foothold and compulsion would become interesting again. I closed my eyes and felt the knot of self-hate in the pit of my stomach. I said, "I recognize you. You are a visitor from my past. I give you my attention without believing what you have to say."

> *There aren't words to describe the joy that floods your being when a formerly hated and feared part of yourself is met within your heart.*

While exploring this sadistic urge to reject myself when I was the most vulnerable, my heart opened. Underneath these voices, I could feel the very scared part of me that was afraid it would never, ever feel better. This thought was irrational in relationship to what was happening at that moment, but it wasn't irrational in relation to when it was created in my childhood and then lived year after year.

Never in my life had this depth of vulnerability been met with that depth of understanding and compassion! I was not rejecting myself when I was scared and I was not rejecting myself when I was rejecting myself! My closed heart was pointing the way to an open heart, and because of that, the urge to be compulsive faded away, leaving me fully accepting of my thoughts, my feelings and my body. Such sweet relief!

There aren't words to describe the joy that floods your *being* when a formerly hated and feared part of yourself is met within your heart. It leaves you spacious, alive, and so very glad to be given the gift of reconnecting with yourself. There is also no reason to run off to your compulsion, for there is nothing to run from and no comfort to run to. You are already giving yourself the comfort that you need – a merciful heart.

A few days after this experience, I went to the conference where I met Emily. She revealed to me the aliveness and joy that is always there underneath the locked doors of my heart. Her presence also reminded me that my tears and my pain could now dance and sing in the safety of my own mercy.

◇ An Invitation

Before we begin cultivating a merciful heart, it is important to recognize that most people have at least some difficulty meeting themselves in mercy. For many people it is practically impossible. In order to discover where you are in your ability to see yourself through the eyes of your heart, I invite you, after reading these two paragraphs, to go to a mirror and not only look at yourself, but really *see* yourself. Look beyond all of those ancient beliefs that you are too much of this and not enough of that and for these few moments recognize yourself. Don't get caught by this society's narrow idea of beauty. See yourself as you were created by Life. Drink it in.

You are a totally unique expression of the mystery of Life. You have been brought forth out of Life's longing to express itself *as you*. If the old stories about 'what could or should be better' try to take over, look beyond them and truly see yourself. And there you are, in all of your glory, a magnificent, multifaceted, absolutely necessary expression of Life. Now look into your eyes. Look directly into your eyes. There is *you* looking back at *you*. SEE yourself. Stay with this for at least a few moments, receiving yourself at your depth.

Were you able to go to the mirror? And if you were, were you able to see yourself with respect and mercy? Even if you couldn't go to the mirror, know that you are not alone. Most people would either not go to the mirror in the first place or, if they did, all they would see is what is wrong. For the people who can make contact with themselves in the mirror, many of them still have difficulty acknowledging their own magnificence.

Know that whatever you could or couldn't do, it's okay. You are on the pathway back to reconnecting with yourself, with Life, and with the Love that you are. Everything grows and blooms in its own time and its own way. That includes you. One day you will recognize who you really are and rejoice in loving yourself from the inside out.

So how do we allow our hearts to open? Let us explore this step by step.

Meeting Ourselves in Our Own Hearts

You can't force your heart open but you can begin to cultivate an open heart. There are a million ways to do this, each one as unique as the person who created it. Here are a few techniques to get the ball rolling. Play with these skills only if they call to you. For, again, we come across that great paradox of Life. We need to do everything that we can to open our hearts, *and* we need to understand that they are being opened by forces far greater than ourselves. It is skillful to cultivate an open heart, *and* it is skillful to know that in the perfect time and in the perfect way, even if it takes longer than you think it should, your life is bringing you back into a deep and loving relationship with yourself.

The intent of each of these practices is to open the door of the heart. As you listen to what calls to you, your own pathway will reveal itself.

◇1〉 Watching Self Judgment

◇2〉 Deep Listening

◇3〉 Accepting Yourself As You Are

◇4〉 Making a Gratitude List

◇5〉 Really Seeing Yourself

◇6〉 When Your Heart is Closed

◇1〉 Watching Self Judgment

The first step in returning to a spacious heart is *to notice how closed your heart is.* All of us experience this to some degree. We live in an inner conversation that is constantly checking out how we are doing. For some, these voices are subtle. For others, they have solidified into shame and have become voracious demons. Most of us have some of each. But we all live, to a greater or lesser degree, from the idea that we need to be different than what we are in order to be *okay*. This never brings us the results that we desire. The truth is that trying to be *good* never brings us the results we desire because being *good* is based on the supposition that we are *bad*!

If we try to get rid of or run away from these voices in our heads, we stay stuck to them like glue. If we wake up to them instead, learning how to *see* the voices in action rather than believing what the voices are saying, there is

107

the very great possibility of becoming free from their spell.

The first time I was able to *watch* the shaming voices in action inside of me rather than *believing* what they were saying was a red-letter day. I had thought everything those voices said was Truth! I bowed before these caustic and critical voices when they said; "I screwed up again. I will never get it right. Everybody else does it better than me. I am too fat, too stupid, too clumsy, too ugly, too needy, too selfish. I am too much of this and not enough of that." Of course, I also got caught in the exact opposite voices. "I am better than you. I am smarter, more beautiful, skinnier, (only when I was dieting!) And I don't need anybody, because I am above all of that!" Ah, the pain that comes from believing those voices! And of course, compulsion was a handy buffer between me and the pain of self-rejection. But only temporarily, for compulsion always made it worse.

It took me a while to learn how to relate *to* these voices because they were so seductive! It felt like they had written a doctoral dissertation on how to judge me. Not only that, they had gotten a law degree in order to argue their case! Most of the time, I experienced them as a foggy, relentless feeling of just not being okay. But at times they flared up into cruel monsters that shook me to my core. As I discovered how to be free from these voices, there is something that I learned that I want to share with you. *They don't know what they are talking about! They are just ancient patterns in your head that don't have a clue about who you really are.* They are like an eight-year-old saying it knows how to run a corporation!

Just a moment of recognizing this truth will give you the courage and the curiosity to turn and watch these voices rather than believing what they are saying. If you would like to explore this in depth, I have written an entire chapter called *Disarming the Judger* in my book, *Belonging to Life*.

We can dismantle the core voices of self-judgment and shame through a powerful but simple exercise called Watching Self Judgement.

For this exercise, carry around a little notebook and whenever you catch yourself judging yourself, write down what the voice said. This is a very clarifying experience. When you see the words of the voices written on paper, it becomes easier to realize how cruel and ridiculous they are. This realization gives you the curiosity and the space you need to not fall under their spell.

When I did this, I took it one step further. I wrote the words of the voices on a big piece of paper taped to a wall in my bedroom. As I looked at this paper, I was able to not only see the words more clearly, but I could also see the themes these voices were using. It

> *took time, but eventually I came to a place where a voice could*
> *scream, "You never do anything right!" and I could say to the*
> *voice. "Oh, you must be having a bad day!"*

Watching these voices can sound scary at first. The suggestion to watch can make you feel like somebody is asking you to get into a cage with a man-eating tiger. There is a powerful mantra you can use when the voices are near so you can watch without having to fall under their spell. The statement is, "If it is unkind, it's of the mind." This statement reminds us that all of the stories in our heads that put us down, no matter how seductive they are, are just old voices. They are learned patterns of relating to ourselves through expectation and judgment rather than from the vast healing of our hearts, and they don't have a clue about who we really are!

Deep Listening

In this exploration of our self-judgment and our shame, we will come across parts of ourselves that are difficult to accept. Not knowing that everybody else has his or her own unacceptable parts, our only option seems to be to reject ourselves. As long as we hide these unacceptable parts of ourselves away from ourselves and the world, they will still have the power to make us believe that they are true. They will also continue to fuel our compulsions from underneath our everyday awareness.

In order to open our hearts to these seemingly unacceptable parts, it can be very helpful to find a person or a group with whom we can speak our truth. There is great healing when someone listens to our most unacceptable parts from a place of understanding and mercy. At first we may have resistance to this for we are absolutely certain that if somebody knew about these parts of ourselves, we would be thoroughly rejected. But the power of sharing our truths is very healing.

I was working with a woman recently who was on a trip with a friend from work. My client had been having panic attacks for a number of years. Because she was very ashamed of them, she had gone to great lengths to hide them from everybody, including her co-workers. Slowly and surely she was healing herself to her core. But since she was on a trip, some of the old feelings surfaced again. She woke up the first morning with panic racing through every part of her body. She was certain that to reveal what she was experiencing to her friend would be a disaster. But the more she tried to hide her panic, the worse it got. Finally the pain was so great that she shared her experience, expecting judgment in return. Instead, she not only received

> *There is great healing when someone listens from a place of understanding and mercy.*

understanding, but also a closer connection with her friend!

Being heard can break the cycle of hating and hiding, but we need to carefully choose our listening partner. Just as we explored in the last chapter, this needs to be a person or a group where you feel you won't be judged for your perceived imperfections and where what you say won't be broadcast to the world. It also needs to be understood that you are not asking for opinions or advice. You just need to be heard. If you have never done this you may not know the power of complete, non-judgmental attention. I assure you, it is far more powerful than anything we have done as we have tried to fix, change, and rearrange ourselves.

It is also helpful to have this practice be a two way street. First one person listens in complete attention and trustful acceptance to whatever the other person is experiencing and then the other person listens. To listen while others share their vulnerable places not only helps us understand that we are all in this together, but it also teaches us how to listen without judgment.

Since many of us have been caught in a glut of self-rejection, we might not have a friend or a group such as this. So we may need to contact a professional, such as a counselor or a minister. This is what I experienced. There was no way I could speak my deepest hates and fears to friends or loved ones. I so completely hated my so-called defects that I absolutely knew and expected that I would be rejected. If they so much as sneezed as I was expressing my deepest pains, I knew that the sneeze was an indication of their loathing of me!

This even happened when I first started working with my mentor. Many times I had the fear that upon arriving on her doorstep, I would find the door locked in complete rejection of who I was. Much to my amazement, she never rejected me! Her willingness to accept the full range of my feelings and experiences showed me how to do this for myself. That is the power that comes from being deeply listened to.

People who have been listened to are not only healed, but also become healers in the world. Having learned how to listen to themselves, they can then be present for the grocery store clerk, the agitated bus rider, the rebellious teenager, the grieving loved ones, and the scared child without turning it all into an emergency. One moment when a person is present for another is a transformational moment for the entirety of Life.

Accepting Yourself As You Are

The first two skills allow us to see and acknowledge how closed our hearts are, so we can develop a relationship with ourselves that is based on under-standing and mercy. For many people, the idea of loving themselves is too big a leap. It can feel so scary and alien that it shuts them down. So we need to take baby steps by first learning how – for a moment here and a moment there – to accept ourselves just as we are. Just as we needed to do addition and subtraction before we could do multiplication and division, we need to start with self-acceptance in order to learn how to love ourselves from the inside out.

Accepting ourselves comes from the understanding that all of Life is a dance of opposites. Nature needs the cold fury of winter in order to become the riotous blooming of summer. It needs raging lightning storms to ignite the fires that clear the forest for new growth. It needs volcanoes erupting from deep within the oceans to make new islands in paradise.

Just as Life has interwoven the opposites of dark and light in order to birth itself into more creative expressions, it has done the same with us. We each have positive and negative attributes. Even though you are not a Hitler, you probably have been very cruel toward yourself in attempting to remake yourself into a *perfect* human being, in much the same way that he tried to create what he perceived to be a *perfect* race.

We also have things we do well and things we don't. In fact, if you listed all the things that a human being is capable of, the odds are that you could probably only do a small percentage of them. Can you win the Tour de France four times? I thought not. How about being able to wiggle your ears without moving any other muscles? The odds aren't with you. So there are far more things you can't do than you can!

When we look at ourselves in this way, we can see that we are nutty as fruitcakes and completely inept at most things in our lives. The only conclu-sion we can come to is that our perfection lies in our imperfection! One of the truest truths I have come across as the clouds in my mind have dissolved in the clarity of my heart is that, with all of the mistakes I have made, I never made a mistake. Each and every one was a necessary part of the unfolding of Life.

A wonderful image that illustrates this is an exquisitely woven tapestry. If you look at the under side, all you see are loose threads and lots of

> *Your imperfections are a part of your perfection!*

knots. The closed heart only looks at the bottom and misses the perfection of the weaving that shows on the other side. The open heart can look at both the top and the bottom and not only see the exquisite art work, but also recognize the necessity of the jumble of threads and knots.

Can you feel the relief that your imperfections are a part of your perfection? If we can accept that, then we can stop struggling so much. We can see that *the most powerful place where we learn about loving ourselves is in what we don't do well. In fact, we have been given our weaknesses and vulner-abilities specifically as a training ground for the heart!* We fall in love with ourselves as we learn how to embrace ourselves *as we are* rather than always trying to be what we think we should be. If we can grasp that for even a moment, the doorways to our hearts can open just a little more and we can take another step into loving ourselves from the inside out.

The wonderful thing is that we don't have to *get it together* in order to cultivate this type of relationship. In fact, it doesn't matter what is happening in our lives. *We can do this when our hearts are completely closed, for we can open our hearts to how closed our hearts are!* If we are afraid to accept ourselves, we can accept ourselves for being afraid of accepting ourselves. If we are sure we are unworthy of this kind of Love, we can accept our feeling of unworthiness. The key is to accept ourselves for whatever we are feeling and experiencing at that moment. *Whatever is happening is all right.* It is occurring in the vast dance of dark and light that is Life. This makes it so effortless for we don't need to be any different from what we are in order to love ourselves from the inside out.

The Healing Power of Acceptance

Because we have been trained to believe that fixing, changing, and rearranging ourselves will bring us the peace that we long for, hardly any of us knows how to tap into the powerful healing of acceptance. We haven't yet discovered that true acceptance is magic!

Jon Kabat Zinn, psychiatrist & author of *Wherever You Go-There You Are,* began a pain clinic at Massachusetts General Hospital in the 1980's that was based on teaching patients how to be curious and accepting of whatever was happening in their bodies. The doctors laughed behind his back and sent him all of their worst cases, figuring he would fail. Instead, he had phenom-enal results that changed many people's lives, including the doctors.

Basically what he taught was how to not fight pain. As they learned how to do this, many of the patients discovered that *most of their suffering was the result of resistance to their pain!* The power of softening around pain and accepting that it was there brought so much relief that when they researched how many people were still using the techniques 15 years later, most of them were!

> *True acceptance is magic!*

The challenges in our lives can reveal to us the power of acceptance. I learned it through having a very sensitive body with a digestive tract that gets easily out of balance. There was a time when nothing I did seemed to make it any better. The doctors didn't have a clue about what to do and neither did I. Besides being very uncomfortable, imagine what kind of fear that brought up!

One of the worst feelings was an almost constant queasiness that would flare up into nausea. If you saw me when I was reacting to this discomfort, you would have seen tight shoulders, a deep furrow in my brow, and a scowl upon my face. For a long time, the only thing I knew how to do was react, lost in hate and fear of this unpleasant and scary experience. This always made it worse.

It took me awhile, but out of desperation I learned how to go toward the experience – to open up around the nausea and actually be present for it. All I was doing was acknowledging the truth of my experience and then moving toward acceptance of it! This always made things easier. When I wasn't fighting what was going on, the queasiness lessened and sometimes it even left. The most important thing was that my whole relationship to the nausea changed, making it much easier to live with when it returned. In those moments when I could accept exactly what was happening rather than fighting it, I could act from a much wiser place. It all became workable.

As my body taught me that resisting what I was experiencing usually made it worse, it made sense to me that my feelings would also respond to acceptance. Let's take fear for example. I used to hate the level of fear that I lived in. I was always trying to deny it, fix it or get away from it. When I learned how to accept this part of myself, I brought it out of the shadows of my self-hate. Fear could be present, but I didn't have to be afraid!

Over time, I learned that the very thing I was resisting, whether it was a physical feeling or an emotion, was the very thing I needed to accept. As I met all the various parts of myself in understanding and mercy, I began to accept the totality of who *I am!* – both the light and the dark. It is thrilling to be able to love myself that much. It is also a joy to see how much easier my life is than when I am constantly trying to fight my way to my healing. When I meet myself in understanding and mercy, I am like a wilted plant that has the water of Life poured upon it. I also see this healing acceptance transform the lives of clients, friends and loved ones. It then ripples out from within them, touching and healing the people in their lives.

To meet ourselves in understanding and mercy is the greatest act of a lifetime. To move beyond judgment and expectation and accept ourselves *as we are* is so radically healing that it transforms every aspect of our lives, both inside of ourselves and outside.

A Simple Skill: Self Acceptance

Because we have been so deeply trained in self-judgment, it is skillful to cultivate self-acceptance. It is woven through practically every page of this book and we will be exploring self-acceptance in depth in the *Treasure Hunting* Chapter. In order to taste the healing power of acceptance now, pause for a moment and think about something that you wish were not a part of your life. At the beginning, choose something not too big, like a slight headache or irritation at your dog. Accept that it is a part of your life right now. Accept that Life is not bad, nor are you *less than* or defective for having this experience. Take a few deep breaths and say to yourself, "For this moment, I let this be here." The flavor of this statement is acceptance. It says: "I accept that this is part of my life right now. It's okay. I'm okay." You can amplify the statement by placing your hand over your heart.

Feel how acceptance softens your stance and makes everything more workable. This kind of acceptance isn't about being at the mercy of the challenges in our lives. It is about letting go of the inefficiency of resisting them so that we can see the challenges through the clear eyes of our hearts. We then become able to act from wisdom rather than reaction.

I was working with a client once who had a very difficult boss. She would get lost in her fury at him. Also she got lost in how furious she was for being furious! When she could accept that she felt rage around this person, she stopped fighting it and her whole body softened. When she went back to work and the rage showed up, she wasn't surprised. She could even begin to have a little humor around it! Her willingness to accept her rage changed her whole work environment.

To move beyond judgment and expectation and accept ourselves as we are is so radically healing that it transforms every aspect of our lives, both inside of ourselves and outside.

We have been deeply taught to resist our emotions, our pains, our lives, and our selves. We have been taught it for decades! Then we begin to react to our resistance and then we react to our reactions. That is the world of struggle that we live in most all of the time. Yet one moment of acceptance is much more powerful than millions of moments of resistance. Take the question, "For this moment, can I let this be?"

into your life. Another way you can say this is, "I accept that this is part of my life right now. It's okay. I'm okay." Use one of these whenever you find yourself resisting something. You will find that moments of acceptance can open your heart again, allowing you to live from the clarity, wisdom, and love that come from your truest self.

 ## Listening To Yourself

Elizabeth Kubler Ross, Swiss psychiatrist and author, as a take-off on the transactional analysis book *I'm Okay and You're Okay*, once jokingly said that she was going to write a book titled, *I'm Not Okay and You're Not Okay and That's Okay*! If we even get a glimmer of how powerful it is to accept ourselves as we are and then let our actions come from that acceptance, we will satisfy one of the deepest longings that we all feel – the longing to be heard.

Having somebody else listen to us is powerful, but to give this to ourselves is phenomenally healing. This is what was happening with the woman who had the anxiety attack while traveling with her friend. After resisting and denying her experience, she finally listened to what was happening and spoke the truth of her experience. This is also what I did with my queasiness, and what my client did with her fury.

We don't have to go through as much heartache as the woman with the panic attacks. We can draw upon the simple technique of speaking the truth of our experience that we explored in the first skill. Acknowledging our truth can re-train our attention so that when an unacceptable part of ourselves makes itself known, we can turn toward it rather than away. This dramatically lessens its power over us. Let us explore this technique again.

After you read through this exercise, take a few deep breaths and close your eyes. If your mind is easily distracted, stay with some deep breathing, allowing your body to melt with every out-breath. Then let your attention stabilize on the rhythm of your breath, riding the waves as they swell and recede.

When your attention is stabilized, broaden your focus by including your whole body. Ask yourself the question, "In this moment, what am I experiencing?" Your body is a constantly changing river of sensation and it is different now than at any other moment in your life. Without wanting to change anything, be curious about what you are experiencing and name it silently to yourself. Are you warm or cold? Is your body comfortable or uncomfortable? Is there any pain in your body right now? Is there a place of pleasant

> *sensations? Can you feel tingles, pressure, moistness? Stay with*
> *this for a few moments and then open your eyes.*

The technique is that simple. Do not be fooled by its simplicity. *In these few moments you were listening to yourself.* You weren't trying to change yourself and you weren't expecting yourself to be any different than what you are. This is one of the most powerful gifts you can give to yourself – your own undivided attention. We did this with just sensations, but as you strengthen your ability to listen to yourself, you can do this with the deepest of feelings and the cruelest of thoughts.

This is the doorway out of struggle. A moment here and a moment there when we are listening to ourselves *as we are* rather than as we wish ourselves to be allows us to discover that the *enoughness* that we have longed for our whole lives is with us right here and right now.

As we listen to our compulsion to struggle with ourselves, we can make contact with our inner radar. As we explored earlier, there is a part of us that knows how to make kind and wise choices in our lives, especially with our compulsions. I call it our inner radar because it knows when to say "Yes" and when to say "No." It knows when to be firm and when to be merciful. It knows when to open and when to close. And it definitely knows how to act for the good of the whole, for it contains our empowered *No* that truly is a *Yes* to Life.

Instead of listening to our own wisdom, we try to make all of our decisions out of our struggling mind. This is the kind of mind that says, "Let's have an ice cream cone." Then five minutes later it is berating us for having done it! We live so deeply in the land of *shoulds, ought tos*, and their opposites *I can't* and *I won't* that we have forgotten that we truly do know what is the wisest and kindest thing to do in any situation. Listening to ourselves will reveal the wellspring of wisdom and clarity within us so that we can live from its nourishing presence.

The invitation is to add moments throughout your day where you listen to yourself and name what you discover there. You can do this at the beginning of every meal or even at all of the stoplights you come across throughout the day. You can do it for a few moments after you wake up in the morning and again as you go to sleep at night. Know that these precious moments of being with *what is* are many times more powerful than any moment of trying to be different from what you are.

> *One of the most powerful gifts you can give to yourself is your own undivided attention.*

Making a Gratitude List

Another wonderful thing to do to open your heart is to make a list everyday of three qualities you appreciate about yourself. Appreciation is the sunlight of human life and a little bit goes a long way. This is a take off on a gratitude list, but it is all about you. It is so powerful because we are trained to look at what is wrong about ourselves. This re-grooves our focus into looking for what is right. When we start doing this, we see how much we have overlooked our own magnificence.

When I first started making a gratitude list on the advice of my counselor, I couldn't think of even one thing to write down. When I told him that I couldn't find one good quality about myself, he asked if I had taken a shower before I came to see him.

I said, "Yes."

"Did you pick up the bath mat when you were done?" he asked.

I said, "Yes."

So #1 on my list was that I pick up bath mats. Now that may seem so very small but it became a doorway into looking for what was right about myself rather than always focusing on what was wrong.

This gratitude list is about taking another step into your magnificence. Thomas Merton once said, "It is a glorious destiny to be a member of the human race. Now I realize what we all are. And if only everyone could realize it! But it cannot be explained. There is no way of telling people that they are all walking around shining like the sun."

Even though there is no way of telling people, I am telling you: You are beautiful beyond your wildest imagination. For this moment, let that in. Let your heart open and then write your list from that place. You can even put Merton's quote on the top of each page of your notebook to remind you why you are writing this list. Slowly, like a thousand veils lifting one after the other, you will discover that you are *walking around shining like the sun*!

 Really Seeing Yourself

I also use my reflection as a place for opening my heart. As we move throughout our day, there are an abundance of mirrors and reflective surfaces where we can see ourselves. If we can move beyond the act of *looking* at ourselves to the act of *seeing* ourselves as we did earlier in this chapter, we can take these moments to pause, connect, and open our hearts.

When I was first invited to see myself in mirrors, I was usually repulsed by what I saw. I went to amazing lengths to ignore the mirror while I brushed my teeth and even when I put on mascara. But I kept at it, and there were brief moments where I could see myself and keep my heart open.

The first time a true burst of Love wiggled its way into my perception was when I turned off the light by my bed late one night and I saw my reflection in the window. Much to my amazement, my heart melted in tenderness, just like a lover's heart. Oh the joy of that moment. My heart was open to me! I now consciously cultivate that kind of connection with my reflection to keep the juices of respect and Love flowing. Whenever I wash my hands, I always look into the mirror and say, "Hi." I sometimes even wink!

So the invitation is to be willing to see yourself whenever you look into a mirror. This is not just a glance. This is looking at yourself in the curious and open way you would look at the face of a lover or a child. And if it brings up self rejection, take your attention there and give that old voice a dose of tenderness and mercy.

When Your Heart is Closed

The techniques we have explored so far work when the door of our heart is open enough to let in the light of mercy. What do we do when our hearts are closed down tight and we are absolutely sure that the mean and nasty voices are correct? There are three things we can do to open the doors again:

◆ The Lost Child Meditation

◆ Ball of Love Meditation

◆ The Voice of Kindness

◆ The Lost Child Meditation

Breathing deeply in order to calm your mind and body, close your eyes and imagine walking down a street in a residential area. From a distance, you hear the faint sounds of a child crying. As you come around the corner, you see the child sitting on the curb, crying her heart out. Imagine that whatever you are experiencing, she is experiencing the same exact thing.

If you are feeling all alone, imagine that her daddy has just moved out because of a divorce and she is heartbroken. If you feel very confused, not knowing your way out of a particular situation, imagine that she is lost and doesn't know her way home. If you find yourself hating yourself, imagine that all of the neighborhood kids have just told this child that she is a dork and they don't want to play with her.

Allow your heart to open to her pain. Now imagine how you would comfort her. Then give that to her, whether it is a hug, a kind word, or a hand to hold. Feel the feeling of your heart touching hers in understanding and compassion.

Whatever you imagined and whatever you felt is exactly what you want from you. Turn the light of this mercy toward yourself. Place your hand over your heart and give to yourself whatever you gave to this child. Say the words; imagine the touch; and feel this experience as deeply as you can. You are worthy of acceptance and love.

◆ The Ball of Love Meditation

After you breathe some deep and open breaths, imagine a beautiful ball of radiant light floating in the air a foot or so in front of your heart. Take a few moments and be fascinated by its beauty. As you look closely, it becomes evident that in the center of this ball is the face of someone who loves you unconditionally. It could be a loved one, a religious figure like Jesus or Buddha, or even a pet.

The closer you look, the more you can recognize the unconditional Love that is flowing out of that being's eyes toward you. Their eyes twinkle as they radiate a complete acceptance of you exactly as you are. As you gaze into those eyes, allow your heart to open and receive this precious gift. With every in-breath, breathe this Love straight into yourself and let a sweet warmth begin to glow in your chest. With each out-breath, send it to every cell of your body. If your struggling mind starts to take over, focus deeply on the radiant Love pouring out of that being's eyes.

When you are saturated with this tender warmth, on the next in-breath, breathe the ball of light straight into your heart and see it vibrating and pulsating there. Know that it will always be there. Whenever you are caught in your judging mind, you can bring your attention to your heart area and ask this ball of Love to help you open your heart again.

◆ The Voice of Kindness

The third aid to opening a closed heart is to think of someone who deeply loves you. Imagine what that person would say when you share with them what is happening inside of you. A friend of mine once said that she opens the door to her heart again by imagining what Jesus would say about her. If you don't have a connection to a religious figure or a person who loves you unconditionally, imagine what I would say if you shared with me the depth of your closed heart. If what you imagine is kind and understanding, then you would be close to the truth.

All of these skills are about bringing us back into the most important relationship we will ever have – the relationship with ourselves. They are also bringing us back to the most important *type* of relationship we can have with ourselves – loving ourselves from the inside out. I want to stress, to underline, to highlight that it is *okay* to fall in love with ourselves. For even more than we need food, we need to rest in our own hearts. Remember the baby monkeys? We need connection, and we need it most with ourselves.

To fall in love with ourselves is not a selfish act. In fact, it is the least selfish thing we can do. For as we learn how to meet ourselves in our own hearts, our actions can come from the wisest part of ourselves. As Jack Kornfield, meditation teacher and author, once said, "The only question to ask on your deathbed is, 'Did I love well?'"

All of the love we give to the world stems from the love and acceptance we have for ourselves. We learn how to love our friends, our loved ones, the Earth, and even our enemies inside of ourselves. We can't love *out there* if we haven't learned how to love *in here*. We can't stop fighting the world and thus adding to the problems of the world if we haven't yet learned how to stop fighting ourselves and accept ourselves instead.

Yes, it takes courage to cultivate an open heart, and you may need to open your heart hundreds of times in a day. But every time you do, you become a part of the healing of the Earth. Your loving yourself makes a difference to every single human being that lives and will live on this planet. In this opening of your heart, you can let go of focusing on all of the hatred and fear that has been gripping human consciousness for thousands of years. Instead, you can shift out of your struggling mind and see it all through the eyes of your heart.

> *All of the love we give to the world stems from the love and acceptance we have for ourselves.*

As you meet yourself in deep understanding and mercy, you will be able to open your heart even to criminals. For no matter how lost a human being gets in violence, conflict, hatred, and fear, all human beings long to know their source, which is Love. As more of us see Life through the eyes of the heart, humanity will finally fulfill the purpose for which it was brought forth out of Mystery, and Life on this planet will know itself at its fullest potential.

Core Ideas in Skill #2 – Loving Ourselves from the Inside Out

❖ All people live, to a greater or lesser degree, from the idea that they need to be different than what they are in order to be *okay*.

❖ Trying to be different or better than what you are in order to be okay will never work, for it is based on the belief that you are not okay right now.

❖ Your self-judging voices can eventually permeate your entire relationship with yourself, removing you from the essential comfort of being at ease with yourself exactly as you are.

❖ The *enoughness* that you seek isn't about changing anything. It is about discovering the *enoughness* that already is!

❖ There is no better place to learn about self-acceptance than around compulsions.

❖ Forgive yourself for being compulsive. It is the way you figured out how to survive.

❖ Imperfections are a part of your perfection. The most powerful place to learn about loving ourselves is in our imperfections.

❖ All of the wild hunger of your compulsion is really a longing for *you*. It is a longing for a tender and respect-filled acceptance of yourself.

❖ Compassion unites rather than divides; it *dissolves* problems rather than trying to *solve* them.

❖ The most courageous thing human beings can do is fall in love with themselves.

✦ SKILL 3: OPEN BREATHING ✦

If someone told you there was a magical thing you could do that would bring an exhilarating sense of aliveness, a deep feeling of calm, and a grounding that allows you to feel safe in your life – and it is always with you – would you be interested? Of course! The wonderful thing is that it is true! There really is something with you right now that can bring all of these healing gifts into your life. And you don't have to purchase anything or go anywhere else. This magical thing is your breath.

To open to your breath again is to open to yourself. To open to yourself is to open to Life. *This is what you are truly hungry for when you are compulsive – a deep and open connection with yourself and with Life.* Let's explore this now.

> *As you are reading, soften your belly and take a deep breath. Feel the opening of an in-breath – how it lifts your body making more space within. Now ride the wave of the out-breath, speaking a deep and resonate ahhhhh. Allow it to open you to the delicious experience of melting back into Life. And again, there is the in-breath, ready to fill you with its healing presence. Take a little time and enjoy each facet of your breath – the opening of the in-breath and the letting go of the out.*
>
> *Now put the two together by consciously riding the circle of your breath – in-breath turn, out-breath turn – and feel the joy of being fully connected to your breath. If you let go enough you can even feel the experience of being rocked by the breath of Life! Ride this ancient rhythm for a few minutes, giving yourself the gift of simply being. When you are ready, continue reading.*

It is amazing when you truly recognize how wonderful it is to breathe consciously in an open and relaxed way. The word *inspiration* literally means *in-breath* for the breath opens us, filling us with much more than just oxygen. It brings more spirit into our bodies, our minds, and our emotions. And there is no accident that the sound of a deep and satisfying out-breath is *ahhhhh*. It is the sound of satisfaction. We express it when we have just finished a great meal, seen a newborn baby or are trying to let someone know we understand. This sound points us to the release that is a full out-breath. It is a release that allows us to let go and trust ourselves to the living process of Life.

Notice that you have probably already gone back to more shallow breathing. This cuts you off from some of the best things in Life: aliveness, connectedness, deep peace, safety, openness and centeredness. Because you live in a society of shallow breathers, I want to inspire you with all of the gifts that open breathing can bring to you. As you read about the deep healing power of breath, I invite you to come back over and over again to a deep and slow breath.

The Gifts of Open Breathing

There are six core gifts that Open Breathing brings to us:

 **Aliveness**

To breathe is to live. We can survive a month or more without food and a number of days without water, but only a few minutes without breath. Even though our bodies can survive on shallow breathing, they long for deep and open breaths and the aliveness they bring.

To breathe fully is to be *really* alive! Every cell in our body is a little factory that needs raw material in order to keep on working. A lot of the food we eat is turned into glucose, a core fuel for our cells. But it takes many molecules of oxygen for every one molecule of glucose in order for a cell to function efficiently. In other words, the main nutrient for our body is oxygen!

When we don't get enough oxygen, the body doesn't work efficiently. (And we wonder why we are tired!) The body is like a wood burning stove. If we close down the dampers of the stove, stopping the flow of oxygen, the fire will eventually burn out, leaving a lot of ash. But if we open the dampers, the fire will burn brightly. The same is true for our body. When we breathe deeply, we bring in more oxygen and our cells glow with aliveness. Often when I thought I was hungry for food, I was truly hungry for some deep breaths!

This vitality comes not only from the oxygen in the air. Breath contains a healing essence beyond its physical components. Many religions, cultures, and healing systems have studied and cultivated this essence for thousands of years. It is called by a variety of names: *prana* (India), *chi* (China), and *num* (the Bush people of Kalahari) to name a few. But they are all pointing to the same thing.

> *To open to your breath again is to open to yourself. To open to yourself is to open to Life.*

It is understood that this healing force is in all

forms of matter, but is not matter and is taken up with every breath. Research done with respected *T'ai Chi*, meditation, and *Chi Kung* masters has shown that this energy can not only empower a person, but can also heal. To breathe normally is to receive some of this energy, but to breathe consciously and freely is to replenish and store this vital substance.

Soften your belly and allow a deep and slow breath.

Connectedness

Living in shallow breathing supports the notion that each of us is an island unto ourselves. Nothing could be further from the truth. Every time we breathe in, we take in trillions of atoms that were once a part of eagles and butterflies, dinosaurs and stars, slaves in Egypt and mighty kings. When we breathe out, we send on their way particles that were once an integral part of our own body, letting them go to a life of infinite adventure. To take a full and complete breath is to open to Life on multiple levels, intimately connecting us to the web of existence throughout time and space.

This kind of breath also brings us back to the joy of being in our bodies and reconnects us with the love affair of rhythm that is Life. The world pulsates with the ebb and flow, the rising and falling of rhythm. It is evident in the tides, the seasons, in our hearts, and even in the peristaltic waves of our intestines. Each of us, being an integral piece of the planet, is joined with the larger rhythms through the pulsations of our bodies, especially our breath. The tides of breath rise and fall every moment of our lives, connecting us to the whole of creation.

Soften your belly and allow a deep and slow breath.

Deep Peace

An easy, open breath brings deep peace to our whole being. It turns on the parasympathetic nervous system whose job is to calm us down. Yet we live mostly in its companion, the sympathetic nervous system. This system says, "Go, go go; do, do, do; see Jane run!" The difficulty we are faced with is that we live in a society that is addicted to the sympathetic nervous system. We love scary or violent movies. We live our lives at break neck speeds. We ingest coffee and sugar to stimulate our bodies. (It is probably a good bet to invest in coffee stocks!)

The great rhythm of doing and being, fast and slow, rest and work is broken by our love affair with speed. This speed always takes us away from ourselves, leaving us more vulnerable to the ravages of compulsion. This is one of the main reasons why we are usually more inclined to be compulsive at the end of the day. We have spent our time running as fast as we can and moving further and further from ourselves, and to stop feels uncomfortable at first. To breathe deeply turns on the calming part of our nervous system. This brings us back to ourselves and to the sanity of calm even in the middle of a busy day.

Soften your belly and allow a deep and slow breath.

 Sanctuary

The breath is a sanctuary that is available to us no matter where we are or what is happening in our lives. Whenever my mind is restless, searching for peace *out there* in another mouthful of food, or in *getting things under control*, or in some other heart numbing activity, I now have a place where my attention can return – the rising and falling of my breath. It brings me back into my body, into the here and now and into the wellspring of wisdom and support that is within.

Every morning and for a number of times throughout the day, I allow my attention to rest in the experience of this ancient rhythm. Because I have become friends with my breath, I actually feel like the great Mother of Life is rocking me in a cradle. Those moments are like mini-vacations that allow my mind to quiet down and insight to flood my awareness.

Soften your belly now and allow a deep and slow breath.

⟨5⟩ Opening What Has Been Closed

Open breathing also minimizes the deepest pains of human life. This is most evident on the physical level, but it also works like magic on emotions. With physical pain, we have a tendency to tighten down around it. When we do, it only makes the pain worse. Imagine somebody squeezing your hand until it hurts and then, when you say it hurts, they squeeze more. We do this to ourselves with headaches, backaches, injuries, and even with the dentist. Our muscles tighten down around the pain. We can reverse the process by breathing into the experience, allowing our breath to expand into it much like blowing up a balloon. It not only frees up the cramping; it also opens space for the blood vessels to bring the necessary ingredients for healing.

We can breathe into our emotions as well. Over and over again, I have watched people in the throws of a deep emotion react to what they are experiencing, and then react to their reaction. When I invite them to bring their attention to the part in their body that has tightened down because of the emotion and then to breathe into the sensations instead, most people are amazed at how this lightens the experience.

When you are being overtaken by an emotion – whether it is anger, fear, sadness or a variation of one of those – a few deep breaths focused right into the physical sensations of that emotion can transform your experience. What we fail to see is that emotions are amplified when we resist them. When we participate with them instead – and one of the simplest and most profound ways we can do that is through breathing into them – many of them become like clouds moving through us rather than a storm that 'rains on our parade'. I call this the Balloon Breath and I invite you to try it after you read the following:

> *After you take a few deep breaths, bring your attention into your breath, feeling it from the inside. Feel how the in-breath expands and opens your body and how the out-breath carries with it a sense of letting go. Now find a tight spot in your body and imagine your breath is a balloon that you are blowing up inside of you, right at the experience of tightness. Gently push against the tension you find there and then let go on the out-breath, saying out loud a long and slow ahhhhh. Do this for a number of breaths, each time expanding a little bit more the area of tension. Muscles respond to the gentle but opening pressure of the breath.*

Now soften your belly and allow a deep and slow breath.

⟨6⟩ Centeredness

An open breath also brings the center of gravity down into your body, tapping you into the wellspring of wisdom that lies in the belly. The belly is an amazingly powerful and healing place to live from. Just as there is evidence of the umbilical cord that connected us to the source of our nourishment when our bodies were being created in our mother's womb, there is an energy umbilical cord in our belly that connects us to the wellspring within us.

When we were little, we were grounded in our bellies and this energy umbilical cord still pulsated with vitality. This is one of the reasons we were able to be so alive in our play. Rooted in the nourishing soil of our own bellies, we could whirl and twirl, leap and dance with a sense of balance that is lost to most adults. It is also why we were so resilient in the face of deep emotions.

Can you imagine twirling and tumbling like you did when you were a child? As adults, our center of gravity is usually up in our heads, and we keep it there by shallow breathing. Having lost this sense of balance that comes from being connected to our bellies, we are like top-heavy trees, vulnerable to the storms of our lives and the unconscious illusion that we can take care of ourselves through our compulsions. Cultivating an open breath takes us back into the safety of being connected to our bellies and all of the spontaneity and trust that lives there.

To watch somebody who naturally breathes from the belly is a thing of beauty. Whether it is a postman or an accomplished ballerina, when someone is connected to their belly through their breath, their movements are a thing of beauty. They could be making lyrical movements or wild and crazy ones, but whatever they are doing we recognize something – an alive connectedness that touches us to the core.

Now soften your belly and allow a deep and slow breath.

As you can now see, to give ourselves the gift of a full and open breath is one of the most healing things we can know, for healing is about opening what has been closed. It is about softening what has been hardened. The wonderful thing about breath is that it does this on all levels of our being – all the way from physical pain to the pain of feeling disconnected from Life.

I can't describe in words how much I love a deep breath that comes from my belly. It puts me in contact again with those times when I was laughing so hard I almost peed in my pants. It also reminds me of lying under the stars with nothing to separate me from deep reverence for Life. It can even bring back the essence of those moments when I was looking into my lover's eyes, giving and receiving love with every cell of my being.

In all these experiences, my belly was soft, my breath was free, and I was animated from my core. As we learn how to connect with our breath again, it can become both our teacher and our healer, taking us back into what we are truly hungry for – intimate, alive and loving connection with ourselves and with Life.

Soften your belly and allow a deep and slow breath.

Breath and Compulsion

As we become more intimate with our breath, it not only brings us all of the gifts we have explored; the breath also assumes the role of a wise and benevolent teacher. It is full of valuable information that can show us how to *relate to* a wave of compulsion rather than being *lost in it*.

From our very first breath until the last and final one, our lives are a continuous river of breath on which the experiences of Life are hung. When we first learned to ride a tricycle, this river was breathing us. When we laughed and when we cried it was there. Every time we were swimming, showering, shopping, kissing, singing, and sleeping it was there.

Every single breath has been different, influenced not only by the needs of our body, but also by our thoughts and emotions. It is fast when we are excited and slows down when we are resting. It has a tendency to be shallow when we are angry and deeper when we are at peace.

If we watch the ever-changing nature of breath, it will tell us how close or far away we are from ourselves. Whenever we are caught in our heads, with its continuous addiction to control, we tighten our bellies and breathe more shallowly. This contraction indicates that we are cut off from the nourishment of being *connected* to ourselves and thus are vulnerable to a wave of compulsion. As we learn how to be attuned to breath, it can point out to us very early in a wave of compulsion that we are in need of connection. As we become more in tune with ourselves, it can alert us even *before* the wave begins.

As we learn how to breathe down into our bellies again, our open breathing awakens our wellspring of deep knowing. In this awakening, we find that it becomes easier and easier to make wise and skillful choices, even in the face of the urge to be compulsive. For, as we touched on earlier, our empowered *No* is a part of the wellspring of wisdom in our bellies. At the heart of this type of *No* is a *Yes* to Life – a *Yes* to balance, skillful living and peace.

Notice what your breath is doing right now. Are you holding onto it or letting it freely rise and fall? I first became aware of how much I held my breath while watching cartoons with my children. Now, as far as I can see, to watch TV is usually not life-threatening. But, in the middle of the Road Runner approaching a cliff with Wily Coyote hot on his trail, I saw that I had pulled up and con-

> *Whenever we are caught in our heads, we are cut off from the nourishment of being connected to ourselves and thus are vulnerable to a wave of compulsion.*

tracted my whole body, especially the right side, and was hardly breathing at all.

I had had enough contact at this point with the joys of an open breath that I was curious about this old pattern of contraction. As I began to watch my breath throughout the day, to my amazement the only time I had an open breath was early in the morning when I was by myself and felt completely safe. As the day wore on, my breathing usually got tighter

> *What I was really hungry for was myself – immediate and intimate contact with me exactly as I was, no matter what was happening.*

and my connection with myself became dimmer, making me more vulnerable to a wave of compulsion.

I wanted to stay in contact with myself, nourished by this connection for more than an hour or two in the morning and my breath became my biofeed-back ally. Whenever it was tight, I was again disconnecting from myself. I began to retrain this ancient response by softening my body and taking a deep breath whenever I noticed how contracted I had become. This brought my attention out of the narrowness of my mind, into the spaciousness of my body. At the beginning, I could only do this when I was sitting still as when driving or watching TV. Slowly I became able to breathe myself back into myself as I moved throughout my day.

As my awareness became more receptive to the experience of my breath (and the joy of an open one), I saw this contraction was always present when a wave of compulsion was here. At first I couldn't do anything except watch this. The grip my struggling mind had on my breath during a wave of compulsion was too strong. But as I played with my breath when my compulsions were quiet, I began to feel the profound satisfaction of my breath going all the way down to my belly. It not only felt right, but I could see that a deep hunger inside of me was satisfied when I allowed my breath to be that open – the hunger for being connected to myself.

When I got to the place that I was able to watch what was going on during a wave of compulsion, I was stunned to realize that I wasn't hungry for the food. *What I was really hungry for was myself – immediate and intimate contact with me exactly as I was, no matter what was happening.* I had thoroughly learned how to abandon myself whenever the slightest discom-fort appeared on my inner radar. Needless to say, this was a stunning and very healing recognition.

It took me awhile to learn that when a wave of compulsion would appear, rather than heading down the ever-tightening spiral of reaction, I could feed it with a few deep breaths. These breaths reconnected me with myself and often the wave would pass through me leaving hardly a ripple.

Other times, when the wave needed more than just a few breaths, my open breathing put me in contact with exactly what I was experiencing, which was usually something uncomfortable that was fueling the compulsion. Through this contact, I took back my power. When I turned toward the experience, using my breath to open to exactly what was going on rather than being devoured by the experience (the main fear of the mind), I could now recognize what was happening.

In this recognition, *I had the choice either to be present for what I was experiencing, allowing my undivided attention to transform these tight places within me back into the free flowing energy they came from, or I had the choice to close down and run away again.* All of my life I had been running, and at the beginning of being present for myself when I was compulsive, I still ran sometimes. But shallow breathing was always there to remind me that running away just made the experience worse.

We will thoroughly explore in the chapter on *Treasure Hunting* how to be present for whatever we are experiencing without being at the mercy of it. Until then, soften your belly and allow a deep and slow breath.

Breath and the Wellspring of Wisdom

Open breathing also puts us in contact with a source of Intelligence and Wisdom that, thankfully, is much smarter than anything we can figure out on our own. If we watch carefully, we will see that whenever a wave of compulsion knocks us over, it feels like we are David facing Goliath and there is no help for miles around. Nothing could be further from the truth. In our bodies lies our wellspring of wisdom that is connected to the very Intelligence that gave us Life in the first place. This Intelligence is waiting to help us with our compulsions.

We can begin to understand the depth of the wisdom that is waiting for us in our bodies by looking at the intricate creativity it took to bring forth human beings in the first place. It is astounding that Life has been able to bring the light from the origin of the universe into the living, breathing being that is you, a person that can see and touch and hear and celebrate the awesome wonder of Life. We could say that each of us is light that has learned how to see, hear, taste, touch, and now describe itself! Our limited little minds can't even begin to comprehend this, let alone explain it. Nonetheless, we get all the benefits from the imaginative inventiveness of Life – we get to be alive!

You are not only a recipient of this Intelligence; you are a field of Intelligence. It resides inside of every single cell of your body and is most evident in the ribbon of information called DNA. This is the blueprint that makes you *you*. Each cell is less than 1/1000th of an inch across and

> *You are a field of Intelligence, residing within a greater Field of Intelligence.*

yet it contains enough information to fill 1000 books with 600 pages each! If you uncoiled the ribbon from every cell of your body, it would stretch to the moon and back 100,000 times!

Before you go on to the next sentence, let that sink in. It is over 230,000 miles to the moon. And yet this ribbon of Intelligence from all of our cells would stretch all the way back and forth to the moon 100,000 times! I think we can safely say that the Intelligence that orchestrates our body is greater than all the knowledge that human beings have ever gathered.

Not only does this Intelligence operate inside of individual cells, but also, when these cells come together into communities called bodies (or organisms), it orchestrates a complexity of processes that boggles the mind. Imagine driving a car, talking on a cell phone and trying to listen to directions from a passenger. This is almost impossible to do, and yet it is only three tasks. Your body administers zillions of tasks every moment of your life! It is so many that it is impossible to comprehend. And yet it hardly ever misses a beat.

How does the body do this? While each cell is an individual unit of Intelligence, all cells reside within a greater field of Intelligence that permeates our entire body (and all of Life). This Intelligence is what keeps the planets spinning as they do, orchestrates the dance of the seasons, and is the wellspring of each person's existence. This is the Intelligence that has brought you forth out of Mystery, beats your heart, breathes your breath, and resides in the space inside of every atom of your *being*. *You are a field of Intelligence, residing within a greater Field of Intelligence.*

As humanity has crawled up into the attic of the mind, we have learned how to rely upon our own resources, cutting ourselves off from the vast sea of Intelligence that is Life and the wisdom and support that is always with us. Feel your body as you are reading this book. There are myriad sensations – pressure, heat, itches, and pain. If you pay deep attention, encompassing all of those is a vibration, an *aliveness*. That is the Field of Intelligence.

This Intelligence is often given the name God and then all sorts of definitions and rules have sprung up around it. Stephen Levine once said, "I can use the word God because I have absolutely no idea what it means, but there is nowhere that I see it not!" Contrary to many popular religious beliefs,

> *Compulsions are here to invite, cajole, push, and prod us back into our bodies and into recognition and connection with this Greater Intelligence.*

contact with this Intelligence is not in some far off place (usually after you die) and is only granted if you have done your life 'right'. The doorway to immediate and intimate contact with this Intelligence is *inside* of you right now.

One of the many gifts of compulsions is that they won't let us off the hook until we stop trying to live our lives all by ourselves. Compulsions are here to invite, cajole, push, and prod us back into our bodies and into recognition and connection with this Greater Intelligence. A little later in the book, we will explore how to ask for help from the wellspring of Wisdom that is within us. Until then, know that open breathing brings us back into our bodies, making us receptive to the awesome field of Intelligence that resides there.

Soften your belly and allow a deep and slow breath.

Breathing Yourself Back Into Yourself

To be in contact with our breath is a wondrous thing. As we have been exploring, deep and open breathing brings a vitality *and* a calm into our bodies that is positively delicious. It also nourishes the deep hunger we have for an intimate relationship with ourselves.

As we cultivate an awareness of what our breath is doing, it also becomes our friend, signaling us when we are disconnecting from ourselves. The breath can then be used as a great healer, transforming our formerly frozen feelings into the joy of flowing energy. Yet most of us aren't even aware of the healing rhythm of our breath that is happening right under (and through!) our noses. Breathing unconsciously and shallowly, we are cut off from the friendship of our breath.

The most important thing we can do to access the joy of alive and open breathing is to simply notice how much we hold our breath. And, in some ways, that is enough. We can't force ourselves to breathe openly again. That kind of struggle is exactly what caused us to close down our breath in the first place! But we can begin to become curious about how much we not only hold our breath but how wonderful it

> *The breath can then be used as a great healer, transforming our formerly frozen feelings into the joy of flowing energy.*

feels when we aren't. That noticing begins to seed a process where we *want* to be in contact with our natural breath rather than feeling that we *have to* make our breath be different than what it is.

From this longing to know free breathing again, you can begin to cultivate your Deep Natural Breath. Let us play with it right now as you are reading.

The next time you breathe out, when you come to what you think is the end of your out-breath, keep on breathing out, slightly pulling in around the region of your belly button. When you do this, you will discover that there is a lot more air left in your lungs and this slight pressure can gently push out the rest of the air.

When you come to the completion of the out-breath, let your belly go and feel the in-breath come flooding in, lifting and opening your body. As the in-breath turns again into an out-breath, watch how you can let go of much more air when you bring your belly into the equation. When your lungs are emptied again, feel the joy of softening your belly, making space for the in-breath. The more space you make in your lungs through a full out-breath, the deeper your in-breath will be. Keep breathing deeply as you are reading, getting a sense of what it is like when your belly is again involved with your breath.

This is the art of full and open breathing, the kind of breath that nourishes you from the inside out. At first it may feel a little awkward, a little like trying to rub your tummy and pat your head at the same time. But the body knows how to breathe this way, and with a little bit of coaching your natural breath can begin to make itself known again. You can then let go of consciously pulling in your belly as you are breathing out, for the body will deeply exhale on its own.

You aren't trying to make the breath stay in the belly. That would just be more struggle. But moments of consciously cultivating a deep and full breath retrain your breathing from shallow to open and from tight to free. You can then remember the joy of open breathing and in that remembering, become more attuned to when you are again holding your breath.

Notice your breath again. It has probably left your belly and is again in the upper part of your chest. Don't try to change it. Just notice how different this breath is from the open breathing you played with a few minutes ago. Stay with your shallow breathing, becoming familiar with how it feels. It is important to know both extremes of breath – the open, free breath and the shallow, contracted breath.

> *To spend even a few minutes a day in curiosity about the breath creates a relationship with this wise and wondrous teacher, a relationship that will guide you in healing and being healed by your compulsion.*

To know full and open breathing is to bring a center of vitality, safety, and creativity into our lives. Familiarity with shallow breathing attunes your awareness so that when you are holding your breath again, that familiarity will wake you up, indicating that there is something that needs your attention. With this familiarity, you can begin to use your breath to signal yourself when you are heading down the path to compulsion.

To attune yourself to the nourishment of an open breath and to be able to use the shallow breath as a signal that you are disconnecting from yourself, it is helpful to have times in your day when you simply pay attention to your breath. I do it every morning. For a few minutes, I breathe the deep and open breath that we explored earlier. This always quiets my mind and brings a sense of vitality to my body. I then allow my breath to be exactly as it wants to be and I bring my attention to the experience. To spend even a few minutes a day in curiosity about the breath creates a relationship with this wise and wondrous teacher, a relationship that will guide you in healing and being healed by your compulsion.

It is also skillful to pause throughout the day and simply take one full breath. If it moves into a number of deep breaths that is great, but just one will do wonders for your life. I do this every time I wash my hands. Because it is so easy to forget to breathe open breaths, it can be skillful to connect a deep breath to something that you do repeatedly throughout the day, giving yourself these nourishing moments where you are returning to yourself. All our moments of waiting – at the doctor's office, in rush hour traffic, or in all the lines we stand in throughout our lives – can become moments where we cultivate a deep and open breath.

It is very important not to make either open breathing or paying attention to your breath into *shoulds*. That would be using the same struggling mind that created compulsions in the first place. These words are an invitation, and for some of you that will be enough. If you don't force these practices, they will become seeds that will grow into full and open breathing in your own time and in your own way. Trust where you are. At the same time, trust that a free and open breath is your destiny, for it is an essential component of a deep and nourishing connection with yourself and with Life.

Soften your belly now and allow a deep and slow breath.

Core Ideas in Skill #3 – Open Breathing

❖ To open to your breath again is to open to yourself; to open to yourself is to open to life.

❖ To breathe fully again is to energize the natural radiance of your body.

❖ Open breathing provides us with an immediate sanctuary that is available to us no matter where we are or what is happening in our lives.

❖ To breathe into your belly is to awaken the wellspring of deep knowing within you.

❖ Breath can gently open your contractions from the inside out, transforming even the deepest of emotions.

❖ When you are feeling compulsive, often what you need is just a few deep breaths.

❖ Pause and take a long, slow, deep breath, for one deep breath makes a difference.

❖ Every time that you pause for just a moment, take a breath and check-in with yourself, you take another step along the path of healing.

✦ SKILL 4: COMING HOME TO ✦ OURSELVES

If we watch closely when we are compulsive, not only are we trying to get away from a feeling or sensation that is uncomfortable, we are also trying to go toward the experience of feeling good again. Take for example a difficult day at work when your boss yells at you and your co-workers go out to lunch without asking you along. For most of us, deep and uncomfortable feelings would build throughout the day until, without a moment's thought, we find ourselves lunging toward our compulsions. If it is drinking, we find ourselves buying a six-pack even though we have sworn off all alcohol. If it's eating, we discover in our laps enough food for three people after we have gone through the drive through.

As we plunge into over-eating, over-drinking, over-shopping, unconscious sex or another cigarette, for a few moments the tension eases and everything seems okay. That hazy glow that comes after a couple of beers or the safe feeling that comes from having a full stomach seems to take us out of the pain and back into ease again – that is until the consequences of our actions and the ensuing self-judgment rear their ugly heads. We pay such a heavy price for taking care of ourselves this way, a price that becomes more and more expensive the older we get. There is another way to bring ourselves the peace that compulsions seem to promise and it is not a temporary peace. It is the peace that is always with us, no matter what is happening in our lives. For right underneath the story in our heads is what we are truly longing for – an immediate and intimate connection with ourselves and with Life.

We reconnect with this kind of connection by cultivating the power of simply *being*. Let me give you an example:

I was writing the other day, sitting on the couch in the room I use for counseling, when all of a sudden I became aware of warmth on my foot. As I looked up, there was the morning sun, caressing my leg. Joy burst forth from deep within me as the past and the future faded away and all that was left was the sun on my leg, a deep sense of delight cascading through my body, and a keen appreciation for the gift of Life. In those moments, I was *here*, fully present for myself and for my life. Oh, the joy of that! The joy of simply *being*!

> *There is a peace that is always with us, no matter what is happening in our lives.*

The healing that we long for comes from relearning how to be and this is what we are truly hungry for whenever we reach for our compulsions. *Being* is about discovering the safety and the nourishment of opening to Life as it is right now. It is about trusting ourselves and trusting our lives so that we can open again like a flower opens to the sun. *It is about being at home within our bodies and within our lives.*

Underneath all of our busyness, what we truly long for is to just *be*. Even though it is one of the most profound things a human being can do, most of us don't know how to *be*. Our minds are usually planning what is going to happen,

> *When we relearn how to simply be, we begin to discover moments in which our minds, our bodies and our hearts are all in the same place at the same time. These moments hold the power to heal us at our core.*

rehashing what did happen and struggling with everything else in between. We love to acquire and do, fix and achieve, attain and figure out. There is nothing wrong with all of these *except* that when they become our primary mode of existence, they cut us off from the astounding healing of simply *being*.

When we relearn how to simply *be*, we begin to discover moments like I had with the sun in which our minds, our bodies and our hearts are all in the same place at the same time. These moments hold the power to heal us at our core. The more we cultivate them, the more connected we become. The more connected we become, the more we live from the wellspring within that holds all of the clarity, peace, wisdom, and joy that we long for. We then learn how to *use* our doing, fixing, achieving mind when we need it, allowing it to fade into the background again as we discover the truth and the beauty of Life *as it is*, right here and right now.

We have been so far away from our lives, lost in the attics of our minds, that most of us don't know how to do this. In all of our doing, acquiring, and becoming, *we have forgotten how to simply be*! We don't know how to be present for ourselves. We don't know how to be present for Life. Living in the memories of the past and the fantasies of the future, we make problems out of most everything and rush through our lives trying to get to the solution.

In our disconnection from ourselves and from our lives, compulsions become a substitute for the joy of *being*. But nothing from the outside can truly quench our deepest longing. What we are hungry for is to be truly awake for Life and to experience the joy of *being* at home within ourselves and within our world. What we are hungry for is the experience of *being*.

Barriers to *Being*

What I am saying probably strikes a chord deep within you. We all recognize on some level that we are not connected to ourselves and to our lives, and yet we are afraid of the kind of connection I am talking about. *We are afraid of simply being!* Try to live a day without your favorite distraction – reading, talking or watching TV. Instead, simply open to Life. If you do this, you will see what I am talking about. You will probably get anxious, frustrated, bored or depressed. You will be caught in your mind, unable to simply *be*.

And yet in *being*, all the wonders of Life reveal themselves. Gilda Radner, the comedian who died of ovarian cancer, once said that if it weren't for the downside of cancer (possible death), everybody should experience it because it teaches us how to deeply appreciate and open to the miracle of Life! Gilda is not the only one who discovered this truth. Many people living under a terminal diagnosis describe it as one of the most alive times of their lives.

Why, when *being* is so wonderful, do we insist on staying caught in the attics of our minds? We touched on one of the core reasons in the house analogy we explored at the beginning of the book. We all lived in *being* when we were young and yet were scared out of it by the overwhelming feelings and experiences of our childhood. We retreated to the attics of our minds as safe havens from Life, and for a while that worked. But it all changed when we locked our doors from the inside and wrote on the back of the door, "Do not ever open this door again or you will die!" The fear of Life was that deep! Our minds, rather than being safe havens, then became prisons, and our jailers were the signs on the back of the locked door that remind us to never again open to Life.

We are not made to live just in the attic of the mind! It is our destiny to know the full house of our *being*, and all the joy, trust and peace that this brings. It is the birthright of every single human *being* to be at home within themselves and within their lives. In order to open the door again, we need to look at three core beliefs we took on while caught in the attic of our minds, beliefs that keep us locked away from the healing of simply *being*.

1. It is Not Safe to Open to Life Again

2. My Body is Not a Friend

3. Cultivating *Being* is Selfish

It is Not Safe to Open to Life Again

Having sat for long periods of time in silence, breathing myself back into myself and back into Life, I have discovered a deep and lasting truth. *Life is for you*. Our everyday experiences aren't a series of disconnected events in which it sometimes seems that God has fallen asleep on the job. In fact, the exact opposite is true. There is a powerful and benevolent intent behind absolutely everything that happens in our lives. Life wants us to awaken into its full presence even more than we do, and it is giving us all the experiences we need in order to relearn the safety and the exhilaration of being open to our own lives.

So the first belief we need to dismantle in order to open the door to *being* is the belief that it is not safe to open to Life. For most of us, this was true when we were young. We didn't have the skills nor the wisdom to meet Life as it was. But we are not children any more and to stay caught in the narrow room of the intellect is where the *unsafety* is. All the stories in our head put a veil between ourselves and our lives so that we don't truly see what is going on. In other words, we walk through our lives blind! We live in the past and in the future, rarely present and alert for what is happening right now. To live our lives caught in our head is like walking along a path on the edge of a cliff with a blindfold on. If that isn't unsafe, I don't know what is!

Not only that, this veil says it is keeping us safe through control. But if we watch closely, we will see that the lions and tigers and bears of our lives live mostly in the exact place we have gone when trying to hide from Life – in the attic of the mind. Throughout the ongoing conversation we have with ourselves all day long are the lions of our hatreds and fears, the tigers of our compulsions and the bears of our despair. And since there is very little space up there, it is very easy to tumble from one struggle to another, completely cut off from the living experience of Life and all the support and wisdom that is waiting for us there. I am not saying that there aren't challenges in our lives. What I'm saying is that we are much more able to respond to our challenges from an empowered and skillful place when we are present for our lives.

> *There is a powerful and benevolent intent behind absolutely everything that happens in our lives.*

It is important to understand that cultivating *being* is not about being powerless. It is not about being out-of-control. Even though at first glance *being* seems like just rolling over and passively letting Life do with us as it will, it is the exact opposite. We are less able to respond to circumstances effectively when caught in our heads because we don't notice what is going

> *Life is speaking to us all the time. It is giving us the clues that will take us out of our reactive mind and back into the joy of being truly connected to Life.*

on! In our unawareness, we live from *reaction* rather than *response*. This is what compulsions are, a reaction to the unpleasant in our lives and a lunging toward the pleasant.

Cultivating being *is a very active place where you are passionately alert, listening and learning from every experience you are given.* Something happens when we stay this open and listen. We begin to realize that Life is speaking to us all the time. It is giving us the clues that will take us out of our reactive mind and back into the joy of being truly connected to Life. Remember those connect-the-dot puzzles from childhood where, when we followed the numbers with our pencil, the picture then became clear? That is very similar to the experience of being present for our own lives. As we learn how to listen, really listen, to whatever we are being given, it begins to make sense.

In order to trust Life at that level, we need to look at our whole relationship with pain for this is why we closed off in the first place. It hurts to be alive. It hurts to stub your toe, to be rejected, to lose a loved one. When we were young, the pains of our lives were amplified dramatically. Time is different for a child. Five minutes felt like an hour; an hour like a day; and a day like a week.

The only skill we learned around pain was to resist it. So we held our breaths and tightened our muscles, hiding feelings deep in our bodies and retreating to the attic of our minds. For a while that worked, but that didn't mean that what we were trying to run away from would go away. In fact the opposite is true. Pain fermented inside of us, turning into pure fuel for our compulsions and exploding all over our lives in the most unpleasant ways.

It took me a long time to see that when I resist pain, whether it is physical, mental or emotional, it always gets worse. As a wise teacher once said, "Pain is a given in human life. Suffering is our resistance to our pain." We can understand what this means when we see that Life is a dance of duality. One day we feel clear as a bell and the next day confusion reigns. One morning we get up and our body feels light and alive. The next morning we don't know how we can make it through the day. For a time, our new relationship is easy and full of fun. Then it turns into a war that seems to have no origin. That is what Life is like. One day is very stormy and then we wake up to sunshine the next day.

When we try to have only the pleasant stuff, it all turns into a struggle.

When we try to run away from the pains of our lives, we also cut ourselves off from our joy. We can't have one without the other. (You can explore this further in the chapter called *The Fertility of the Dark* in my book, *Belonging To Life*.)

It also took me a while to discover that if I open to my pain in curiosity, I bring it out of the shadows into the light where I can work with it in kind and skillful ways. Pain is so much more workable when we stay open to it. The easiest place to see this truth is in your body. Even physical therapists and doctors now know that if you teach a person how to open around their pain, it not only lessens, it also hastens the time of healing.

This has certainly been true in my body. I have had much physical pain in my life, and for years all I did was resist. I took pills. I overate. I tried to distract myself in every way, and my pain stayed stuck to me like glue. When I learned how to open to it and acknowledge it in a non-resistive way, it not only became much more bearable, I discovered that right in the heart of the pain was all of the wisdom that was needed to bring it back into balance. Oh, the joy of learning how to listen! The joy of being present for my pain!

This technique not only worked with my physical pain, it also did wonders with all of the emotional pain that I had run from my whole life. I have also seen it work like magic with friends, clients, and loved ones. When they share with me the depth of their suffering, they are usually holding their breath, tightening their bodies, and their minds are spinning out of control. By inviting them to go toward the experience rather than running away, I take them into their bodies, asking them to name and then experience what is going on. Invariably they take a big breath, discover that it isn't as scary as they thought, and whatever is happening becomes workable again.

We will be exploring this in depth in the *Treasure Hunting* chapter. Until then, know that just taking a few deep breaths when you are in pain, whether it is physical, mental, or emotional, and softening your belly can lessen the pain. As you open, you can then discover that, rather than being your enemy, your pain is a wise and benevolent teacher, revealing to you the place where you are caught in struggle. If you listen, it will show you the way beyond the struggles of your mind.

> *As you open, you can then discover that, rather than being your enemy, your pain is a wise and benevolent teacher, revealing to you the place where you are caught in struggle.*

This is why I call my pain my noble adversary. As I grappled with the great challenges of my pains, they sharpened my attention, opened my heart, and taught me how to truly listen. They invited me to be open to my own life – the pleasant and the unpleasant, the joys and the sorrows. They then showed me that when I can meet myself as I am and open to my life exactly as it is, the joy that is my birthright would make itself known.

It is not only safe to open to Life; it is only in opening to whatever is right here and right now that we will discover the connection and the peace that we long for. Let us practice opening in the following exercise:

After you read through this exercise, I invite you to close your eyes and take some deep breaths. Every time you breathe out, let go. Let go of the tension in your neck, your shoulder blades, your belly, and even your feet. Let it all go and amplify this letting go by saying the sound ahhhhh. Now let go of all of your thoughts about the past and about the future, and ground your attention in your immediate experience. Feel warmth and coolness , along with the pulsating and vibrating that is your body.

As you settle into your body, feel yourself sitting here. Feel the pressure on your legs, your buttocks and your back. When you make contact with the experience of sitting, with every out-breath, melt into whatever you are sitting on and let it hold you. If it is hard to make this shift of perception from sitting 'on top of' to being held, imagine the support beneath you all of a sudden evaporating. You would fall to the floor! So it is true that you are sitting on top of something, but you are also being held. For these few moments, let go of sitting 'on top of' and allow yourself to be held!

Now expand your awareness. Whatever you are sitting on is being held by the floor beneath it. And the floor is being held by the foundation and the foundation by the Earth. Now, what is the Earth being held by? Allow your awareness to expand so that you can imagine looking down through the floor, the foundation, the crust of the Earth, and even the center of the Earth. Keep on going, and as your awareness pops out on the other side of the Earth, you see with astonishment that the Earth is being held by space! It isn't stuck on a stick or hung by a string. It is allowing itself to be held by nothing more substantial than space. And yet it is fully supported.

Now bring your awareness back to yourself sitting here. Recognize

> *that as you sit here, you too are being held by the same space that is holding the Earth. Let go to that. Allow yourself to trust Life enough for this moment that you see that wherever you are, whatever is happening, you are being held by Life.*

The safest thing you will ever do is open to Life. This opening pulls your attention out of the story in your head that loves to struggle with Life enabling you to discover that this moment is a part of the river of your own life. *And it is for you.* In all of its ups and downs, pleasures and pains, it is a benevolent and trustable process that is taking you step-by-step home.

② My Body is Not A Friend

Since *being* is about immediate contact with ourselves and with Life, it means we have to be *in* our bodies. But most of us don't live here. We have been hijacked by the style of mind that says the body is just a vehicle for maneuvering through our lives - a piece of meat that is supposed to do the bidding of the mind. We have been brainwashed into riding around inside of a mind that *sits on top of a body*, never aware that what we truly long for is to live *in* our bodies again.

James Joyce, Irish novelist and author of *Ulysses,* wrote the wonderful line: "Mr. Duffy lives a short distance from his body!" When we were young, we were naturally in contact with how delicious it is to have a body. We lived inside of our bodies, inside of ourselves, and were in contact with our wellspring within. Over time we learned that it wasn't safe nor accepted by the adults around us to be this open and alive. For survival we turned down the dimmer switch of our free-flowing energy, holding our breaths and tightening our muscles. As adults, retreating to the attic of our minds (which is for most of us a very long distance from our bodies!), we discovered that we rarely, if ever, feel at ease with ourselves, at home in our bodies.

Lost in the ivory towers of our intellects, we are almost completely out of touch with our bodies, and at the same time are obsessed with their appearance. The average model is 5' 11" and weighs 110 pounds and we try to emulate them! Who weighs that much when they are that tall? Only people in countries that are facing starvation - and models! Are

> *Lost in the ivory towers of our intellects, we are almost completely out of touch with our bodies, and at the same time are obsessed with their appearance.*

143

we brainwashed or what? In fact, we have carried this unhealthy relationship so far that we value people in this society by how they appear on the outside rather than what they are on the inside!

Looking down from the ivory tower of our minds, not only do we judge our bodily appearances, we also load much of our self-hate onto our bodies too. Think of all the self-destructive behaviors that are acted out on the body: over loading it with food, drugs, and alcohol, biting our fingernails, meaningless sex, picking our skin, expecting the body to work endless hours fueled only by coffee, sugar, and high-fat foods.

We also draw most of our swear words from our body: *shit, asshole, cunt, fuck you.* Just writing these words brings up a wave of grief inside of me. Here is this wondrous creation that we have been given, narrowed down to disregard and disrespect. From Christian theologians such as St. Augustine, who was caught in his own struggling mind, and our misinterpretation of the writings of the Apostle Paul, we bought into the belief that the body and its emotions, needs, and feelings were *beneath* the world of the spirit. From the writings of the Greek philosopher Plato, came the idea that "we must avoid as much as we can all contact and association with the body, except when they are absolutely necessary."

All one has to do to see the effects of disconnecting from the body is to compare the face of someone who really believes in *the evils of the flesh* with the face of a child who is still connected to him or herself. A person who believes that *pleasure* and *sin* are compatible words is often a study in tension (think of the monks who punished themselves with prickly hair shirts and self-flagellation in the Middle Ages or the dour and dark countenances of the Puritans.) Their mouths are tight, their brows are furrowed, and their eyes are dead. Then remember the aliveness of a child who has just danced their favorite dance for you – the flush in their cheeks, the light in their eyes. To be in our bodies is to be home!

> *All one has to do to see the effects of disconnecting from the body is to compare the face of someone who really believes in the evils of the flesh with the face of an innocent child who is still connected to him or herself.*

It wasn't only religion and philosophy that cut us off from our bodies. Science didn't help either. It divided Life into parts, missing the interconnectedness of it all. As science explored the various parts of the body, it missed the deep intelligence of the body as a whole. In scientists' urge to divide in order to understand, they reduced all of Life down to a mechanistic universe made up of inert atoms, separate unto themselves, with no spark of spirit within them.

> *To love, honor, and celebrate your body is to celebrate Life. And it has been waiting since your childhood for you to come back home.*

Nothing could be further from the truth! Our bodies are an unfolding sea of creativity that is more intelligent, more ancient, and more alive than we can possibly imagine. Even those so-called static building blocks of Life called atoms are pulsating with Life. If you blew up an atom to be the size of a baseball field, the nucleus would be just a grain of sand out by the pitchers mound and the electrons would be dancing beyond the outer edge of the field. What is it that fills up the rest of the space? Nothing less than the creative urge that spilled out of the unfolding we call the Big Bang. It showed up as light – as vibrating, pulsating, creative waves and particles of light. This is not just fanciful thinking. This is the conclusion of many of our leading edge scientists.

Ponder this amazing fact. The vast space inside of every single atom that makes up every single thing in the universe is filled with the creative light from the Big Bang! Every one of your 100 trillion cells is made up of 100 trillion atoms. So you are nothing less than a field of creative light! The more you are present in your body, the more it shines! Mathew Fox, in his book *Sins of the Fathers, Blessings of the Flesh,* reported that if we were able to harness all of the light in one human *being*, it would be able to turn on all of the flood lights it takes to light a major league baseball field and keep them lit for three hours!

There are two core gifts we are given as we relearn how to be *in* our bodies:

a Joy and Aliveness

It is so delicious to be *in* our bodies. This *in the body* experience connects us to a river of aliveness that, when we are present for it, nourishes us to our cores. In fact, aliveness is what we are hungry for whenever we are compulsive. When we make contact again, we enter the web of joy that is Life. Everywhere we look Life celebrates the joy of existence – the beauty in the unfolding of a flower, the dance of dandelion seeds on the wind, the purr of a cat, or the music of a waterfall. *Joy is nothing less than the energy of Life celebrating itself freely.*

Sit quietly and watch a tree long enough that you can begin to feel it stretching its branches out in a love affair with the sun. You can *feel* this same propensity for joy in the sound of water cascading across the rocks and in the play of the wind in the leaves. It is also evident in many babies of this world, whether the baby is a kitten, a foal, a human or a chimpanzee.

The same is true for your body. When you are truly *in* your body, you can feel joy radiating out of every cell. The body is a river of free-flowing energy that loves to be animated from its core. This energy wants to leap and soar, being as expressive as the sun and as still as a clear mountain pool, infusing us with the glow of radiance. As I write this, I can feel it pulsating throughout my whole body. When I was disconnected from my body, this level of joy was scary. Now that I am grounded fully in my body, I can allow this energy to flow through me, seeking the full expression it so deeply longs for.

We are starving for the glow of *being*! Think of the eyes of someone in love. They are glowing because their inner light is shining too. We often think of great spiritual leaders down through the eons with halos around their heads. This is how we symbolize the truth that the dimmer switch of their light field has been turned up full volume. We can know this glow too as we make friends with our bodies again.

Deep Knowing

The field of light that is our body is also highly intelligent and can guide us through the ups and downs of Life. We call it gut instinct or intuition, but most of what we label this way has to literally shout from the deep regions of our *being* in order to get our attention. *When we begin to listen, really listen to the deep knowing inside of us, we finally realize we are traveling down the path of Life with a wise and very dear friend!*

This deep knowing is the *inner radar* of our wellspring. It knows much more clearly how to live our lives than any idea our intellects can come up with. It knows when to say "yes" and when to say "no" in every experience. This inner radar also holds all the missing pieces to the puzzles of our lives. And it most definitely knows how to make wise choices in every situation, especially around compulsions.

We tap into this inner radar by *being in* our bodies. I discovered this while doing massage many years ago. I had learned numerous techniques and was busily applying what I thought I should be doing. My massages were good, but not great.

I then began to notice that some massages were more *alive* than others. When I became curious, I realized that with the clients who were having a *wow* kind of experience, I was massaging from a different place. Rather than thinking about what I should be doing, *I was listening to what <u>my</u> body* *was asking for*! My inner radar was telling me exactly what was appropriate for the person to whom I was giving a massage! And the more I listened, the more people left feeling truly connected to themselves.

I then began to apply this in other aspects of my life, especially with my children. I would listen in my body for the appropriate words or actions in any given situation. When I spoke from this place, a place that felt *right* inside of me, it always brought clarity and lessened dramatically the normal resistance of teenagers. They respected what I said when they recognized that I was speaking from this clear and clean place.

Your body is your friend. To come back to it is to tap into your wellspring of wisdom and joy. To love, to honor, and to celebrate your body is to celebrate Life. And it has been waiting, since your childhood, for you to come back home.

In order to become more at home in your body, there is a powerful meditation you can do. It can stand on its own or you can add it at the beginning of your daily *returning* practice. This meditation opens up the *I am not knots* in your body so that your energy can flow freely. Let us explore it now.

After you read through this exercise, close your eyes, take a few deep breaths and let go as deeply as you can on each out-breath. Then allow your breath to be as it wants to be. As you settle into its rhythm, feel your body. It is a constantly changing river of sensation, different right now than it ever has been. Simply feel what it is experiencing in this moment.

Now, using your attention like a flashlight, bring it to the top of your head. As you let it rest there, the sensations in your head will reveal themselves, just like a Polaroid picture developing. If the sensations are hazy, ask yourself, "How do I even know there is a head there?" This invites the mind to be curious, exploring what is there. Stay there for at least 30 seconds – more if it is an area that intrigues you today.

Then bring your attention to your face and see what is happening there. Again, use your attention like a flashlight. There are numerous sensations - tickles, warmth, pressure, moisture. Slowly work your way around your face just as if you were exploring a brand new country. When you come to your lips, wet them with your tongue and see what happens. Then come inside your mouth and recognize your tongue. Allow it to explore all of the varied surfaces in your mouth.

Now move down into your throat area. Again, it will be different from your face. As you settle in, what do you discover there? Is there tightness? If so, is it more on the right or on the left? Go around to the back of your neck and see what is there. Again, whenever you move your attention, let it settle in the new spot for a few moments. Rather than trying to find the sensations, allow them to reveal themselves to you.

There is no set pattern to this mediation. If it intrigues you, explore both of your arms and your hands with your curiosity. Or maybe your back interests you today. Wherever you go, notice if you have any areas that you like more than others and any areas that you are resistant to being with. If you find an area with a lot of tension, know that you have been resisting whatever is there.

One of the very powerful areas to make contact with is your belly. We hold a lot of tension in the belly, both on the surface and deep within. There is also a tremendous wellspring of aliveness there, and as you pay attention, the wellspring will reveal itself.

Be sure to explore the whole pelvic floor too, for as it opens, energy can cascade down your legs, grounding you right here and now. As you explore your legs, see if there is any tension that blocks this energy. As you explore your feet, check in with one first, exploring it as intimately as you can, and then go to the other. Notice both the similarities in sensations and the differences.

When you are done, take your attention back to the body as a whole and notice how it has changed now that you have spent intimate time with it.

This is a wonderful gift to give to yourself – the gift of *being* fully present for your body. The miracle of your body is being touched by the healing power of your attention! You can take two minutes to do this meditation, just exploring your face, or you can take an hour, exploring every nook and cranny of your body. You can also explore the more surface sensations or you can go deep inside, feeling the rhythm of your breath from inside the lungs and the pulse of your heart throughout your body. Know that every time you check in with yourself this way, you are taking another step into living *in* your body, connected to your wellspring within.

Cultivating *Being* is Selfish

Deep in our collective mind is a belief that to spend time with ourselves –to cultivate *being* – is selfish. This idea holds great power in our society, exerting pressure on us to prove that we are not just standing around taking up space and, heaven forbid, enjoying ourselves. Most people are so terrified of being labeled as selfish that they run around like chickens with their heads cut off trying to prove their worth. Even with all of that doing, they still carry secret fears deep inside that they are selfish and self-absorbed. In this disconnection, their actions become *reactions* rather than *responses* coming from their wisdom within. The more a person disconnects from himself or herself, the more that person becomes like an untuned car, driving down the freeway of Life with black exhaust trailing behind.

Thich Nhat Hanh, the Buddhist monk and insightful author, did a wonderful twist on the old phrase, "Don't just sit there, do something," which is the hallmark of our society. He said, "Don't just do something, sit there!" What he is inviting us into is the truth that our value comes not from what we *do* or accomplish but from who we *are*. We can only know the depth of who we are when we spend time with ourselves. When we listen, we become a healing presence in the world for we live from our deep knowing within.

This means that, far from being selfish, taking time to be with ourselves is essential. It is essential to step out of the ongoing pell-mell speed of our society so we can have time just to *be*. For many of us it means that we need to simplify our lives, for to live from the joy of *being*, we need to make self-time a priority. Self-time is the kind of time where we let go of the past and the future, cultivating a connection with the immediacy of Life.

I live in a beautiful 1914 cottage that looks out on a magical garden. Once a month, people come for a day of silence. They climb the maple tree and feel it holding them. They sit by the waterfall, allowing its music to soothe them to their core. They swing on the swing, watching the multitude of birds dance through the yard. By the time they leave, their eyes have regained their sparkle and their skin is glowing again.

Far from being selfish, to cultivate *being* is the healthiest thing we can do for ourselves and for our world. The most primary relationship we are given in our lives is the one with ourselves. We are the person we go to sleep with every night and wake up to every morning. We are also the person we were born into at our birth and we are the person we will be with on our

> *Far from being selfish, taking time to be with ourselves is essential.*

deathbed. Doesn't it make sense to cultivate *being* time, learning how to listen to ourselves? Doesn't it make sense to learn how to tap into our essence so we can live connected to our own inner radar?

Our *being* time is not only for ourselves but also for everybody else in our lives. How can we possibly live skillfully if we are not connected to ourselves? Rather than being self indulgent, cultivating time where we can just *be* supports everybody else in our lives. Rather than being selfish it is the greatest gift we can give to others – to listen to and live from our own center. As we learn how to nourish ourselves in this way, we can then give from a *full tank* that blesses everybody we touch. Learning how to *be* includes learning how to be with *both* the joys and the sorrows of Life. We can't have one without the other.

Let's get a sense of how powerful it is to spend time just *being*, listening to, and meeting the pains of our lives in the following exercise:

> *After you read through this exercise, close your eyes and take a few of those precious deep breaths that invite your whole body to let go. As you settle into the rhythm of your breath, allow yourself to become aware of one of the deeper pains of your life. It could be the sorrow of death, a cloud of depression, a feeling of being an outsider, the deep grief of being abandoned by a loved one, a debilitating physical challenge, a core feeling of shame. Choose one challenge and then open to it. Don't just think about it; allow yourself to identify the feelings that go along with it. Feel how, when you get close to these feelings, you want to react, to run away, to close off, and shut down.*
>
> *Now expand your awareness out and recognize that right now there are tens of thousands of people who are experiencing exactly what you are experiencing. Take the feeling of abandonment for example. Allow yourself to know that without a doubt, somewhere on the Earth, there are young children right now that are being abandoned on a city street, left to fend for themselves. Feel the overwhelming terror, confusion, and grief of these children. Allow yourself to recognize the truth that you are not alone in your pain, no matter what it is.*
>
> *What can you do? You can come back to yourself. Feel this same pain inside of you, but for these few moments, don't react. Become conscious of your pain. Become merciful with your pain. Meet it right here and right now. As you touch your pain through your merciful attention, you can finally recognize that this is not just*

> *your pain. It is the pain of humanity, and as you heal your pain*
> *with your merciful attention, you take the collective mind of*
> *humanity another step into healing. Now find others on the Earth*
> *who are experiencing the same pain. There are many. You are not*
> *alone. Feel their pain inside of you and know you can truly make a*
> *difference by being present for yourself, exactly as you are.*

At first glance, this may not seem to make much of a difference. Instead, you may want to go buy an airplane ticket and go help all those people in pain. But when you meet the pain within you – the pain that we all carry, the pain that causes each one of us to live in unskillful ways – you literally help to heal the pain of the world. This may seem like only a drop in a mighty ocean of pain, but drop-by-drop it can be healed.

This meditation also works with our joy. Because you are a part of the web of Life, every time you are present for your life, tasting your food, seeing your lover's face, feeling the cool evening air on your cheek, you bring the collective mind of humanity another step into conscious and loving connection with Life. It is empowering, not only for yourself but also for every single person on the face of this Earth and for the Earth itself, for you to take time to *be* with yourself exactly as you are.

May all beings be free from suffering. May all beings know peace.

As we see through all of the ideas that keep us separate from *being,* it becomes clear that we not only have the right to *being* time, it is one of the core responsibilities of our lives. The more we become connected to ourselves, drinking from the wellspring of *being* that is always with us, the less we are vulnerable to a wave of compulsion. The less we are caught in compulsion's grip, the more we can know the joy that is our own true nature. We then become *Life celebrating Lif*e, and everyone benefits from our knowing and our glowing!

Cultivating *Being*

Now that we know that it is safe and important to cultivate *being*, let us explore how to bring this wonderful healing experience into our lives. It is all about bringing our attention to our lives, not as we wish them to be, but exactly as they are, right here, right now. Remember the little girl at the beginning of the book who kept on being drawn back to the wonder of the river? She was *here,* connected with her life *as it was in that moment.* Because of that, she could *feel* the joy of the water in her body! As adults our attention, rather than being *here*, usually follows the ever wanting and fearing mind around on its crazy pell-mell course throughout the day.

To know ourselves again with our birthright of aliveness and joy, we need to retrain our attention into fascination with the experience of being alive. It is possible to do this in the middle of our busy lives. It is not about *doing* anything. It is just about *being* curious about Life as it is right now. It is about *being in* our bodies; it is about *being in* our lives. It is relearning how to wash the dishes when we wash the dishes, eat when we eat and hear when we are listening, so we can tap into the river of aliveness that is Life.

Moments where we are fully here for Life are powerfully healing. Jon Kabat Zinn in his book, *Full Catastrophe Living,* speaks about a study done at the University of Ohio. Exploring the effects of a high fat, high cholesterol diet on rabbits, researchers put these cuddly bundles of Life in cages stacked one upon the other. When the test results came back, the rabbits in the lower cages had much less heart disease. This didn't make sense. They were all genetically identical, were on the same diet, and, it was thought, were being treated in the same way. That is until it was discovered that the rabbits in the lower cages were periodically being taken out of the cages by one of the members of the team to be stroked, cuddled, and talked to!

A few moments of connection made a huge difference in the cholesterol of the rabbits. This amazes us, but that is what *being* is all about. It is about connection. It is about choosing to be open to Life, right here, right now – not an idea of it, but the real thing. And whether it is connection with a bunny hug, the beat of our heart, the taste of our food, the sound of a bird, the face of a loved one, or the warmth of the sun on our leg, this kind of connection *heals*.

> *Being is about relearning how to wash the dishes when we wash the dishes, eat when we are eating and listen when we are listening, so we can tap into the river of aliveness that is Life.*

Since we have been contained and controlled for so many years, how do we open to Life again, cultivating the exhilaration of *being*? We laid the foundation by exploring a returning practice in the chapter on *Curiosity*. Every time we bring our attention back into *what is*, we are cultivating *being*. We then learned to soften and open the contraction in our minds and bodies by touching whatever is there with the mercy of our hearts.

> *We won't relearn how to be present for ourselves and for Life overnight. But know that every time we return to what is, we strengthen the muscle of our attention, increasing our capacity to be present for Life.*

In the beginning, most of us return and open to *what is* only sporadically, and when we do, we become like bouncing balls – a moment of pure connection with Life then off we go back into the dream of the mind. For a while, this is all we can do. We didn't learn how to walk overnight. We won't relearn how to be present for ourselves and for Life overnight either. But know that every time we return, we strengthen the muscle of our attention, increasing our capacity to be present for Life. Then there comes a time when we are ready for more, ready to truly open to Life again. It is when our *whole body* begins to remember that it is safe and healing to open to Life that we can begin to *live* from *being*, tapping into its many treasures.

I once had an experience that shows what I am talking about. Having just returned from a full weekend of teaching, I had a few hours the next morning to write. I found my mind fuzzy and my body very tired. I knew what I wanted to say, but it wouldn't come out in an orderly fashion. In the middle of my muddle, my cat jumped up on my lap, asking for my attention. Of course, my response was resistance. "I am doing some important work now," I said, "and I don't have time for you!"

As I continued to go round and round in my mind about what to write, my cat gently but persistently kneaded my legs, saying to me, "Take a break! Get out of your mind and come back into your body." When I finally was able to see that I was a ball of resistance and then could recognize the invitation my cat was giving me, I started to chuckle as I turned off the computer and curled up with her. Her purrs vibrated in my body, inviting me to soften my belly and come back into the delicious rhythm of my breath.

As I settled in, letting go of all the struggles in my mind, my attention filled my whole body and there to meet me from the top of my head to the bottom of my toes was pure aliveness. The best word I can use to describe what I was experiencing was *delight*. That is such a wonderful word – de-light -

meaning *from light*! That was truly my experience. When I was back in my body, the radiance of the wellspring within filled me with its presence. As my kitty and I purred together (with a few kitty kisses here and there), the deep knowing that permeates this radiance revealed to me what wanted to be written with such clarity that I became amazed that I stayed caught in my struggling mind so long!

It is astounding how just a few minutes of dropping into our body and connecting with ourselves can open us to the river of joy that is always waiting for us right under the struggles of our mind. Sourcing ourselves through the vitality and aliveness that is our body grounds us in the flow and the glow of Life. Try this for yourself in the following exercise:

> *After you read through this exercise, close your eyes and take a number of long, slow breaths. Then bring your attention into the river of sensations that is your body. Go beyond the aches and pains, the coolness or warmth, and feel the aliveness. If it is hazy, put your attention a few inches away from your body and notice if you feel anything there. Then bring it back into your body and feel the tingle that resides there.*
>
> *If it is still hazy, shake your hand to get your energy flowing again and, when you stop, rest in how good it feels. If you are ready to go for the gusto, put the book down and shake your whole body like we did earlier in the book. When you sit down again, close your eyes and feel! When you are ready, open your eyes.*

This is the river of aliveness that comes from *being*. It is not only delicious, it is intelligent, benevolent, and it nourishes us to our core. The more we make contact with it, the more we will see that there really is something there – a field of wisdom and love that is waiting for us right beyond our struggling mind. You don't have to go around shaking your body to know this. All you need do is relearn how to bring your attention back into your body, allow it to rest there, and watch the aliveness grow. It takes time to relearn, but as far as I can see, it is one of the most powerful gifts we can ever give to ourselves and to Life.

◇ The Skills of *Being*

What would it be like if you could learn how to fill your body with *delight* rather than food, drugs, hectic busyness, or alcohol? That is what you are truly longing for anyway. Woven throughout all of the skills we have explored so far are techniques that I want to bring together now in a simple

3 step process that will allow you to begin to open to yourself and to Life again and reconnect with the river of joy within.

The three steps to cultivating *being* in order to access the field of aliveness that we are so hungry for are:

◆ Bring curious attention to the body.

◆ Let go of any tension that dims the field of aliveness.

◆ Open to Life.

◆ Bringing Curious Attention to the Body

The first step is to become curious about what is happening right now in your body. At some time, you may want to go back and reread the chapter on *Curiosity* in order to deepen your ability to bring your attention out of *what was* and *what will be* into *what is* right now.

Your body is a constantly changing river of sensations and the body you are in right now is different than at any other time in your life. Everything is new in this moment. With your attention, become curious about the river of sensations that are happening there.

You can deepen by asking the question, "In this moment, what am I experiencing?" This is what I call a Check-In Question. It helps you to let go of everything that has happened up until this moment of your life for it all belongs to the *already lived*. This question also invites you to let go of whatever may happen in the future, because it isn't here yet. Instead, it fully focuses your attention on what is happening right here and right now. Whenever you drift off, you can use this question to bring your attention back. To keep your mind curious, see if you can find at least two distinct and different sensations.

◆ Letting Go of Tension

As you scan your body, if you are like most people, you will notice a lot of tension. These are *I am not knots* that dim the full expression of your joy. The second step is to let go of any tension you find that is dimming the full experience of *being alive*. This shows up as tightness in your shoulders, pressure in your chest, knots in your stomach, contraction in your belly.

As we explored in *Open Breathing* (see page 122), breath is a marvelous friend in opening us up again. The best breathing technique I have discovered for opening and relaxing the chronic holdings in our body is to take a deep breath and then hold it for a moment. As you let it go, keep on breathing out until all the air is gone and then pause again for a moment. As you take in the next breath, contract your entire body – really, really tighten it from your nose to your toes – then pause at the end of the breath, and as you breathe out, let go. Let go of the clenching in your jaw, the tightness in your shoulders, the contraction in your stomach, the tension in your feet. Imagine them melting like an ice cube placed in the sun. Really enjoy this letting go. Ahhhhh, such sweet relief.

Feel how this subtle softening into Life turns up the volume of your aliveness. Allow yourself to melt into the free-flowing energy that is Life.

We are so used to focusing on the contractions and struggles of our lives that we are not familiar with making contact with the field of aliveness that our struggles are floating in. When we turn our attention away from our struggles and toward our aliveness, it becomes amplified by our attention. It then expresses itself as joy.

◆ Opening to Life

The third step is to open the focus of your attention to include the fullness of your life right here right now. This is a unique moment of your life. Life has never been like this before and it will never be this way again. See it; taste it; feel it; recognize it for the precious gift it is. *Be* as present as you can for this living moment of your Life.

Moments in which we bring our attention into our immediate experience, let go of any tension we discover, and then open to Life nourish us with the power of *being*. Let us try this in the following exercise:

After you read through this exercise, breathe deeply for a few moments and then check into your body, asking yourself, "In this moment, what am I experiencing?" What does this moment of your life feel like? Are you sitting, standing or lying down? Notice what is happening.

Now bring your attention to your breath and on the next in-breath, tighten your whole body. As you then breathe out, allow your body to melt, saying out loud a long and slow ahhhhh.

Check the hot spots of neck and shoulders, jaw, and belly. Is there any place where there is still tension? If so, on the next in-breath, amplify that tension by tightening the area, really exaggerating the tension that is there. Then on the out-breath let it go. You can even add visualization on the out-breath, seeing the tension flow down your body, into your legs, and out through your feet. Take this breath to every pocket of tension and work with it until it lets go.

As you open your body, feel the tingles and aliveness that are there. Open to the joy that is fueling this aliveness. Then expand your attention to include everything around you. This is it! This is your life! Every single moment of your life has brought you to this moment, and this is the only one that matters. Receive it. See it. Hear it. Feel it. Be present for yourself and for your life.

Moments such as these are powerful beyond your wildest imaginings. You are nourishing yourself in the deepest way a human *being* can – with pure connection. The more you connect in this way, the less interesting your compulsion will be. In the middle of your day, you may not always be able to make full contact with Life, but know that your aliveness is there, waiting for you. Just taking a few deep breaths, holding them for a moment and then letting them go will pave the way to a full and complete connection.

As you practice moments of *being*, your attention will become more finely tuned. No matter where you are, you will be able to feel the river of aliveness that fills your whole body right there underneath your chronic holdings. And you will discover that, just like the tension you found in your physical body, this field of energy wants to soften too, opening and expanding into Life. You don't need to *do* anything for this opening to happen. It happens naturally as you soften back into your body and into Life. In the beginning, don't spend too much time looking for the joy. Just be willing to breathe through your tension and come back to yourself as you are. The joy will make itself known when it is ready.

The more you know this field of joy, the more you will see that every bit of that tension in your mind, body, and heart turns down the river of aliveness that you are hungry for. Don't fight your tension. Let it become an ally in your awakening. Whenever your body is tight, you will be reminded that you are caught in struggle, far away from the nourishment of simply *being* and then, for at least a couple of breaths, let go and open to Life.

> *In the beginning, don't spend too much time looking for the joy. Just be willing to breathe through your tension and come back to yourself as you are. The joy will make itself known when it is ready.*

Whenever I find myself contracting, I do a few of these breaths which bring my attention to the here and now. As the tension releases, my energy field expands and as I let go of any limits to my right for joy, my energy begins to flow again. It always amazes me how safe this is, how nourishing, and how freeing. As I have discovered the healing of making immediate contact with Life, I look for pauses throughout my day where I can let go again and allow my body to glow. And that is what *being* is all about.

Being Throughout the Day

As you pay attention to Life, you will see that it gives you moments of down-time throughout your day. These are moments where you can cultivate pauses that refresh, connecting you with the healing of simply *being*.

❖ You may be waiting at the Post Office, frustrated with how long the line is, and suddenly you remember to connect. Close your eyes, take a few deep breaths, and let your tension melt as you feel your body. Listen to the symphony of sounds swelling and receding all around you, listening as if this is your first day on Earth. You can then open to whatever Life is giving you in that moment.

❖ If you are in a bathtub, close your eyes, giving yourself to the water. Really melt. Then move your legs so the water swirls around you and open to the experience of its soothing embrace.

❖ When you are exercising, stop for a moment here and there and bring your full attention into your body. Really feel how exercise amplifies the river of aliveness.

These pauses are moment of pure experience – immediate contact with Life. You don't need to make a big production of this. Just a few breaths is often enough to get the ball rolling. For underneath all of your wanting and fearing, trying and doing, is a longing to simply be present for Life!

Because softening and opening back into pure contact is so alien for most of us, it is skillful to expand our capacity to *be* in more ways than just a few deep breaths here and there. It can be very helpful to set aside some time every day where we let go of all of the outer demands and use our attention to connect. If your mind says you don't have enough time, that is just gobbledygook! Everything works better when we connect. If you truly feel that everything on your To Do list is absolutely essential, ask yourself if it will matter in a hundred years. It is amazing how that idea can cut through so much superfluous activity, bringing us back to the most essential thing – connection with Life right here and right now.

I try every day to have *timeless time* in my garden. I swing on the swing, allowing my body to feel the joy of the rocking just as I did as a child. I will often close my eyes and just revel in these moments of pure connection. As I keep on swinging, I listen to the music of Life – airplanes appearing and disappearing, birds calling to one another, the pleasant cacophony of passing cars, the thrill of the wind playing with the trees. In these moments I am truly *being*! There is no leaning into the future or wandering back into the past. There isn't any need for Life (including myself) to be any different than what it is. In these moments, I am truly *being* nourished by Life.

In cultivating *being* time, choose something you enjoy. The word *enjoy* means *in joy*! Look for whatever brings more space into your mind and more lightness into your heart. What is it that makes you feel warm and safe? What is it that brings a smile to your face? What is it that causes your belly to soften? (A soft belly is one of the clearest indicators that we are opening again to the river of aliveness that is Life.)

A wonderful question to ask is *"Right now, what do I truly need?"* This is another Check-In Question, one that will open the door to really listening to yourself. What you are looking for is not what you want (that may be your compulsion) or what you should do (that is just the *doing mind*) but what you really *need* right now. This is a very powerful question to ask. Ask it even if it's not at all clear what it is that you need. For the power is in the asking. (We will be exploring this in depth in the next chapter.)

❖ Is it curling up under the covers with the electric blanket on high?

❖ Is it renting a rowboat early on a Sunday morning and floating in the sounds and sights of Life awakening to another day?

❖ Is it asking your lover to give you a massage that won't lead to intercourse so you can practice melting into your body?

Whatever it is, be willing to give yourself the gift of pure experience. As you discover the joys of *being*, give yourself at least a few minutes every day that are all about purely connecting with yourself and with Life.

As we follow the river of pleasure that is true experience, our breath becomes freer and the river of aliveness begins to move again. This is why we often find ourselves saying the healing sound of letting go – ahhhhh - after we have had a delicious meal, made contact with a new baby or had a wonderful orgasm. In those moments, we are making ourselves available to

159

one of the most important nutrients we can know for a healthy life – the joy that is our essence! As we understand how important it is to cultivate *being* and that it is okay to give ourselves its many gifts, we can feed ourselves from the inside out, making our compulsions much less interesting.

Helpful Hints

Know there is a difference between *doing being* and *being being*. Usually when we have tried to cultivate *being* in the past, we have experienced it just in our heads. How many times have you had a massage where you were up in your head wishing that it was a little different than what it was? Or what about sex – are you really present? And how many times have you floated in a warm bath, with candles no less, and read a book? I am not saying that is bad. *All I am saying is that who you are is not a thought, it is an experience!*

When you understand that, then you will be ready to take another step – a step into truly experiencing what you are experiencing! Whether you know it or not, you crave pure experience and all of the healing that it brings.

It is important to know that the intellect will try to take over. Before opening to *being,* it may say:

- ❖ "I am afraid to be with me."
- ❖ "I can't hear what I need."
- ❖ "I don't have time."
- ❖ "I had an awful day."
- ❖ "I don't know how to do this."
- ❖ "I won't do it right."
- ❖ "I am too depressed."
- ❖ "I am too empty."
- ❖ "I don't know how to say no."
- ❖ "I am too sick."
- ❖ "I am too out of touch."
- ❖ "I am too tired."
- ❖ "I am too unworthy, fat, or ugly."
- ❖ "I have too many people depending on me to take care of me."
- ❖ (And the big one) "I do not deserve to feel joy in my life."

We will always be running up against the next reason why we can't or won't open to *being. All of our resistances are actually very good reasons to be present for ourselves.* When we are pressed to the max by our lives and disconnected from ourselves, we all feel vulnerable whether we can acknowledge it or not. Just as an overwhelmed or overly tired child needs to be taken care of, so does our vulnerability. It is soothed and supported when we come back to ourselves. If we are stretched to the max, it is important to return to ourselves in simple and nourishing ways.

> *It is world-changing for one person to open to the river of joy that is Life.*

The intellect will try to take over in the middle of your *being* time. It may be so enamored with the joy of *being* that instead of *being present*, it is planning how you can do more of this in your life. It may even get sidetracked into judging how well you are doing. Or it may tell you this is boring and isn't doing anything for you. Rather than listening to the *content* of your thoughts, see them as an indicator that you have again lost contact with *you*. Pause. Take a few deep breaths and come back to being curious about what you are experiencing right now.

Remember, you have *permission* to feel this good. You not only have permission, it is world-changing for one person to open to the river of joy that is Life. It nourishes you in the most essential ways, tapping you into your own deep knowing that will skillfully guide you through Life. Also, know what you do is not so important as adding pauses throughout the experience and feeling what is happening right now.

It is important to cultivate a nourishing connection with ourselves before we are starving for it. My experience is that as the day goes on, my attention moves more up into my head, making it much more likely that I will disconnect from my body and all of the wisdom and joy that reside there. I then become more vulnerable to compulsion. So before I get into trouble, I ask myself throughout the day, "In this moment, what am I experiencing?" and "What do I <u>truly</u> need right now?" These are my Check-In Questions that bring me back to myself.

As we cultivate the river of joy and aliveness that is Life, the final thing we need to remember is that we may be afraid of *being*. We have been contained and controlled for so long that we have forgotten the safety, the nourishment, and the exhilaration of opening to Life. We are not only unfamiliar with it, we don't know what to do with it. The mind often turns on the *control mode* when aliveness floods us with its truth. "Hold on for a minute. Where is the shut off valve? I need to be in control here."

So we need to explore opening to Life in little bites, slowly expanding our capacity for the joy of *being* alive. It is also important to recognize that our capacity for free-flowing joy is like a clogged up old pipe. When you start allowing the water through it again, it will happen in fits and starts as it pushes out all of the contraction in our bodies, minds, and hearts. Remember that as you are clearing out your *pipes*, what you are heading for is the clear-flowing water of your own vitality.

Invitations to *Being*

Give yourself permission to at least contemplate your right to the joy of *being*. In this contemplation, if you don't see clearly how you could cultivate *being*, I offer a few other ways to get the juices flowing. Each one of them is about time away from outer demands so that you can cultivate a deep and nourishing relationship with yourself and with Life.

I am not giving them to you as another thing to add to your already full To Do list. We have tried that before only to become very resistant. These ideas are offered more as triggers to get your imagination going. If you choose to explore one of them, see them more as invitations into yourself rather than just another *have to*. Listen carefully to your body as you read them and it will show which ones it wants to explore.

- ❖ Give yourself a face massage. Every single inch of your skin has 19,000 sensory cells! Soothe your brow, cradle your cheek, tap your forehead, ruffle your eyebrows, explore your lips. Or ask for a foot massage from a friend. In a study of touch with rats, the ones that were touched were calmer, more curious and much more able to get their needs met. The ones that were kept in isolation experienced immune deficiencies, retarded bone growth, and the slow maturation of their central nervous system!

- ❖ If you want to overeat, listen to yourself and discover what food you are craving and place it in front of you. If it isn't clear exactly what you want, choose any food. Smell it, explore it with your eyes, and discover it with your touch. When you are ready, allow yourself to take one bite and play with it like you did when you were a child. Roll it around in your mouth and explore it with your tongue. (Tongues love to play!) When you are ready, bite into it and allow its essence to cascade across your taste buds. Become enamored by the pleasures of taste.

  Be stunned by how delicious and satisfying one bite of food can be. If the part of you that has been denied food feels that to eat slowly is just another form of control, tell it that it can eat as fast and as unconsciously as it wants to after you are present for at least two bites. Often that amount of pleasure makes bolting our food uninteresting. People often speak about how satiated they are by a small amount of food when they are present for the experience.

- ❖ Pause throughout the day, take one deep breath and open the field of your attention into the fullness of Life, right here, right now. This is it! This is the only moment that matters. Experience it as deeply as you can.

❖ Whenever you find yourself waiting in line, bring your attention back into your body, take a few deep breaths, and open to the preciousness of this moment.

❖ Turn off all the lights and bathe or shower in the dark.

❖ Get close to the Earth. Lie on the grass and allow yourself to be held by the Earth. Make sand castles at the beach. Buy an air mattress and go float on the water. Climb a tree.

❖ Rather than a sick day, take a *well day* from work. Pretend that you are your best friend who wants to give you a day full of delight, whether it is a day in nature or a day in bed.

❖ Have an *I don't have to do it* day. Don't exercise, don't floss your teeth, don't return phone calls. Disconnect from the enslavement of *doing*.

❖ Move your body without thinking of it as exercise. Do log rolls down a hill, go swing on a swing, go dancing, fly a kite, jump on a trampoline. Our bodies love to move!

❖ Go to a public place that has sights and smells that bring you joy. It could be a playground with the happy sounds of children, a coffee shop filled with warm smells and the delightful murmur of people connecting with one another; a library with the wonderful smell of books and the fullness of silence. Imagine that tomorrow you will suddenly become blind and deaf. Allow this idea to open you to really savoring this experience for the preciousness that it truly is. Nothing is ordinary!

❖ If there are certain feelings that are blocking your access to simply *being*, exaggerate them. If you are mad, stomp around and get wild. If you are feeling sorry for yourself, turn up the whine dial and ham it up. If you are afraid, comfort yourself as if you were your only child. If you are grieving, rent a sad movie, get a box of Kleenex and have a good cry. Don't minimize even the smallest of griefs. And if you're just stuck, go howl at the moon or make wonderful belly opening sounds in your car.

❖ Make a comfort nest somewhere in your home. Nourish your body with soft, cushy, warm stuff. Then breathe yourself back into openness, using one of the breath techniques we have explored.

❖ Nourish your sight with beauty – a picture or a tiny vase of flowers. Discover what would nourish your ears – wind chimes or maybe a tape of ocean waves. Remind yourself that whenever you see or hear a gift of beauty, you will pause and reconnect with Life, right here, right now.

❖ Have a day where you don't speak. Silence can be very nourishing, grounding and connecting.

❖ One of the most powerful methods for *being* is the simplest. Slowly, with great tenderness, bring your hand over your heart and touch yourself with mercy.

The intent of cultivating pure experience is to make deep and intimate contact with the free-flowing field of joy and aliveness that is our essence. As we consciously cultivate it, we discover that we don't necessarily need to add anything like a bathtub or go anyplace else like a playground. Just with our attention, we can enhance the free-flowing energy of our vitality, giving ourselves permission to glow.

Gift Yourself with Yourself

We have been exploring the art of opening to Life and experiencing it! To e*xperience or not experience, that is the question.* When we learn how to open, we discover that *absolutely everything we have ever longed for is right here, right now.* As you cultivate *being*, you will again be flooded with loving yourself from the inside out, in contact again with the river of aliveness that is Life.

Learning to be present for Life is very much a forgetting and remembering and forgetting and remembering process. We will leave ourselves only to come back to ourselves only to leave ourselves again. The river of aliveness is always here no matter what is happening in our heads, waiting to be amplified by our attention. As the juices get flowing, and as you see all of the healing and empowerment that comes from making immediate contact with Life, you will be able to access it no matter where you are and no matter what is happening.

Don't ever forget you are worthy of this kind of time and attention. As you learn how to feed yourself from the inside out, filling yourself with the joy of being, the temporary pleasure of compulsion that so quickly turns into devastation will take a back seat. You will finally be free. Enjoy the ride!

Core Ideas in Skill #4 – Coming Home to Ourselves:

❖ When we feel disconnected from ourselves and our lives, compulsions become a substitute for the true joy of being at home inside of ourselves and in our lives.

❖ We have forgotten how to simply *be*!

❖ There is a big difference between being lost in a story *about Life* and being *with Life* as it is.

❖ *Being* is about moments where your mind, your body, and your heart are all in the same place at the same time.

❖ Absolutely everything you have truly longed for is right here, right now.

❖ Opening to Life is the safest thing you will ever do.

❖ As you learn how to feed yourself from the inside out, filling yourself with the joy of *being*, the temporary pleasure of compulsions will take a back seat. You will then know the healing that you long for.

❖ It is never selfish to take time to be with ourselves, for *being* time nourishes us to our core so we can be fully present for our lives.

❖ Your body is a gift from Life. It is nothing less than magnificent, no matter what shape, size, color or age.

❖ When you were young, you were naturally in contact with how delicious it is to have a body. You lived inside of your body, inside of yourself, and on a daily basis you were in touch with your wellspring within.

❖ When you begin to listen to your body again, you will realize it is a messenger that is always talking to you.

❖ Tightness in your body is where your free-flowing aliveness is bound up, and it is trying to speak to you.

❖ As you return to your body, you will know your rightful heritage of joy and aliveness.

✦ SKILL 5: LIVING IN QUESTIONS ✦

We now come to the fifth and final skill where we will explore the power of living in questions. We are only beginning to realize the healing power of asking questions. No matter where we are, no matter what is happening, living in questions can bring clarity when we are confused, courage when our strength has failed us, hope when despair is all that we see and vision when we don't have a clue about which way to go.

You may have noticed that I am talking about *living in* questions. That is different from just asking a question. Our old way – ask a question and look for the answer – is necessary in our day-to-day lives. But asking questions in this way can often bring us frustration, especially when we ask them around our compulsions. That was certainly my experience. Looking for answers as to why I was compulsive and how I could stop was exhausting, confusing, and frustrating. Most of the time, I couldn't find the answers that I was looking for. If I did, I usually couldn't hold on to them or my answers became obsolete! It was when I learned how to ask questions in a different way that the clouds began to lift and I was able to heal and be healed by my compulsions.

This chapter is about a new way of working with questions, a way in which we discover that the power of questions is not in finding the answers that we are looking for. *The power of questions is in the questions themselves!*

There are two ways to tap into the power of questions rather than always looking for an answer:

❖ The first way is what I call *Check-In Questions*. This type of question is about bringing our attention into our immediate experience so that we can calm down our reactive mind. In this calming, enough space is created within us so that we can listen to the wellspring of deeper knowing that is always there.

❖ The second way of tapping into the power of questions is what I call *Open-Ended Questions*. This type of question is about asking questions without looking for an answer. Through this powerful way of working with questions, answers come to us from way beyond our own limited understanding.

We will explore these two different ways of being with questions by working with three specific questions. We will first look at them as Check-In Questions. We will then explore how you can transform each one into an Open-Ended Question that can be asked no matter what is going on in your life. We will also spend time working with the intent of each of the three ques-

tions so that you can better
understand how to use them to
heal and be healed by your
compulsion.

> *The power of questions is in
> the questions themselves!*

Even though living in questions is
a very fluid and alive process, for clarity and simplicity we will work in this
book with three basic questions. I have worked with these three questions
with many people over the years, and, based on this experience, the questions are carefully worded to bring forth the core intention of each question
in any situation. When you are clear about the intent of each one and have
become familiar with practicing living in questions, you can draw from the
list of other questions at the end of this chapter, listening for the ones that
call to you.

Let us now begin by exploring the three questions, what their intentions are
and how they can be used as Check-In Questions.

Check-In Questions

There is a famous story that has been around for years about a man who
lost his house key. While he is searching for the key under the streetlight in
front of his house, a stranger comes by and begins to help in the hunt. After
a futile search, the stranger happens to ask the man where he lost the key.

"I lost it right by my front door," he said.

"Why then are you looking out here on the street?" asks the stranger.

"Because that is where the light is," the man replies.

This story speaks directly to how we try to heal ourselves. We look outside
of ourselves for the answers to our compulsions. *In all of our searching, we
have never even considered the possibility of exploring our immediate
experience, which is where the keys to our healing are hiding.* We listen to
experts out there but we don't know how to listen to ourselves!

In order to unravel the tangled web of compulsions, *we need to learn how to
listen to ourselves*. We need to learn how to bring the light of our compassionate attention into whatever we are experiencing so that the clouds of
reaction can lift, and we can hear again our wellspring of deep knowing that
is always with us.

The three questions we will be using in our explorations, along with their
intentions are:

◇1◇ **In this moment, what am I experiencing?**

The intention of this question is to invite our attention to be curious about what is going on right now in our body, our mind and our heart.

◇2◇ **For this moment, can I let this be?**

The intention of this question is to move us beyond *reaction* into *response*. It reminds us that if we resist whatever we are experiencing we empower it even more. As we let go of struggling, we can explore what is going on in a spacious and eventually merciful way. It is this spaciousness and mercy with whatever we are experiencing that will transform even the scariest of feelings back into the free flowing aliveness that we truly are.

◇3◇ **Right now, what do I <u>truly</u> need?**

The intention of this question is to open the door to the wellspring of deep knowing within us which always knows what will bring balance, clarity and peace in any situation.

We have touched on each of these questions in the first 4 skills. Let us now take an in depth look at each one so that we know the healing of living in questions. In the *Treasure Hunting* section we will learn how to apply these questions to all sorts of experiences in our lives, most especially when we are compulsive.

◇1◇ In This Moment, What Am I Experiencing?

As we have explored all the way through this book, the healing that we long for begins when we can be curious about what is happening right now. That is why the First Question, "In this moment, what am I experiencing?" is so powerful. It dips the finger of our attention into the river of our experience. Rather than being lost in struggle, it invites us to be curious about what is happening right now so we can see the truth of what we are experiencing.

We are not usually very curious about what is going on. In fact, we have been deeply trained in the opposite. We have a tendency to look at what is wrong and then we get lost in how we can make it better. In other words, we are geared to make things into problems and we have the capacity to struggle with practically everything in our life. We want what is not here and we usually don't want what is. Constantly wanting things to be different than they are, we don't see that our lives, rather than a random series of events, are living adventures, giving us the exact experiences we need in order to grow into the fullness of our potential.

This question cuts through our reactivity. It allows us to let go of the story about what we are experiencing so we can actually experience it. Then, rather than living in reaction, we can passionately listen to our lives. In this listening, we discover that every experience contains valuable information that can help us immensely in our healing.

When we are willing to look at, and then experience what is going on, everything that happens adds to our healing rather than feeding our old urge to struggle. The tight fist in your stomach, the lump in your throat, the anger that feels like it is going to explode are all trying to tell you something. They are messengers from the deepest and wisest parts of yourself, and they come bearing information and insights that will help you unravel the web of reaction that fuels your compulsion.

Also, the simple light of our attention is very transformative. It can clear up the most challenging experiences of our lives – especially compulsions. Most of the suffering that we experience comes from our knee jerk propensity to react. Living in reaction, we then react to our reaction and sometimes even go on to reacting to our reaction about our reaction! This stirs up huge clouds in our minds and bodies - the clouds of anger, sadness and fear, which are the core fuels for our compulsions.

This question is about *turning our attention toward what is going on* rather than living in endless cycles of reaction. As we learn how to be curious, the clouds of our reactions, which formerly felt as solid as rock, calm down and become workable. We then discover that most of what we are afraid of ceases to have power over us when we simply pause and look.

It is very important to see that most of us are highly resistant to experiencing what we are experiencing. We are either ashamed of what is going on within us or we are afraid of it. It does take time to calm down our reactivity so that we can respond, and I assure you, it is the safest and most merciful thing we can do.

We will explore this question more deeply in the *Treasure Hunting* section (Page 198), but for now I invite you to play with it. One of the ways you can do this is to be willing to make a commitment for just one day to, over and over again, dip the finger of your attention in

> *The tight fist in your stomach, the lump in your throat, the anger that feels like it is going to explode all are messengers from the deepest and wisest parts of yourself, and they come bearing information and insights that will help you unravel the web of reaction that fuels your compulsions.*

the river of your experience by pausing for a moment and asking the question, "In this moment, what am I experiencing?" Be fascinated about what you are experiencing. It helps to add this question to something you do a number of times a day – using the bathroom, waiting at stop lights, eating a meal – just as we explored in the chapter on *Curiosity* (Page 73).

As you ask this question, it is skillful to pause for a moment and focus on whatever is the most predominant experience of that moment. It could be something outside of you or inside of you. It could be the sounds of the cars around you or maybe it is heartburn from overeating at lunch. It could be the wonderful taste of a strawberry or it may be anger at a friend. Whatever you notice, name it to yourself and then go on about your day.

As you begin to be interested in exactly what you are experiencing, it will become clear that both your outer world and your inner world are a part of a constantly changing river of experience. *As you begin to show up more for your own life, seeing what is going on becomes more interesting than trying to make this river be any particular way. And* when you can see what is going on, it can be healed.

For This Moment, Can I Let This Be?

The first part of the deep healing we are exploring here is to *see* what we are experiencing right now, and that is what the First Question is all about. Many of the experiences in our lives that keep us caught in struggle will be dissolved in the light of our pure seeing. Remember, most of what we experience is just the story *about* life that fills up our heads – a story that is made out of wanting things to be different than they are (especially ourselves!) This story is like a cloud that is laid over the wonder and the mystery of the present moment of our lives. And when we can see the clouds, rather than being lost in them, they lose their power over us.

When we experience something that does not let go in the face of our undivided attention, it is time to open to the intention of this Second Question – to *be with* whatever is happening. *The quickest and most powerful way to dissolve our struggles is to let them be!* We are only beginning to understand that when we resist something we are experiencing, it gives it energy. *It is our reactivity that keeps us caught in struggle.* If we can accept our experience, and then be willing to look and listen, whatever we are experiencing loses its power over us.

Letting something be is certainly not what we are used to doing. We are inclined to react – trying to fix, change, rearrange, deny, defend, and generally get rid of anything that feels uncomfortable. And yet letting something be as it is – even for a moment or two – is where lasting healing happens.

> *The quickest and most powerful way to dissolve our struggles is to let them be!*

The Beatles captured the essence of this Second Question in the song, *Let it Be*. Deep truth is woven into the words, "When I find myself in times of trouble, Mother Mary comes to me, speaking words of wisdom, 'Let it be'." The healing power of letting something *be* is built upon the truth that when we tighten around life and resist, we hurt more; when we soften and open, we hurt less.

Our controlling minds resist this new way of being with ourselves only until they see the magic that can happen when we let things *be*. The first place where I was able to see real evidence of the power of letting something *be* was around physical pain. I was in a head-on automobile accident when I was 24 and came out of it with a lot of pain. I fought the pain for years, and this only made it worse. When I learned how to stop fighting and instead allowed the pain to be there, softening around it, it began to get better.

I then began to explore the willingness to give the emotions that fueled my compulsions permission to be. I discovered that, *when I was really hurting, if I could allow myself to be exactly as I was, I immediately felt better.* In a moment of meeting myself as I am – letting myself be exactly where I am – my body usually breathes a spontaneous deep breath, my heart lightens, and everything begins to flow again.

There are two important points to understand in order to tap into the phenomenal power of letting something *be*.

a Letting something be isn't about being a helpless victim.

Rather than being helpless in the face of whatever is going on, letting something be gives us our power back. It does this by *taking us out of struggle mode so we can look and explore, becoming fascinated with what is going on.* As the clouds of struggle calm down through our willingness to give our experience the space to be, we can then *listen, deeply listen,* to ourselves. Our lives are not a random series of events that are here to confound, upset, or even please us. Each and every experience we have is tailor-made to highlight the story of struggle that we live in most all of the time and to show us the doorway back into the joy of pure being. The truth is that whenever we are compulsive, what we are truly longing for is this depth of listening and connection with ourselves.

ⓑ Letting something be is not about not doing anything.

In fact it is the exact opposite. It is about letting go of the *reactive mode* so that we can *respond*. As the clouds of reaction calm down through the power of this second question, we can then make contact with the wellspring of wisdom within us that knows how to bring balance and healing into every challenge of our lives – especially compulsion. When we react, we create clouds of reaction in return. When we respond, we set healing forces in motion. And response isn't about being a wimp. It can have a clear sharp edge to it that cuts through unclarity like a Samurai's sword.

To open to the intent of this question is much like being in a room with very loud music filling up the entire space and then all of a sudden, the music stops. There to greet you is the song of the bird outside the window, the hum of the refrigerator, the beat of your heart. All of those were still happening even when the music was loud, but you couldn't hear them. The same is true for the deep knowing of our wellspring. It is always speaking to us, but we can't hear it because of the static of our reactions. Letting something *be* calms this static down so we can listen.

A great example of the power of the question, "For this moment, can I let this be?" came from a woman in one of my groups, She began working with this question in her challenging relationship. Her partner was a very controlling man, and this would bring up deep rage inside of her. Because he wasn't yet a safe person with whom she could speak her rage, she found herself constantly on *pre-boil*. This subterranean anger was beginning to show up in physical difficulties in her body.

When she began asking the questions, she was amazed at the depth of her anger. The First Question allowed her to take the attention off of the idea that everything her partner was doing was wrong. As she let go of the story, she could become curious about what was happening inside of her. At first, the idea of letting the anger *be* was alien to her because she had been taught to fight it her whole life. But with a little coaxing, the Second Question made enough space inside of her that she could begin to listen to her anger.

> *Letting something be is not about not doing anything. In fact it is the exact opposite. It is about letting go of the reactive mode so that we can respond.*

The next time we talked, her eyes were dancing in joy. "I have never listened to my anger before. I could truly experience it without getting lost in it! As I acknowledged it and listened to what it had to say, I watched it fade away. I was then much clearer about what I needed to say and do in the relationship that would be healing for both of us."

This story again shows us that cultivating the ability to let things *be* isn't about being powerless. It is about moving out of *reaction* so that we can *respond* clearly and cleanly to Life. We are highly-tuned reactors, and our reactions are constantly muddying the waters of our lives. But if we let muddy water sit quietly, it will become clear. If we can pause, bring our attention into our immediate experience and then make space for exactly what is happening, there is a far greater chance that the muddy waters of reaction will calm down and we can then skillfully *respond* to the circumstances of our lives.

> *If we can pause, bring our attention into our immediate experience and then make space for exactly what is happening, there is a far greater chance that the muddy waters of reaction will calm down and we can then skillfully respond to the circumstances of our lives.*

When you begin working with the question around the challenges of your life, you may find yourself answering it with a no. "No. I don't want this headache or this anxiety or my craving to be here!" But this is workable too. That is the beauty of the questions. If you answer no, simply go back to the First Question and ask, "What am I experiencing now?" What you will recognize is that you are resisting being with what you are experiencing! You can then ask the second question again for if you can let go of struggling with your resistance to being with your experience, whatever you are experiencing loses its power over you!

You may even need to let go of resisting your resistance to experiencing your resistance! You simply go back and forth between the two questions until you can find something you can allow to be. When you answer is yes, the clouds of reaction can calm down.

There are times that you won't be able to find a *Yes*. But that is okay. You then have the option of the Open-Ended version of this question, "For this moment, how can I bring compassion to this?" We will be exploring this question in depth in the next section. Until then, it is important to understand that the core intent of the question, "For this moment, can I let this be?" is to clear the pathway to compassion. In order for this to happen, we first need to accept our experience. Once we can accept something – even if it is for just a moment or two – this opens the doorway to compassion and mercy.

If you find that you are completely resisting your experience, you can ask a variation of the Second Question, "For this moment, can I not struggle with this?" Remember, whatever you resist persists. To fight with something gives it power and always makes things worse in the long run. To accept that this is what you are experiencing right now gives you your power back.

Play with these questions. Take a deep breath whenever discomfort comes into your life – whether it is an overly long stoplight, an upset stomach, a financial fear – and say, "For this moment, can I let this be?" If your answer is "No," go back and forth between the first two questions until you can accept where you are. If no acceptance comes, work with the optional question, "For this moment, can I not struggle with this?" Know that the inclusion in these questions is magic. It can make bearable and even transform the hardest heart, the deepest grief and the sharpest pain. Under the true power of these questions, our bodies soften, our hearts let go, and our attention becomes a healing force that is for our highest good.

Right now, what do I <u>truly</u> need?

We first explored the question "In this moment, what am I experiencing?" in order to transform our attention into a laser beam, taking us into the truth of our experience. We then moved from *reaction* to *response* with the question "For this moment can I let this be?" This question allows us to give whatever is happening the spaciousness and, eventually, the mercy that it needs in order to heal.

The Third Question, "Right now, what do I <u>truly</u> need?" not only invites us into a deeper level of listening to ourselves, but it also awakens our wellspring of deep knowing. *This is not a listening with our heads; it is an internal listening – a listening to the wellspring of wisdom within us that knows what needs to happen in order to bring balance into our lives.* That is why we use the word <u>truly</u> and why it is underlined.

There is a very important distinction that needs to be made here. We are not asking for what we *want*. Wants come from the desire for immediate gratification, based on a limited perspective. Needs come from a deeper place that is in alignment with what is for our highest good.

The most important thing about this question is the willingness to ask it. It is a doorway into hearing what is the kindest and most skillful thing we can do in that moment. Because most of us have not been taught how to truly

listen to ourselves, at first nothing
may come clear. If it doesn't, don't try
to figure it out. That will just take you
back up into your head. Know that
turning toward yourself and asking
this question is powerful in its own
right. *It trains you into listening to
yourself.* Also, the asking of the
question awakens the wellspring
within you, making it easier over time

> *This is not a listening with
> our heads; it is an internal
> listening – a listening to the
> wellspring of wisdom within
> us that knows what needs to
> happen in order to bring
> balance into our lives.*

to hear exactly what it is that will bring peace into your life.

One of the first times I understood the power of truly listening to myself was
early one morning after a very busy week. Upon waking, my body was still
tired and my mind was in a very high level of anxiety. Today was to be my
one day off before I started another very busy week and instead of being a
peaceful, recharging day, it was full of all the things that stack up in my life
when I am very busy.

My mind also used to have a tendency when I was this tired to entertain the
belief that life would come to an end if I didn't get everything done! In this
situation, I scared myself even more by looking at the week to come,
deciding that I was tired enough that I needed to pull back and resist Life (a
very painful way to live, especially when you have known and lived its
opposite!)

For a few minutes I was lost in the grip of an ocean of feelings. I then closed
my eyes and asked the question, "In this moment, what am I experiencing?"
It brought my attention to the anxiety that was ricocheting through my body
and the deep feeling of overwhelm in the pit of my stomach. As my attention
settled, I asked the question, "For this moment, can I let this be?" My
resistance said "No! This overwhelm will just make a mess of my day." But
wisdom within me said, "It only makes it worse to resist. Let it be, so it can
begin to come back into balance."

After taking a deep breath, I somewhat hesitantly said to this feeling that it
was okay that it was here. Having cultivated the power of the Second
Question many times in my life, it lifted the clouds and I felt more grounded
and connected to myself. I then moved to the Third Question, "Right now,
what do I truly need?" As I listened, it was suddenly very clear that at that
moment all I needed was to be fully present for myself. Rather than getting
out of bed, I stayed there for awhile, opening to my experience. My heart
melted and my whole experience lightened. As I allowed myself to be
exactly where I was, meeting myself with understanding and mercy, waves

of joy began to fill my body. I was astounded and overjoyed with the simplicity of touching my experience with my heart.

Just out of curiosity, I then withdrew my heart and could feel the intensity of the anxiety building and my body contracting. I then opened my heart again, saying to the feelings that it was okay that they were here. Each time I said it, my whole being melted more and joy flowed through my body.

This clarity of heart not only opened me to joy, it helped me to see clearly what needed to be done in order to bring balance back into my life for the rest of the day. Then, from a non-reactive place, I made some choices that made everything much easier.

Because we are not trained to listen to ourselves, it can be very helpful to work with this question when our lives are calm. Make a game of it. If you are sitting on the couch after dinner, check in with yourself and then ask "Right now, what do I truly need?" Or maybe it is a hectic day at work and the candy machine is looking very interesting. Instead, you pause, check in with yourself, and then ask the question, "Right now, what do I truly need? Remember, this is not about what you *want*….it is what you *need*. In the beginning, when all is not clear, know that just asking sets the answer in motion.

The Three Questions happen in a progression. The first brings our attention into our immediate experience; the second opens a space around it and the third connects us to the wellspring of wisdom within us. But you don't have to use them in that order. You can use just one or even just two. Often all I need to do is ask the First Question and everything comes back into balance again. I lived in that question for years before the other two revealed themselves to me. Listen to yourself. Get creative, and let questions work their magic for you.

Open-Ended Questions

The second way of working with questions that can heal us to our core is to ask Open-Ended Questions. These too, just like the Check-In Questions, are different than the kind of questions we are used to asking. We usually ask a question to get an answer. And while these types of questions are necessary for maneuvering around in our lives, if an answer is not forthcoming – and often it isn't – it throws us into frustration and struggle. *The difference with Open-Ended Questions is that we don't look for the answer.*

> *Lost in the search for the answers to our lives, we have totally missed the power of the questions themselves.*

When you first hear about this kind of question, the controlling mind may say, "You must be crazy. Ask a question and not look for an answer? That is insanity. I don't have time for this. I am too busy trying to figure it all out." But if you watch carefully, you will see that a quest for answers keeps you caught in your head, left with only your own limited understanding. *Lost in the search for the answers to our lives, we have totally missed the power of the questions themselves.*

The power of Open-Ended Questions comes to us when we realize that Life is a field of Intelligence. Everywhere we look, we see its handiwork, whether it is the exquisite balance of the web of Life or the amazing healing that happens in a body if it suffers a major accident. All that we see appears out of this field of Intelligence. This goes all the way from the dance of an electron, to the play of the wind, to the laughter of a child.

The Intelligence that permeates absolutely every particle of Life is beyond our limited human minds' ability to comprehend. If you doubt that, check-in with your body. It is made up of over one hundred trillion cells and they all work together with barely a thought from you. In order to even begin to grasp this astounding cooperation and creativity, imagine every single person on this Earth working with everybody else for the common good of the whole. Hard to imagine? Yes! But that wouldn't even begin to come close to what your body does. It would take 15,000 Earths, each with 6 billion people, all working together, in order to come even close to what your body does every day.

How does your body do that? It is possible because it is permeated and penetrated by this field of Intelligence out of which all of Life unfolds. So whatever it is that keeps the planets spinning as they do, that brings spring forth out of winter that beats your heart and heals your wounds, permeates every single nook and cranny of your being. In other words, *you are not alone.* There is an Intelligence that is with you every step of your way, an Intelligence that is bringing you the exact set of experiences you need to move out of your isolation into a true and abiding relationship with your own true nature.

◇ How Open-Ended Questions Work

We may not be able to comprehend the working of the vast Intelligence at the heart of Life, but we can partner with it through Open-Ended Questions. It needs to be understood that, with these questions, we don't look for the answer, but we can *expect an answer.* In fact, asking Open-Ended Questions *guarantees* an answer. But if we look for the answer, we gum up the works. Let me explain.

When we ask a question without looking for an answer, it creates a vacuum that has to be filled. It is much like the process of canning peas. We put them in the jar, screw on the lid and then place them in the boiling water in order to create the vacuum that seals the jar. Asking a question and then continually looking for the answer – "Is this it? No. But maybe this is it. I don't know the answer. This is too confusing."— is like lifting the jar out of the boiling water and taking off the lid to see if the vacuum had been created. Of course, now we have broken the seal and lost the vacuum.

To ask a question and to not look for the answer literally creates a vacuum in the universe. It is a law of physics. The Intelligence of the Universe rushes into the vacuum of an Open-Ended Question, and the answer automatically, in its own time, condenses out of the void and into our lives.

Rather than asking Open-Ended Questions of the vast Intelligence of Life, we usually narrow ourselves down to our own limited resources and understanding. Give us the simplest of challenges in our lives, and rather than going into the spaciousness of an Open-Ended Question, we go into struggle and a sense that we have to do it ourselves. We scrunch our shoulders, furrow our brows, and tighten our breathing, cutting ourselves off from the sea of creativity in which we live.

With the problems of our lives, we are like students sitting in a classroom doing a difficult math problem while an extraordinary teacher stands in front of the room (the Intelligence of Life). Instead of even recognizing the teacher and asking skillful questions, we sit doubled over our books, struggling with the problem. Without even looking up, we desperately search for the answer, exhausting all of the information we know and grappling with ever-increasing frustration. The greater the challenge, the more it feels like trying to climb a steep and slippery slope. Just think of your endless struggle with your compulsion and you will see the truth of this.

> *When we ask a question without looking for an answer, it creates a vacuum that has to be filled.*

If we have been trying to find the answer for a long time, we also have a tendency to slip into overwhelm with all of its self-judgment and despair: "I'll never get through this." "I'm always stuck." "Every-body else gets it and I don't." Rather than engaging with the resources that are available, we struggle with the struggle, never asking the teacher for help. All the while the teacher is there in the room with

> *The more I asked Open-Ended Questions, the more I discovered a true partnership with an Intelligence that was a lot smarter than I.*

us waiting for us to ask. All the while, no matter what problem we are facing in our lives, it has been given to us by the Creative Intelligence that gave us life. This Intelligence always responds to the spaciousness of an Open-Ended Question.

When I began to live in Open-Ended Questions, a wonderful truth became clear to me – that problems and solutions are two sides of the same coin and they always show up together. The resolution to every problem we have ever had or ever will have is nestled in the heart of the challenge. *Life waits for the question. Moments of Open-Ended Questions signal the Universe that we are willing to listen to the truth and the wisdom that comes with every challenge in our lives.*

This type of question doesn't work in linear time – ask a question and get an answer. Answers will come in their own time and their own way. I've received them while reading a spy novel where one sentence stands out from the rest, almost as if I were reading the whole book just to receive those few words. I've also overheard conversations in the grocery store in which a few words pierced my unknowing and answered my question. Answers come in dreams and even while taking a shower or cooking dinner. All of a sudden an answer comes burbling up from within, stunning us with its simplicity. It can arrive with the blinding clarity of the early morning sun as it floods us with light; or it can come as gradually as an inner knowing that reveals itself much as the sun does when it penetrates the fog.

Until I learned the power of Open-Ended Questions, I was like a fish out of water in my own life. In so many situations, I didn't know what to do. I was raising two children all by myself and, as I once told my daughter, "I have never done this before!" I was also being stretched in my work in ways that sometimes scared me to my core. The more I asked Open-Ended Questions, the more I discovered a true partnership with an Intelligence that was a lot smarter than I.

It became clear that the Intelligence of Life was waiting for the spaciousness

> *The art of trusting that the Intelligence of the Universe will answer our questions comes to each of us in its own time and in its own way.*

of an Open-Ended Question. The clarity that living in questions brings was most evident in difficult situations. Whether it was a teenage daughter who decided she wasn't going to listen to anything I said or a client who was on the verge of suicide, when I asked for help through Open-Ended Questions, these questions dropped me out of the panicked mind that was certain it didn't know the right thing to do or say. My favorite Open-Ended Question was, "What do I need to do or be in this situation that is for the highest good of everybody concerned?" This opened me up to a greater Intelligence, and to this day, I am still amazed at the clarity of the wisdom I receive. Once I created a partnership with Open-Ended Questions, I wondered how I ever survived without them.

I then began to ask Open-Ended Questions around my compulsions. It is astounding to me now as I look back on my history with this type of question that it took me so long before I was able to bring them to my compulsions. Reflecting on this, I realized that my doubt that anything could heal my compulsion was so great, that it probably would have chewed my questions up and spit them out in a flash. But by the time I started using questions when I was compulsive, I had had enough direct proof of their power that I knew that they were working their magic even when it didn't seem like the questions were making a dent in the process.

The art of trusting that the Intelligence of the Universe will answer our questions comes to each of us in its own time and in its own way. Slowly we move beyond the doubt that there is an intelligence waiting for our questions. We then see through the subtle but very strong illusion that we are in charge and finally we discover the patience to wait for the answers to come.

One of the wonderful things about Open-Ended Questions is that you don't have to know what is going on, what you are feeling, or even what kind of answer you want. You also don't have to have a concept of what this Intelligence is that is waiting for the opening of a question. You don't even have to trust that this Intelligence will answer you. All you need do is ask, and let the question go and the answer will show up in the vacuum of your Open-Ended Question.

The beauty of asking Open-Ended Questions and allowing

> *With Open-Ended Questions, you are not asking your mind to do anything or figure anything out. You are asking for help from that which is greater than you.*

the Wisdom of the Universe to answer rather than relying on our own limited intelligence is that we don't just *get* an answer. We *become* the answer itself. There is a huge difference between understanding something with our heads and understanding it with our whole being. Rather than understanding something from our limited framework, the answer *lives* us. We then know a true partnership with Life.

The Three Open-Ended Questions

Now that we understand the power of Open-Ended Questions, let us explore how we can use them to tap into the nourishment, clarity, support, and love that we need on this journey back to ourselves.

What we will be doing here is slightly changing each one of the Check-In Questions. Check-In Questions will take you very far down the path of your healing as they bring you into an immediate, caring, and listening relationship with yourself. But there will be times when your mind is too cloudy to see anything, your heart is too closed to open, or you can't even imagine listening to yourself. This is the time to use Open-Ended Questions where you ask for help from the great Wisdom at the heart of Life. *You are not asking your mind to do anything or figure anything out. You are asking for help from that which is greater than you.* You ask and then let the question go, allowing it to create the space for the answer to live you.

Let us now look at how we can transform our three Check-In Questions into Open-Ended Questions.

What Is Asking To Be Seen?

Our Check-In Question "In this moment what am I experiencing?" transforms into an Open-Ended Question by asking, **"What is asking to be seen?"** With this question, we ask the Intelligence at the heart of Life to lift the clouds of our unknowing so that we can see and then meet what is asking to be met. This question truly understands that whatever is happening is a part of our journey back to ourselves. It may be unpleasant, challenging, scary, overwhelming, frustrating or just simply confusing, *but it is for us!* It is bringing us necessary information that will help us to unravel the web of struggle that we find ourselves caught in.

This question is helpful because there will be times when our minds may be in resistance when we ask the question "In this moment, what am I experiencing?" Rather than clarity, this question may bring frustration or despair.

The question "What is asking to be seen?" cannot be answered by the mind,

> *The question "What is asking to be seen?" cannot be answered by the mind, so it cuts through our confusion and our unknowing and goes straight to That Which Knows.*

so it cuts through our confusion and our unknowing and goes straight to *That Which Knows.* Every time you ask this question, you not only turn toward your experience (even though you may not be able to see anything), but you also signal the Wisdom at the heart of Life that you are ready for the fog to lift so that you can be present for whatever you are experiencing. You just ask and then let it go. Clarity will come in its own time and in its own way.

How can I bring compassion to this?

If you are like me, many times on the journey back to myself, I didn't want to let whatever was happening in my life *be*. I also didn't have a clue about how to meet the unacceptable parts of myself with understanding and mercy. I judged my experiences; I feared my experiences; and so I continued to struggle.

Whenever we are in resistance, we can turn to the healing of the Second Open-Ended Question "For this moment, how can I bring compassion to this?" This question is asked in order to awaken the vast, healing regions of the heart, for that is where all true healing happens. For if we love whatever comes into our lives, it loses its power over us; if we can be merciful and understanding with whatever comes into our lives, we will be free.

In the beginning, your mind may say again, "No way! I can't even begin to imagine being compassionate with my struggles. In fact, it is impossible." But again, the power of this question comes from the asking. This asking opens the door to the Wisdom at the heart of Life that is waiting for the opening of a question. It is important to *just keep asking!* It took years and years for your heart to completely close, locking you into the prison of struggle. It will take time to walk back out of the prison into the healing light of your open heart. Every time you ask this question, whether it feels that way or not, it takes you another step into your healing.

If this question doesn't work for you, you can turn the two check in questions we explored earlier into Open-Ended Questions by simply adding the word 'how': "For this moment, *how* can I bring compassion to this?" and "For this moment, *how* can I not struggle with this?" With each of these questions, we can keep on reaching out beyond our struggling selves, asking for help in opening our hearts to ourselves.

❸ What is the way through this?

The Check-In Question, "Right now, what do I truly need?" transforms into the Open-Ended Question, "What is the way through this?" There are times on this journey back to ourselves when our minds are so confused that we don't have a clue about what is going on and our hearts are closed tighter than a drum. We may not be able to look at what we are experiencing and we may even be resistant to acknowledging it in any way. In fact, at the beginning of our healing, our answer to the Second Question will often be, "No!"

This is when the power of the Third Question, asked in an Open-Ended way, truly reveals itself. I call this the Default Question – it is the one you ask when you can't remember any other question. It is also the one you go to when it feels like there is nothing else you can do.

I had an experience after leading one of my Hawaiian retreats that reveals how healing this question can be. At the end of the retreat, everyone drives to Kona for a few days of play and to swim with the dolphins. Since leading a retreat is wonderful but exhausting, I usually spend a day by myself to recharge and then fly home, rather than traveling with the group. One year I made the decision to go to Kona with the group, allowing no down-time in between. We didn't arrive until after dinner, and I was exhausted. When I woke up the next morning, there was not a hint of the adult within me that had just led a six-day retreat. I felt like I was four years old and I just wanted to go home.

When I asked the First Question, I could see the depth of my tiredness and the extent of my vulnerability. When I asked the Second Question, what I got was raging resistance to this vulnerability being here at all. I wanted to go play now and I didn't want to feel this way. In fact, I was feeling deep self-judgment for being this vulnerable.

Needless to say, my resistance to what I was experiencing only made it worse. I had made some plans later on that day and was beginning to feel a sense of dread about my commitments. When I asked what it was that I really needed, everything was in such an uproar inside of me that nothing was clear about how to bring balance back into my mind and emotions. I then asked the Third Question in an Open-Ended way, requesting help in showing me the way through this.

> *The Third Question is the one you ask when you can't remember any other question. It is also the one you go to when it feels like there is nothing else you can do.*

> *If we are lucky, we will come to a seeming dead-end over and over again until we understand that asking for help is the doorway into the healing that we are ready for.*

I gazed out the window for a few minutes and then noticed a mystery novel on a table across the room. It felt right to crawl back into bed and dive into the book. For the first 30 pages or so, I would surface out of the book into self-judgment for being vulnerable and for being in bed in Hawaii! I would also experience fear of my commitments later on in the day. But about 30 minutes later, when I stopped reading for a few minutes and asked the questions again, my heart finally opened to my weariness and vulnerability. Of course I could allow myself to be exactly where I was! I had just led a Six-day retreat and the tiredness was to be expected.

It is amazing to me that just an hour earlier, I was both afraid of and judgmental of what I was experiencing and that resistance was only making things worse. In fact, I was so contracted that nothing was making a difference. I then asked for help in getting through this very contracted part of myself. As I asked this Open-Ended Question and let it go, it worked its magic from underneath my everyday awareness. As the cramp in my mind and heart melted, a feeling of peace came over me. I then went on to have a wonderful day of play and connection with my friends in Hawaii.

The beauty of this question is that it takes us to the same place that compulsions are trying to bring us into – a deep and nourishing relationship with the great Wisdom at the heart of Life. Compulsions throw us into the belief that, not only are we responsible for being compulsive, but we are also totally responsible for our healing. Nothing could be further from the truth. Compulsions are too deep and too complex for us to heal all on our own. If we are lucky, we will come to a seeming dead-end over and over again until we understand that asking for help is the doorway into the healing that we are ready for.

The strength of the question, "What is the way through this?" is that it works for you no matter how confused and lost you are. No matter what is going on, you are not alone. The Intelligence that beats your heart and gives you breath (and is a lot smarter than you) is right there with you – even though the opposite seems true. This Intelligence is waiting for your request for help. Some people call this *surrender*. I don't like that word, because for me it carries a connotation of defeat. I like the word *open*. Through this question we *open* ourselves to the help that is always there.

Again, this question isn't about looking for an answer. It is about creating a space within you for an answer to come. Sometimes answers will come to you right away and sometimes they will take time. I have lived in some questions for years, and the answers came not a moment before I was ready for them. As I look back on my journey with questions, I am stunned at the absolute perfection of this process, even though many times in this journey I have felt like I lost my way, especially in the beginning. But it was these questions that cleared the fog and allowed me to reconnect with myself and with Life in a trust-filled way.

And one of the truest things I know, after having been on the path back to myself for many years, is that Life waits for our request for help. It wants to know a loving and respect filled relationship with ourselves.

Just as with the Check-In Questions, all three of the Open-Ended Questions can be used together or each can stand on its own. At the end of this chapter will be different examples of how to live in the questions. Until then, be willing to live in whatever question called to you as you have been reading this chapter.

These questions can be asked at any time in our lives, but they are extremely powerful when our compulsions are present. They are magical keys that can unlock the door of our struggling minds. The flavor of these questions comes from the willingness to approach ourselves with curiosity and compassion, allowing us to explore our thoughts and feelings rather than being at the mercy of them. They open the door to more and more moments of purely being present for ourselves and for our lives in a fascinated and compassionate way. And most importantly, they connect us with the wisdom of the wellspring within us that is, thankfully, a lot smarter than we are!

The key is to keep on asking questions, understanding that *challenges come with solutions woven into them.* Our job is to pay attention, listen, and live in questions, for the vast Intelligence of the Universe is waiting for the opening of our questions.

Other Possible Questions

The following are questions that have come from my own process and from the people I have worked with over the years. I have put the questions that you will most likely use as Check-In Questions at the top of the list with the

Open-Ended Questions coming after. But as you will discover, some questions can be used either way. Listen to yourself, and use them in the way that works for you.

As you work with questions, the questions that are appropriate to each situation will come to you. After awhile, the experiences of your life will come with the opening of a question, and the questions that live you will be creative, responsive and a never-ending source of nourishment and wisdom.

So be willing to live in questions. I still live in questions and will continue until my last breath. No, that is not right. *I am the questions,* and they constantly bring me back to a deep and nourishing connection with myself and with my life.

Enjoy!

First Question:

The intent is to focus our minds on what is happening right now.

> What part is here?
> What sits here?
> What is happening right now?
> What are my thoughts doing right now?
> What is happening in my body?
> What am I needing to notice?
> What am I resisting?
> What am I ready to see about myself and my life?
> What is the truth of my experience?

Second question:

The intent is to move from *reaction* to *response*, giving whatever we are experiencing the space it needs to heal.

> Can I make space for this?
> Can I accept this as a part of me?
> Can I accept this as a part of my life?
> Can I not struggle with this?
> Can I let this be so that I can be present for it?
> For this moment can I let myself be exactly as I am?
> What do I need to love and accept about myself?
> Can I be with this?
> What do I need to love right now?
> How can I be with this?

> How can I accept this?
> How can I respond?
> How can I say *yes* to this?
> How can I allow this to be?
> How can I touch this with my heart?
> How can I make peace with this?
> How can I nurture myself?
> What is in need of my heart?
> What is it that I need to love?

Third Question:

The intent is to awaken the wellspring of wisdom within us.

> What do I need to do or be that is for my highest good?
> What am I really hungry for?
> What is the kind choice here?
> What is the wise choice here?
> What is my deeper knowing?
> What is wisdom's choice?
> How can I get out of my way?
> What is Love's wisdom in this moment?
> What is the doorway through this challenge?
> How can this be healed?
> How do I not hate and fear this?
> Where is the humor in this?
> What is the shift in perspective that I am ready for?
> Where is this taking me?
> What is my highest good?
> What are the treasures hidden in this experience?

Working with the Questions

We will now review the questions and explore practical ways in which you can apply them in your life.

The Check-In Questions are about being present for your experience, tuning in to it and opening a space around it so you can listen to the deep knowing within you.

- ✧ In this moment, what am I experiencing?

- ✧ For this moment, can I let this be?

- ✧ Right now, what do I <u>truly</u> need?

The Open-Ended Questions are asked when you don't know what you are experiencing, you can't open around it, and you don't have a clue about the way through.

- ✦ What is asking to be seen?
- ✦ How can I bring compassion to this?
- ✦ What is the way through this?

As you become familiar with living in questions, you can make them your own. You may live in just one question for a while. In my own life, I spent a lot of time in the beginning with just the first question. Slowly my heart began to open as I learned how to be present for my experience. Then the second question became predominant in my life. It was only when I finally knew how to meet myself with compassion and understanding that the power of the third question began to reveal itself. With deep joy I finally discovered how to make wise and kind choices.

You can also blend the Check-In Questions and the Open-Ended Questions together in whatever way is helpful for you. You may ask the first two Check-In Questions and then go directly to the third Open-Ended Question. Listen to yourself. Asking questions is a fluid and very alive process.

The following are some examples of what it is like to use the questions individually and combined together. I will be pulling from the list of other possible questions in order to show you that the most important thing to remember is the intent of each question. If you can do that, then your own individual questions will come clear to you.

- ❖ The intent of the First Question is to pull our attention out of the story in our heads so that we can see what is going on right now.

- ❖ The intent of the Second Question is to stop fighting what is going on so we can give it the space to heal, eventually touching it with our hearts.

- ❖ The intention of the Third Question is to listen to the deep knowing within us that is waiting to help us, through the opening of a question.

Individually

Each of these questions is powerful in its own right. The invitation is to live for a day in one of them. It is healing to train your mind in curiosity, compassion, and listening – the core intention of the questions – at a time when things are fairly quiet in your life. It also helps to anchor them to something you do repeatedly throughout the day, like going to the bathroom, eating, or stopping at stop lights. Whichever anchor you choose, whenever it shows up in your life, stop, take a breath, and ask the question you have chosen for the day. Another way to do this, if you have a timer on your phone or watch, is to beep yourself every hour and ask your question.

Combined

The Check-In Questions and the Open-Ended Questions can be combined in numerous ways. The following are some examples of how this works. There may be some feelings that we explore in these examples that you cannot yet imagine meeting in this way, but follow as best you can. You will learn how to work with this in the next section.

The Scenario: You are driving home after a challenging day at work and you are in a state of complete reaction. All you want to do is crawl into your compulsion.

You ask "In this moment, what am I experiencing?" but everything inside of you is in chaos and you don't have any idea what the answer is.

As you ask it again, you are aware of feeling confused. Then it dawns on you that the answer to the first question is that what you are experiencing is confusion!

You then go to the second question, "For this moment, can I let this confusion be?"

This question reminds you that if you fight with it, it will only get worse and will probably make your compulsion look very interesting. If you can give it space, then it can move through you rather than you getting lost in it. The second time you ask if you can let this be, there is a *yes* that comes up inside of you – "Yes, I can let this be for just this moment."

This opens up a space inside of you where you can *relate to* what is going on rather than being *lost in it*. Immediately your attention is drawn to a knot of tension inside of you. Knowing that this tension is created by some feelings that are burbling within you, you ask a variation of the first question, "Right now, what am I feeling?"

As you keep your attention on the knot of tension, it reveals itself as fear. You hear the voices that go along with this fear saying, "I am afraid that if I don't do my job right, I will be fired."

You immediately ask, "For this moment, can I let this fear be?" This question opens your heart and you now can touch this scared part of yourself with understanding and mercy. You tell this feeling that you are listening and that it is okay that it is here.

You then go to the third question, "Right now, what do I truly need?"

A desire for your compulsion flits through your mind. But because you have been willing to turn toward yourself rather than away, it is clear to you that no matter how much you want to act on your compulsion, it will only make you feel better temporarily and will, in the long run, make you feel worse.

When you ask the question again, you remember the truth that there is a wellspring of wisdom within you waiting for the opening of a question. A few stoplights later, you become clear that when you get home you want to review the report that you were concerned about so that you can discuss it with your boss tomorrow. You will then be more familiar with it and know where your boss stands on the issues. This calms down the knot of fear, but visions of your compulsion are still lingering.

When you ask again, "Right now, what do I truly need?" you feel that you need to do something that will allow you to stay connected to yourself in a comforting and balanced way. You consider the possibility of buying the paper, going to a coffee house, and having a latte while you read. "No," says your wisdom. "It would feel better to be with somebody I am comfortable with and do something fun." So you call a good friend and make plans to see an upbeat movie together.

But suppose you get all the way to the third question, "Right now, what do I truly need?" and there is resistance again. "All I want is my compulsion," demands the scared part of you.

The clouds of reaction begin to take over your mind again, so you go back to the first question, "In this moment, what am I experiencing?" You feel the craving for your compulsion deep inside of you.

You realize that if you fight this craving, it will only make it worse. You then ask, "For this moment, can I let this craving be?" The answer is "Yes," and with this spaciousness, the cravings calm down.

Your mind is now clear enough that you can ask again, "What is it that I truly need?" This question opens your heart and reminds you that it is never your compulsion that you are really longing for. What you truly need is a healing connection with yourself.

You bring your hand over your heart and tell yourself that you understand that it was a very challenging day and that you are here for yourself right now You keep your hand over your heart all the way home, and, as your reactions fall away, you have a wonderful evening.

You ask the question, "In this moment, what am I experiencing?" and nothing inside of you wants to look, let alone listen to what is going on. In fact the question fans the flame of anger within you, and there is not the slightest willingness to explore your inner experience. All you want is your compulsion.

Immediately you go to the Third Open-Ended Question, "What is the way through this?" You then let that question go, allowing it to work for you. This doesn't stop the wave of compulsion but that is okay. It is a shorter wave than usual because very quickly it is clear to you that your compulsion isn't helping you feel better.

While lying in bed later that night, feeling uncomfortable from the affects of your compulsion, the first question pops into your mind: "In this moment, what am I experiencing?" At first glance all you feel is a thick fog. But you stay with the question, knowing that it will clear up the fog so you can see and be with what is going on within you. As the fog lifts, you feel the overall feeling of discomfort in your body.

When you ask, "For this moment, can I let this be?" your immediate response is, "No! I screwed up again." But that contraction is so painful that you are willing to ask this question in an Open-Ended way. "For this moment, *how* can I let myself be exactly as I am?" (a variation on the Second Open-Ended Question)

This question reminds you that if you struggle with where you are, it only makes it worse. If you allow it to be and pay attention, things will lighten up and there will be something to learn. As you take some deep breaths, what comes to you is that you weren't compulsive because you are weak willed or defective. Instead, there is something inside of you that you don't yet know how to take care of in any other way. You also remember that if you focus on what is going on inside of you right now, without judging yourself, you will see more clearly how the price you pay for your compulsion is never worth it.

So you ask the First Open-Ended Question: "What is asking to be seen?" As you bring your attention into your body and begin to explore exactly what you are experiencing, you write down on a pad of paper everything you discover – the ball of dread in your belly, the pounding of your heart, the tight shoulders, the acid stomach, and the empty hole deep within you.

You then ask, "Right now, what do I <u>truly</u> need?" You feel compelled to open this book to a random page and read whatever you see first. What you read opens your heart to yourself again and your self-judgment lightens. As you turn out the lights, you ask for help through the Third Open-Ended Question, "What is the way through this?" knowing that it will work for you while you are asleep.

When you notice you are lunging towards your compulsion and you are too tired and too upset to explore what is going on, you ask, "How can I not struggle with this?" (a variation of the Second Open-Ended Question.) This question creates enough space inside of you that you remember that you can ask for help.

So you go immediately to the Third Open-Ended Question, "What is the way through this?' You know that you don't have to figure anything out or even do anything about it right now. This question will work for you underneath your ordinary awareness. On the drive home, every time the urge to be compulsive tries to take you over, you ask the question again, remembering that your wellspring of wisdom is waiting for the opening of your question. Help is there even though you are not aware of it right now.

You ask, "In this moment, what am I experiencing?" and your answer is an angry, "Nothing!" You ask it again, and you realize you are feeling resistance to even asking the questions. But you know that resisting your resistance will only make it worse.

You then ask, "For this moment, can I let this resistance be?" Again you get a resounding, "No! This is uncomfortable and I don't want to be experiencing this!" But there is a part of you that knows that since you are in deep reaction, there is something within you that has been stirred up by everything that has happened today.

You then ask a variation of the First Open-Ended Question, "What am I resisting?" "Well of course I am resisting all of this unpleasantness," says your anger. "I don't like this feeling of agitation all over my body and I just want to get out of here. Give me my compulsion!"

You don't get lost in the anger, for you know it is only here because you are in fight or flight mode after this very challenging day. Your awareness then asks, "What is this resistance taking care of?" Suddenly all of your reactions fall away and you become very curious about what is going on inside of you.

As you bring your attention into your body, what begins to reveal itself is a deep sense of hopelessness and despair. "If I lose my job, then I will be a total failure," says this despair. This thought is irrational in relationship to what went on today, but instead of judging it, you realize immediately that this is a vulnerable part of you that was triggered by all that happened at work. Rather than trying to deny it, you understand that it is here because it needs the healing of your compassionate attention.

You then ask, "How can I be with this?" Your body responds to this question with some deep breaths and you automatically begin to breathe through your heart. On every out breath you send mercy to this scared one inside of you. As you pull into your driveway, you know that this under-standing and mercy will fill the hole within you that you had previously tried to fill with your compulsion.

When you ask, "In this moment, what am I experiencing?" you feel a knot of fear in your belly. When you ask, "For this moment, can I let this be?" you answer, "No. I have a condo meeting I have to go to and I don't have time for this right now." The fear flares up even more. You immediately go to the Third Open-Ended Question "What is the way through this?" You remember that with this question you are asking for help from the deep knowing within you, and just asking it reminds you that you are not alone. Your body begins to breathe some long, deep breaths.

Through the opening of your breath, you remember that this is an opportu-nity to stand with your vulnerabilities rather than reacting and then reacting to your reaction. When you ask, "Right now, what do I truly need?" what comes first is, "I don't want to go to the meeting." Since that is not a viable option, you come back to the question again and let it work for you.

As you continue driving, what comes bubbling up from your wellspring is the knowing that this is all workable and you can support yourself at the meeting by using the questions. As you enter the meeting, even though there are chips and dips on the table, you realize you don't need to take care of yourself through food. It is clear to you that everything is going to be okay.

Sitting at a stoplight, completely lost in reaction, you notice the first ques-tion, which you have put upon your dash board. It reminds you that the questions can help you move out of this storm inside of you. When you ask, "In this moment, what am I experiencing?" a ball of dread explodes in your stomach. "I don't know what I am experiencing and I won't be able to figure it out. I never do anything right," says the judging voice in your head.

You ask the question again, and it awakens your willingness to be curious about what is going on inside of you. You take a half-step out of the conversation in your mind, and you can see that you are judging yourself. In fact, you can see that since your boss called you into his office for a reprimand today, you have been beating up on yourself unmercifully.

You then ask a variation of the Second Check-In Question, "For this moment, can I bring compassion to myself?" "No," is your response. "I am just a screw up!" Immediately your awareness recognizes the self-judgment rather than believing what it is saying. In order to help relieve the spell of self judgment, you ask this question in an Open-Ended way – "For this moment, *how* can I bring compassion to myself?' Rather than the all consuming self-judgment you begin to feel some mercy for yourself. You know that you are doing the best that you know how at your work. Whenever the self judging voices come into your head, for the rest of the night, you ask this question. Slowly, like the fog lifting, you truly see that you don't have to believe these old voices.

As you ask the question, "In this moment, what am I experiencing?" there is a ball of anger in your belly that feels like it is ready to explode. "In this moment, can I let this be?" "No. It is not all right to be angry. It has never been okay to be angry, and if I allow it, it will consume me," you reply. Remembering that you fuel a feeling by resisting it and calm it down by meeting it, you ask, "In this moment, how can I bring compassion to this?" As you do some deep breathing into the anger, your mind begins to clear.

With this spaciousness you become willing to explore the sensations of anger in your body. As you pay attention, it becomes clear to you that there is something underneath it. You ask a variation of the First Open-Ended Question, "What is asking to be met?" Your attention stays with the ball of anger, and after a few moments, a wave of fear makes itself known. You immediately want to pull away, but you stay open by asking, "Can I meet this in mercy?" (a variation of the second question) This question opens your heart and you begin to breathe into the fear, giving it some understanding and support. You remind this feeling that whatever happens, it is all going to be okay.

You then go to the Third Check-In Question, "Right now, what do I <u>truly</u>

need?" It very quickly comes clear that you need to go back to work and check things out with your boss. This is a little scary, but you know that you don't have to go in there alone. You have the questions to help you.

As you drive up to the building, you ask a variation of the Third Open-Ended Question "What do I need to say and do that is for my highest good?" In the conversation with your boss, whenever you find yourself reacting, you come back to this question. It allows you to respond from your well-spring of deep knowing rather than living from reaction. As the meeting comes to an end, you know that you clearly spoke your truth, and on the way home you now realize that the urge to be compulsive has left.

As you drive away from work, you feel completely shut down. There is a big lump in your throat and it feels like an elephant is sitting on your chest. Your mind is screaming, "This is too much. Everything is always hard in my life and it never gets better!"

Having worked with the questions for awhile, there is a part of you that can immediately recognize that this is your familiar place of despair. You know from experience that, if you can be with this feeling rather than turning away, it will lighten up. So you ask, "In this moment, how can I be with this?" (a variation on the Second Open-Ended Question)

What comes to mind is that you need to soften the reactions inside of you that have been building up all day. So as you breathe in, you tighten your whole body, and as you breathe out, you let your body relax. You practice this at every stoplight you come to, and you can feel the reactions inside of you begin to calm down.

You then remember that this despairing part of you responds to compassion. You begin to talk to the lump in your throat and the tightness in your chest as if they were a lonely child. You say to these sensations of despair, "I see you, Despair, and it is okay that you are here. I understand how you feel and I am with you now. Everything will be okay."

As these words of compassion lighten your mind and your heart, the wiser part of you remembers that this is just a state of mind passing through and everything will truly be okay.

Because you have been working with the questions for a while, when you notice how upset you are, you immediately ask, "In this moment, can I let this be?" Your awareness remembers that this is just a state of mind passing through and you don't need to struggle with it. Things calm down inside of you and you know that, rather than following your compulsion, what you truly need is to go home, crawl into bed, and read a good book.

The art of asking questions is exactly that – an art. As we cultivate this art, it will slowly ripen in our consciousness. A pianist doesn't play Mozart after a few lessons, and you won't master the art of living in questions overnight. Be willing to simply ask questions without expecting anything in return. Know that it doesn't matter if you can only stay in the space of a question for a moment or two. Just like a small pebble thrown into a huge lake, its ripples eventually make it all the way to the shore. One question sets things in motion, moving you farther down the path of awakening.

Core Ideas in Skill #5 – Living In Questions:

❖ The power of questions is in the questions themselves!

❖ We can ask questions when we don't want to know what we are experiencing, when we can't open to what we are experiencing, and even when we don't trust that the questions will make any difference. If we just keep asking, the questions will support us in ways we cannot even imagine.

❖ Check-in Questions invite you to explore what you are experiencing with curiosity and compassion so you can make contact with the wellspring of wisdom within you.

❖ It is very healing to slow down for a moment and experience what you are experiencing.

❖ The quickest and most powerful way to dissolve your struggles is to let them be!

❖ There is a wellspring of deep wisdom within you that is waiting for the opening of a question.

❖ Open-Ended Questions are about tapping into the Wisdom at the heart of Life.

❖ Answers from Open-Ended Questions, rather than coming from your head and then finding yourself struggling to apply them in your life, come from within you and you begin to *live the answers.*

❖ The art of trusting that the Intelligence of the Universe will answer our questions comes to each of us in its own time and in its own way.

❖ The core healing that compulsions are bringing to you is the knowing that you are never alone. There is an Intelligence with you every step of the way that is supporting you in ways you cannot see, and waits for your request for help.

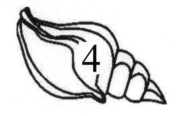

Treasure Hunting

✦ *RESPONDING* RATHER THAN *REACTING* ✦

All of the skills we have explored so far allow us to come out of the struggles of our minds and be present for ourselves and for our lives. And even though you may now be experiencing moments of pure *being* and finally recognize that this is what you have been truly longing for, it is so easy to drift back into your everyday struggles, cut off again from the nourishment, wisdom and support that are always available right here, right now. And whenever we find ourselves reentering struggle mode, we again become vulnerable to our compulsions.

Not only that, some of those habitual thought patterns and the feelings that we get lost in can be pretty darn seductive – fear, anger, confusion, self judgment, despair. And they all fuel our compulsions, usually from under-neath our everyday awareness. As we explored in the *Curiosity* chapter, they are just parts of a story in our heads, a story that has been woven out of the experiences of our lives. Because we don't realize this, we fight with them, trying to ignore, dominate, distract and numb out. We don't recognize that this is exactly what gives them energy – gives them power to tromp through our minds and hearts like an elephant in a tulip patch.

To bring the light of our consciousness to what we are experiencing as we are experiencing it – to explore our thoughts and feelings with curiosity and meet them with mercy – dispels them like the sun on the morning fog. As we explored in the chapter on *Curiosity*, focused attention is one of the most powerful transformers that we have available to us.

I call this ability to bring the light of our compassionate attention into our habitual patterns of perception *treasure hunting*. Why *treasure hunting*? Because as we meet ourselves with curiosity and compassion instead of turning away, all of our struggles transform back into the free flowing aliveness they came from.

Remember what it was like when I invited you earlier to shake your body, and the tingles and aliveness you felt everywhere? That was a tiny glimpse into the kind of joy that is our birth-right. Instead of being fully alive, we are like free flowing water that has turned into ice. As we bring the light of our attention into what we are experiencing, the ice of our struggles begins to thaw into flowing water. Then, as we give ourselves the warm

> *I call this treasure hunting because there is always a treasure hidden in the sensations, feelings and thoughts that we have habitually run from.*

light of our heart, our struggles evaporate into the air just like water evaporating into steam. We then become one again with Life. That is our birthright – to feel that alive and full of joy.

I also call it treasure hunting because there *is always a treasure hidden in the sensations, feelings and thoughts that we have habitually run from.* As we learn how to *relate to* them without being *lost in* them they give us the treasure they have been concealing. Fear brings us trust; physical pain brings relief and release; anger reveals compassion; and despair opens us to a connection with ourselves and with Life that is better than any fairy tale we have ever read.

In the next three chapters we will weave the five skills we explored into a workable system that you can use to heal and be healed by your compulsion:

- ❖ We will use the first skill of *Curiosity* in order to move beyond our ideas of what should be, in order to experience what we are experiencing.

- ❖ We will tap into the second skill of *Compassion* in order to meet whatever we discover with the spaciousness of our heart.

- ❖ We will utilize the third skill of *Open Breathing* in order to open ourselves up again and to nourish ourselves with the wisdom of breath.

- ❖ We will apply the fourth skill of *Being* in order to invite ourselves back into our bodies and a deep and abiding relationship with ourselves and with the present moment. This is what we are truly longing for whenever we are compulsive.

- ❖ And we will use the fifth skill, *Living in Questions*, as a guide on this journey back to ourselves.

As we weave these skills together it will become clear that the core intent of compulsion is to open us to the truth that we are not alone – that there is a presence that is keeping pace with us every step of the way. We are healed by compulsions when we discover a deep and lasting partnership with the Wisdom at the heart of Life.

What we will be exploring here is probably different than anything you have ever done before. It is the art of turning toward ourselves when we are compulsive. It is about *responding* rather than *reacting* so that we can bring the light of our attention to the thoughts and feelings that are fueling our compulsions. Most of us don't know how to do this because we have been taught that if we just stay in control, everything will be okay. Of course this doesn't bring us the lasting healing that we long for. But since we have not been taught any other way, we keep on going back to denying, managing,

> *What we are experiencing isn't as important as <u>what our relationship is</u> to what we are experiencing.*

explaining, dominating and controlling.

If we have gotten beyond denying our experience, we usually spend a lot of time trying to understand where it came from (I had a horrible older brother or my parents divorced when I was three) and while this helps, it only takes us so far. We also try to express our feelings, believing that we can empty them out like we empty a bowl of water (only to discover that the bowl fills up again!) There is also a whole school of thought that says if we just rise above our difficulties with positive thinking and numerous affirmations, then we can leave them far behind.

We have all used enough of these techniques to realize that they may bring temporary respite, but not the deep and lasting peace that we long for. This peace comes when we realize that what we are experiencing isn't as important as *what our relationship is* to what we are experiencing. As we let go of fighting with what is happening, learning how to be present for it instead, the survival system we learned when we were young – made up of all the thoughts and feelings that fuel our compulsions – dissolves under the light of our compassionate attention.

This is much easier, much simpler and much safer than you can even imagine, for there is a big difference between feeling a feeling and meeting a feeling. In feeling a feeling, you can be caught in the middle of it. Let us take fear for example. Part of the fear is that it will engulf you, and so as you begin to feel it, the feeling is intensified by the fear that it may take over and pull you down into a vortex of fear. This is why most of us run as fast as we can the other way when we are told we have to feel our feelings in order to heal.

Meeting a feeling is entirely different. It is the recognition of the feeling without falling into it, giving it exactly what it needs to heal – your undivided, compassionate attention. It is the difference between saying, "I am afraid/terrified" (feeling a feeling) and "Ahh, fear." (meeting a feeling) In that moment of witnessing the feeling – *relating to it rather than from it* – it loses a little more of its power over you and you take another step into freedom.

> *There is a big difference between feeling a feeling and meeting a feeling. Meeting a feeling is recognizing it and giving it exactly what it needs to heal – your undivided, compassionate attention.*

In meeting a feeling, you don't have to figure out where it came from nor do you have to figure out how to get rid of it. Transformation comes from the power of your undivided attention. Do not be confused by its simplicity, for truth – real truth – is always simple. The power of this kind of meeting is so awesome that just a few moments with a feeling that you have formerly run from can change your life.

There is a wonderful story that John Gray, author of *Men Are From Mars and Women Are From Venus,* tells about his 7 year-old daughter that will give you a glimpse into the world of meeting feelings. He was very late picking her up from school and she had been waiting all by herself for some time. At seven years-old this can be quite overwhelming, and when he finally arrived, she was very upset. Rather than ignoring or discounting her feelings, he sat down on the curb and was intensely present for her experience. After rivers of tears, she got angry and asked if he was going to pick her up tomorrow. When he answered "yes," she asked if he was going to be on time. When he said "yes," she then asked him to come early. And he did.

He didn't *react* to her feelings, he *responded* to them. He didn't reject them nor did he become enmeshed with them. He was a neutral witness, honoring her experience and allowing her feelings the space to be heard. Because her feelings were heard and validated, they didn't get boxed inside of her!

All of the boxed up feelings inside of you (that fuel your compulsion) are asking to be met in the same curious and compassionate way that John Gray met his daughter's feelings. In fact, they have been waiting your whole life for you to give to yourself what John gave to his daughter.

In the next four chapters we will be exploring how to bring the light of our compassionate attention into our experience. As we learn how to *respond* rather than *react*, our feelings can join again the free flowing aliveness that is our birthright.

1. In *Healing Our Pain,* you will discover why it is safe and healing to be present for yourself, even in the difficult parts of your life.

2. In *Treasure Hunting 101*, you will be given the basic techniques that will allow you to use the light of your focused attention to transform your experience.

3. In *Treasure Hunting With Feelings,* you will learn how to take these techniques into the thoughts and feelings that have caused you to run to your compulsion over and over again.

4. And finally, in *Treasure Hunting With Compulsions*, you will discover how to bring everything we have explored to your compulsion so that you can heal it and be healed in the process.

We are now getting into the most technical part of the book. The invitation is that the first time you read each chapter in this section, read it to get a feeling for what is being offered. The most important thing you can take from the *Treasure Hunting* section is that it is not only safe, but it is very healing to bring compassionate attention to whatever you are experiencing. Then read each chapter again, listening for the techniques that are appropriate for you. Remember, you are the only person who knows the steps you need to take for your healing.

Core Ideas in Responding Rather Than Reacting

❖ Hidden in the inner experiences that you have habitually run from always lies a treasure.

❖ Treasure hunting is all about bringing your attention to your life, not as you wish it to be, but exactly as it is, right here, right now.

❖ If you aren't aware of what is going on inside yourself, you live in reaction. Reaction creates contraction in your mind, body, and heart. It is this contraction that fuels compulsions.

❖ You have the choice either to be present for what you are experiencing, allowing your undivided attention to transform your contractions back into the free-flowing energy they came from, or to close down and run away again. You can learn from either choice.

❖ Compulsion is here because it wants to teach you how to reconnect with yourself. It is a powerful force from within that is bringing enough discomfort into your life so that the only option left to you is to pay attention and meet whatever you discover with an open heart.

❖ Over time, you will be less and less interested in compulsions as being present for yourself brings you all of the joy, peace, and comfort you have been longing for.

✦ HEALING OUR PAIN ✦

Before we learn the art of bringing our attention to ourselves and then to the feelings and thoughts that are fueling our compulsion, we need to acknowledge how afraid we are of doing this. We have been absent from ourselves for a very long time and a relationship built on listening, compassion and trust can seem alien at first.

As we learn how to meet our feelings rather than being consumed by them, we discover that most of the ones that fuel our compulsions have been hidden down in the basement of our *being* where we imagine it to be very dark and scary. Many of us are afraid of the shadow side of Life – our rage, our terror and our despair – so we demonize our negativity and then project it onto our loved ones, different parts of society, and even other countries.

Since we aren't able to take responsibility for what is within us, we find ourselves living in the attic of the mind, locking behind closed doors everything we are afraid of. These parts of ourselves don't go away when we close the door. In fact, they ferment in there, growing bigger and stronger the longer we keep them locked up. And when any feeling escapes and comes knocking at the door to the attic, off we go to our compulsions rather than opening the door and welcoming our feelings in.

Oprah Winfrey, while talking with Gary Zukav, author of *Seat of the Soul*, clearly revealed our resistance to meeting the feelings we have been afraid of. It was a show on addictions, and she was speaking about the night that she ate lots of macaroni and cheese and bread pudding after seeing the negative reviews on her movie *Beloved*. While sharing with Gary, she began to see that she didn't just want to eat that night. She was also trying to run away from feelings of powerlessness and rejection.

Gary then helped her to see why it is so important to meet our feelings. In the face of an invitation to go deeper, Oprah immediately went to her management techniques by saying that she could have gone for a run or to the gym. Gary invited her to feel what was going on inside of her. In other words, he invited her to engage with her experience rather than trying to manage it.

> *Many of us are afraid of the shadow side of Life – our rage, our terror and our despair – so we demonize our negativity and then project it onto our loved ones, different parts of society, and even other countries.*

Oprah expressed the resistance we all feel to doing this by saying how much even imagining that brought up painful feelings for her. She then said, "Why would I want to sit there and feel all of that?" Gary responded, "Because if you don't, you will need to contend with this very strong impulse to eat, gamble, buy, run drink, have sex."

> *We are afraid of opening the door to our feelings because we have not been taught how to open it in a way that is safe and healing.*

When Gary said that on national television, I was thrilled. He is the first major figure I have heard speak the truth that we need to find out what is fueling our compulsions in order to heal. And Oprah spoke the fear we all have of doing this.

We are afraid of opening the door to our feelings because we have not been taught how to open it in a way that is safe and healing. And we don't understand that those feelings are too painful to bear only when we try to keep the attic door shut. When we learn how to open the door and meet what is there, that is when the formerly scary feelings can transform back into the free flowing aliveness that is our birthright. When this happens, the joy we experience is beyond our wildest imaginations.

Healing is opening what has been closed, embracing what has been most feared. In order to move beyond our highly trained inclination to react and run away, let us explore the fertility and the necessity of our pain and the safety that comes from meeting it.

The Fertility of Our Pain

If we look closely we will see Life's inclination to hide its treasures in the dark. In practically every myth that has been handed down through the ages, both the keys to the adventure and the treasures themselves are usually hidden in the dark: The dragon sits on the golden egg. The princess is protected by a moat full of crocodiles. The evil queen has the magic wand. The necessity of the dark – of the difficult, challenging aspects of our lives – is woven through the *Odyssey, Dante's Inferno* and even in the *Wizard of Oz*. Each of the main characters in that movie became more of themselves through their challenges – the lion discovered his courage, the scarecrow his intelligence, the tin man his heart, and Dorothy found her way home.

Our compulsions and the boxed up feelings that fuel them are the place where the treasures of our true self are hidden. *To discover what lies hidden under our compulsions, we need to make friends with our pain.* "No. No. Never!" we say. And Oprah says, "Why would I ever want to do that?"

Suspend your resistance for a moment and imagine a huge and ferocious lion chasing you. This is what it is like with the boxed-up feelings within us that we have tried to escape through our compulsions. When the *lions* of these feelings come close to the surface, we put on our running shoes and sprint away. We eat more chocolate, figure out more things To Do, get lost on the Internet, get out our credit cards.

Sometimes you can outdistance the lion. Eventually, if you are lucky, you won't be able to run anymore. Falling to the ground, you are sure you are going to be devoured. As the lion screeches to a halt beside you, much to your amazement, he doesn't take a bite out of you at all. Instead, he turns into a pussycat, and as his mouth opens, you see resting on his tongue a gift he has been trying to deliver for years!! The lion is your compulsion and all of the feelings you have been running from. And just like the lion, these feelings hold great treasures. But you have to stop running in order to be gifted by them.

In my own journey, as I was able to meet my terror, it transformed into trust. As I was able to meet my self-judgment, it transformed into compassion. As I met my rage, I finally learned how to use that energy to focus my mind, allowing me to cut through the most contracted states of consciousness. And as I found the courage to meet my despair, I finally knew that I was never ever alone.

The Necessity of Our Pain

The darkness of our pain not only holds great treasures, Life *needs* the dark in order for this great and wondrous adventure to unfold. Every single atom in the universe has a negative charge. Half of the Earth is always enfolded in the night. Plants grow in the absence of light and seeds germinate in the dark embrace of soil. Agnus Whistling Elk, a Manitoba medicine woman, summed up this truth better than anybody I have ever heard:

> *If you look at something carefully, you will always be able to see its dark side. And yet we choose never to look into the shadows. Understand that it is what you choose not to observe in your life that controls your life. Everything begins with a circle of motion; without the positive and negative poles there would be no movement, no creation. Without the dark side your beauty would not exist. Don't be afraid to look at both sides. You need them both. Honor all as part of the Great Spirit.*

This is true for your life. Each of us is a mixture of dark and light. We need

> *It is what we choose not to observe in our lives that controls our lives.*

both polarities in order to exist. We are made up of the uplifting and lighter energies such as joy, faith, and humility. We also carry the heavier and darker energies such as judgment, fear, anger and sorrow. It is not only normal to have both positive and negative traits; it is necessary! The fullness that we are is created out of the dance of dark and light, remembering and forgetting, strengths and weaknesses that we are.

We can expand this truth into our daily lives too. Our days, our years and our lives are a dance of dark and light. We were sold a debilitating bill of goods when we were young – the whole idea that we are here to live happily ever after. The full spectrum of Life includes the difficult. There is an old saying that goes, "Into every life a little rain will fall." For most of us we don't just experience gentle showers. We also know thunderstorms and windstorms and midwinter gales that rip the limbs off of the trees of our souls. But rain makes things grow and windstorms open spaces in the forest of our hearts, which then allow for new growth to appear.

At the opposite end of the spectrum, we also have the times of sweet summer mornings when the air is full of rich, intoxicating smells and the sparkle of dew is more breathtaking than the most exquisite jewel. But these times of ease inevitably move into the storms of winter again, and if we try to hold on, it only causes suffering. Just like the seasons, Life will constantly rock back and forth between the pleasant and the unpleasant. Our peace comes when we realize that our lives will continually move through the full spectrum. If we can learn to ride the waves, we can tap into a deeper peace that trusts it all.

Thich Nhat Hahn, the wonderful Vietnamese monk who was nominated for a noble peace prize by Martin Luther King, once said:

> *I saw my mind and heart as flowers. All feelings, passions, sufferings revealed themselves as wonders, yet I remain grounded in my body. There is no enlightenment outside of my own mind and the cells of my body. Life is miraculous, even in its suffering. Without suffering Life would not be possible.*

> *Our lives will continually move through the full spectrum. If we can learn to ride the waves, we can tap into a deeper peace that trusts it all.*

What would our lives be like if we honored and explored our darker aspects as much as we try to hold onto and cultivate our lighter ones? What would happen if we realized that we will continue to move back and forth between the pleasant and the unpleasant throughout our entire journey? Let me answer that. We would be integrated human beings. Feelings would come and go, dancing through us like the clouds that dance across the sky. There would be no need to get caught in fear or anger, nor any need to hold onto happiness. This would move us into the deep peace that lies behind the dance of opposites, the peace that is our own true nature.

The Safety of Meeting Our Pain

One of the core reasons we run away from our painful feelings is that we are terrified that they will completely engulf us if we get too close. We are also afraid that if we allow them a voice, they will never, ever stop. Not having been trained to pay attention to our feelings in a respectful and honoring manner, when the ones we have rejected burble to the surface, we meet them with hatred and fear.

In this relationship of rejection, our feelings are just like the snakes Grace Wiley worked with. If someone comes into their territory with hatred and fear in their heart, they will attack. So of course we have become terrified of our feelings, for as we have attacked them, they have responded in kind. But just like Grace did with the snakes, we can learn how to *gentle* our feelings with our undivided attention. When we can stand with a feeling without running away and listen to what it has to say, it has been my experience, and the experience of the people that I work with, that it loses its power as we take our power back.

Patricia Sun, a wonderful teacher of awakening, once said to me that the

> *When we can stand with a feeling without running away and listen to what it has to say, it loses its power as we take our power back.*

terror we all feel about meeting these feelings is genuine but it is not real. That terror is just a paper dragon. Andrew Harvey in his book *Hidden Journey* tells of a dream he had which reveals this truth – both the fear we have of meeting our feelings and how insubstantial they are when we finally face them. It opens with Andrew and a famous Russian poet sitting together in a large room. The poet is known for his searing sarcasm and heavy judgment of everything mystical. Andrew has become a disciple of a famous master of the mystical and desperately wants to hide this from this man's cutting judgment.

The poet asks him if he has a master. Andrew denies it. Again he asks Andrew if he has a master. Meeting his fear of being seen as *less than*, Andrew finally tells the poet the truth. With a bang, the door to the bar opens and a horse and rider come into the room. As Andrew looks closely he sees a bloody body lying across the front of the saddle and he sees that it is himself! This was a powerful representation of the fear he had of being seen as inadequate. He felt that if he spoke the truth of his experience that he would be destroyed! A voice from within then asks him to look closely and as he does, he sees that the body is made out of paper-mâché and the horse of plastic!

All of our fears of meeting these feelings do seem very real at times, but if we look at the feelings that we are most terrified of – our rage, our terror, our self-hatred, our despair – we will see that they are just made out of paper-mâché. Initially they look very big, but upon close examination, they lose their power. The intensity that comes from approaching them is sometimes overwhelming, but as soon as direct contact is made, the overwhelm passes and the feelings transform into joy, leaving us feeling opened and vibrantly alive.

Our pain is not the enemy we thought it to be. Instead, it holds many of the keys to our healing. And even though it can be scary at times to go toward our darkest feelings, we do have a light available to us at all times. The skills of curiosity and compassion are both powerful enough to guide our way through even the darkest of times and potent enough to shine the light of healing on anything we may meet along the way. So let us now explore how to bring compassionate curiosity to our experience so that the light of our focused attention can transform whatever we meet.

Core Ideas in Healing Our Pain:

❖ Your pain is a necessary part of you.

❖ To deny your pain does not get rid of it. In fact, it will fuel your compulsion from underneath your everyday awareness.

❖ When you try to run away from the pains of Life, you cut yourself off from the joy. You can't have one without the other.

❖ It is what you choose *not* to observe in your life that controls your life.

❖ Your life will continually move through the full spectrum from pain to joy. If you can learn to ride the waves, you can tap into a deeper peace that trusts it all.

❖ There are gentle ways to open to your pain that are safe and healing.

❖ Your pain is always a guardian of great treasures.

✦ TREASURE HUNTING 101 ✦

Now we are at the heart of the matter, the place where healing and being healed by our compulsion occurs. As we have explored, this happens in the ability to use the light of our attention to discover what we are experiencing when we are compulsive and then the power of our heart to meet whatever thoughts and feelings are running us so that they can be healed. Through our compassionate curiosity, our attention is then freed from our old patterns of reaction so that we can listen to the wellspring of deep knowing within us. In this listening, we can then make wise and skillful choices that will allow us to open again to the joy of being fully connected to ourselves and to our lives.

Treasure hunting is based on the foundation of curiosity that we have explored throughout this book. If we aren't aware of what is going on in ourselves, we live in reaction. Reaction creates contraction in our minds, bodies and hearts. And this contraction within us, left unattended, gets us into all sorts of trouble, the core trouble being that it fuels our compulsions.

If we can learn how to be curious about what we are experiencing, *responding rather than reacting, this loosens the power of whatever we are resisting.* And *response* is so much wiser than *reaction.* When we can fully experience whatever we are experiencing, it puts us into contact with the wellspring of wisdom within us that knows what is needed in any situation in order to bring balance to our whole *being.*

Response heals all levels of pain – physical, mental, and emotional. The easiest place to start working with its healing power is in our bodies, for it is easier in the beginning to work with physical pain. It is not as elusive as emotional pain or as confusing as our mental world can be at times.

When I discovered that acknowledging my pain through compassionate curiosity brought spaciousness and healing; when I discovered that I could ask for help from the wellspring within and that it had been waiting for the opening of my request; and when I discovered that I could trust the process – including the pain – an amazingly wonderful thing began to happen. I reconnected with what I knew when I was very young – that Life is happening right here, right now; that all that I truly longed for was right here, right now; and that I did have the choice about whether I was going to narrow my focus down to my struggles or bring it back to the fullness of Life in this moment.

I could also see how my pain was

> *Responding rather than reacting loosens the power of whatever we are resisting.*

> *Rather than just surviving, I began to thrive. Rather than just doing Life, I was being Life!*

serving me now. Rather than throwing me into an ever-tightening spiral of reaction, it reminded me that I was again struggling with Life. In other words, my pain became a wake up call. Whenever it was present, I would acknowledge it, touch it with my heart and then open my attention into the unfolding river of Life as it is right now. Over and over again it became clear that whatever I was reacting to in my mind, body or emotions was just a small part of the fullness of Life.

Oh the joy of that! I was entering again the great river of Creativity that is Life the moment it appears out of Mystery. *Rather than just surviving, I began to thrive.* Rather than just *doing* Life, I was *being* Life! You may not understand what I mean yet, but it is about coming *home*. It is about trusting ourselves again and trusting our lives. It is about becoming comfortable in our own skins, living our lives from the inside out. And it is one of the greatest gifts that Life can give us.

So how do we do this when we have been trained to *react* rather than *respond*? It may seem impossible at first glance, but I assure you it is simpler and safer than you can imagine. Let us begin by taking a look again at the healing power of simply *being present* for whatever we are experiencing.

To Tell The Truth

In order to cultivate awareness of what is going on and, from that awareness, learning how to have choices about what we are going to pay attention to, we begin by simply telling the truth to ourselves about what we are experiencing. This is the foundation of true freedom. *Telling the truth* is about listening deeply enough to ourselves so we can be real about what we are actually experiencing. *It is the art of letting go just for a moment of all the images we carry about how we are* supposed to be, *and instead reporting to ourselves* what is really happening.

This may seem very basic at first glance, but it is powerful beyond our wildest imaginings. Most people don't know how to do this. They have almost completely lost the ability to be real with themselves. They live in their heads, following all of the *shoulds*, *ought tos* and *have tos* of their minds while many of these images are in direct conflict with how things truly are. This creates a great division between who they think they *should be* and who they *really are*. The grief of this disconnection, usually hidden under layers of compulsion, is enormous.

When people learn how to pay attention to their own experience, discovering what is truly going on, they are often stunned with how completely they have been able to pull the wool over their own eyes – stunned but delighted, for it is such a relief to finally be real about what actually is going on.

Telling the truth taps us into the wisdom of the body, one of the wisest and dearest friends we will ever have. The human body has been around for a very long time and, like all animals, it has developed the capacity to survive by being highly tuned into exactly what is going on. When our head is spinning all sorts of tales about what we *should be* experiencing right now, the body won't lie. If somebody has made us angry and if we are very good at hiding our anger, even though our head is saying that we aren't angry, the body will raise our heartbeat and tighten our stomach.

So let us now look at how our body will teach us how to come out of the clouds of reaction back into the truth of what we are experiencing.

◇ Sensations versus Feelings

The thoughts that run us are very seductive. And the feelings that ensnare us can be either very elusive or very intense. We get so lost in them that we become lost in a story *about* what we are experiencing rather than *experiencing* what we are experiencing. In order to become free, we need to let go of the story (it's all her fault or why does this have to happen to me) and instead, meet what is going on inside of us ("ahh, anger" or "ahh, overwhelm").

So we will start our exploration in telling the truth by focusing on sensations in our body. To do this, we need to comprehend that there is a difference between sensations and feelings. Sensations are physical experiences in our body – a tickle, butterflies in our stomach, a headache. Feelings come from our emotional body – anger, fear, sadness. Sensations may or may not have any emotion attached to them - the butterflies are probably coming from an emotion whereas the tickle probably isn't. But *every single feeling we have ever*

Every single feeling we have ever experienced also shows up as a sensation. You may not always know what you are feeling, but the sensations that come with our feelings are always available to our curiosity.

experienced also shows up as a sensation. Think of what your body does when you are angry or afraid and you will know what I mean.

The power of working with sensations is that *you may not always know what you are feeling, but the sensations that come with our feelings are always available to our curiosity* – tight shoulders, lump in the throat, queasy stomach. Also, because we often don't have a clue about what feelings are causing us to be compulsive, we can discover what they are by listening to the sensations in our bodies – the sensations that correspond with the feelings that are fueling our compulsions.

The ability to bring your attention to your immediate experience is what will eventually unravel the tangled web of compulsions. It may take a while for you to fully understand the phenomenal power of what we are exploring here, for the mind deeply believes in fixing, changing, dominating and understanding. But these compensatory behaviors are nothing in comparison to the power of bringing the light of our focused and compassionate attention to whatever we are experiencing right now.

◇ How to Tell Yourself the Truth of Your Experience

Being invited to tell ourselves the truth of what is going on is a skill that we need to learn. We have all been taught the exact opposite – to not feel what we feel, distracting ourselves instead. Having become so good at drowning out the signals from our bodies (our deep and wise friend), it is no wonder that we are compulsive a good deal of the time.

It is a phenomenal gift to simply slow down for a moment or two and experience what we are experiencing. Tuning into exactly what is going on closes the gap between who we think we should be and who we really are, and it is a gift beyond price. This ability to check in and discover what is going on also keeps our body open and alive. And most importantly, it keeps us from heading down the path to one of our compulsions. For an area of tension in the body, when it is not met and released, turns into contraction. And the more the contraction goes unnoticed, the more likely it will feed reactions in the mind, the breeding ground for compulsion.

In this section we will practice telling the truth of our experience just on the physical level. Our thoughts can be moving so fast that we can't see what is going on. And our feelings can be unclear or overwhelming. But the sensations in our body are always there, available to our focused attention. And as we explored earlier, when we learn how to check into our bodies, the feelings and thoughts that show up as our sensations can begin to come clear to us.

There are six simple steps we will use in order to become curious about what is going on, giving whatever we discover there what it needs to transform – our undivided, compassionate attention. These steps are built upon the Check-In Questions we explored in the chapter on *Living in Questions*:

☆ In this moment, what am I experiencing?

☆ For this moment can I let this be?

☆ Right now, what do I truly need?

Let us now weave these questions into Six Steps that you can use to heal and be healed by your compulsion:

1. The first step is to re-center ourselves with our breath.

2. The second step is to ask the question, "In this moment, what am I experiencing?"

3. The third step is to name to ourselves what we discover there – headache, pain in our back, acid stomach – so that a part of us is not lost in the experience.

4. The fourth step is to open this area through our breath and then bring the healing of spaciousness through using the question, "For this moment can I let this be?"

5. The fifth step is the question, "Right now, what do I truly need?" in order to awaken the wellspring of deep knowing within us.

6. The sixth step is to broaden our attention beyond whatever we have been reacting to, bringing it back into the fullness of Life in this moment.

In this chapter we will practice these Six Steps with just the sensations in our body. In the beginning it is much easier to reconnect with our experience using our body. In the next chapter we will then explore how to use these basic steps with the feelings that are fueling our compulsions.

Working with the Six Steps

Re-center with Breath

As we explored in *Open Breathing*, breath is an invaluable tool in our journey back to ourselves. Because it is so simple and yet so powerful, the best breath to use with these steps is the one where we breathe deeply, adding a short pause at the end of the in-breath and at the end of the out-breath. These pauses turn on our parasympathetic nervous system, the part of ourselves that calms us down. They also signal our mind that we are moving into a deeper level of consciousness. The wonderful thing about breath is that it can be as simple as one deep breath. When we are caught in the middle of an inner storm, one conscious breath can help immensely to calm things down. If you want to work with other breath techniques, reread the chapter on *Open Breathing*.

Bring Curiosity to Your Experience

The question, "In this moment, what am I experiencing?" is used to turn our mind into a flashlight in order to highlight what is truly happening in our bodies right now. It turns our attention from *what was* and *what will be* and makes us curious about *what is happening right now*. As we move from *reaction* to *response*, our focused attention is like a laser beam, transforming whatever it rests upon. Many of the tensions in our body will dissolve under the light of our attention, and the more we do this, the quicker our holdings will melt away. Remember, this is just trapped energy that belongs to the free-flowing aliveness that we are. For those tensions that don't dissolve, we can go on to the next steps.

You may discover that, when you are invited to pay attention to what your body is experiencing, you can't feel a thing. This is not unusual. We have been so educated out of our bodies and so trained to deny our feelings that when we first become curious about what we are experiencing, all we may discover is fog or a blank wall. You may even have quite a bit of resistance to experiencing what you are experiencing. Don't be dismayed. This is very normal on the journey back to yourself. That is where the Open-Ended Questions come in. You can ask the First Open-Ended Question, "What is asking to be seen?" and then let the question go. It will work its magic from underneath the surface of your everyday consciousness, clearing the fog and the resistance until, with simple clarity, you can discover exactly what you are experiencing.

Name What You Are Experiencing

This step is about giving a name to whatever we are experiencing. Naming to yourself what you discover through your focused attention begins to create space around your experience. It allows you to *relate to* what is happening rather than being *lost in it.* And each time we name what we are experiencing, *we are no longer completely identified with it and have begun to disentangle ourselves from its web.*

Usually it's best to begin with a more general name such as *struggle, contraction* or *resistance.* Then, if your mind is willing to be curious and you can make contact with an area of tension, you can get more specific using words like *headache, dry eyes,* or *acid stomach.* You can then amplify your attention by becoming more specific with your naming. Is it hot or cold? Are there shooting pains? Is there pressure, tingles, aching, throbbing? This keeps the light of attention focused there so that the tension can release.

You may find that a sensation in your body seems to become amplified through your focused attention. Especially at the beginning of the journey back to yourself, this is very normal. *It is not that your attention is amplifying anything. What is happening is that you have lifted the fog of your resistance and thus have become aware of what is really going on.*

> *Each time we name what we are experiencing, we are no longer completely identified with it and have begun to disentangle ourselves from its web.*

Stay with it as long as you can, even if it is just for a moment of two. If you want to stay there longer, allow your naming to become more specific. This will deepen your ability to *relate to* what you are exploring rather than getting *lost in it.*

Create Space Around the Experience

This fourth step is about accessing the powerful healing of letting something *be. Remember, our core compulsion is to struggle.* When we let something be we let go of our tendency to fight with it. We can then look, listen and *respond* from a deeper level.

In the beginning, the easiest place to see the phenomenal power of letting something *be* is in our bodies. If we can give our tensions and our pains

> *The quickest way back into balance in our lives is to not fight what we are experiencing.*

space, most of them will pass right through us. For the pockets of tension that are more chronic, we can amplify our willingness to let something be through the Balloon Breath we explored on Page 126. You send your breath to this area by imagining on the next in-breath that you are blowing up a balloon that is at the center of the tension. On the out-breath, you say one long *ahhhhh* out loud, and let your body respond to that sound by letting go. The in-breath opens the tightness of reaction that usually surrounds tension in our bodies. The out-breath invites that tension to release.

After a few breaths, allow your breath to be as it wants to be and then ask the Second Question, "For this moment, can I let this be?" Just the asking of this question signals that you are choosing to *respond* rather than *react*. This takes you out of the realm of struggle that keeps on fueling the contractions and begins to open the doorway to your heart. It is the heart that knows that the quickest way back into balance in our lives is to not fight what we are experiencing.

If nothing is clear, you can ask one of the two optional questions we touched on when we explored the question "For this moment, can I let this be?" These are: "For this moment, can I bring compassion to this?" or "For this moment, can I not struggle with this?" You can also ask each of these questions in an Open-Ended way by adding the word *How* at the beginning. Every time you ask an Open-Ended Question, wisdom will come into the vacuum that you have created. This wisdom will awaken your heart, allowing you to live in the healing of *response* rather than the struggle of *reaction*. If you find yourself closing in reaction, ask your question again. Just the energy of Open-Ended Questions is very healing.

⟨5⟩ Listen to the Wellspring

Once we are present with ourselves in a focused and open way, it may become clear exactly what we need to do in order to bring healing to our experience. If it isn't, we can then ask the Third Question, "Right now, what do I truly need?" Remember, we aren't trying to figure out the answers to this question. That just keeps us caught in struggle. We ask this to the wellspring within us that knows what is the most empowering thing to do in any situation. Then the answers – rather than coming from our heads and struggling to apply them in our lives – come from within us, and we find ourselves *living the answers*.

The mind will have a tendency to get frustrated if it doesn't get an immediate answer. The more you use this question the quicker and clearer the answers will be, but at the beginning this may not happen. You can then ask the Open-Ended Question, "What is the way through this?" Remember, it isn't necessary to receive immediate wisdom. Just the power of the question sets things in motion.

You may get this far and then get pulled back into the vortex of reaction. That is a part of the awakening process. We are like babies, learning how to walk and we will fall down over and over again. Know that this question is awakening your deep wisdom and just like a peach ripens from a hard green nugget to a round, golden globe, you too are being ripened.

Also, you may get a clear answer but not want to act upon it. The pull to stay caught in reaction may be much stronger than the desire to act wisely. At times that is to be expected. We will explore what to do in this situation in the chapter on *Treasure Hunting With Compulsions*. Until then, know that every time you ask this question you are energizing the wisdom within you that knows how to make kind and skillful choices.

And even if you can do this for only a moment or two before you plunge back into reaction, it is enough.

⟨6⟩ Open into Life

The final step is about placing our attention on something bigger than whatever we have been contracting around in our body. Because the mind loves to attach onto struggle, it is powerful to learn that there is always a lot more going on in Life than the struggles we get lost in, and we do have the choice about where we are going to place our attention.

It isn't always easy to pull our attention away from struggle and place it again in the immediacy of Life – especially at the beginning of awakening. Some of the old patterns in our body, mind and heart can feel like they are all-encompassing. But that is not true. Whether it is a pain in our body, a deep emotion or a very seductive mind pattern, these are just a part of the story that we took on when we were little – a story *about* Life rather than the Real Thing. This story keeps us caught in struggle rather than being present for the fullness of Life and the fullness of who we truly are. This fullness

> *We are something bigger than what we are experiencing. We are not our thoughts, our feelings or the sensations in our body. We are that which can see them!*

has never gone away. It has just been covered over by our compulsion to struggle and it is waiting for the clouds to part so we can return home.

Our bodies can help us to see that if our attention keeps on getting lost in reacting to a pocket of tension, all it does is energize it. If we broaden our attention into the fullness of this moment, we energize *being* and that is the truth of who we really are. We are something bigger than what we are experiencing. *We are not our thoughts, our feelings or the sensations in our body. We are that which can see them!* The more we pay attention, the clearer this will be. The more we see this, the more we will know freedom.

Rather than paying attention to our struggles, we can broaden our focus into the rest of our body, discovering that there are many areas in our body that are doing just fine. We are alive; our heart is beating; our breath is rising and falling; tingles of aliveness are cascading all throughout our body. We can even open further, reconnecting with the fullness of Life right here, right now – the music of sounds as they swell and recede all around us, the different variations of light that surround us, the amazing gift of Life.

It is very important to do this last step *after* we have brought our attention to whatever is contracting within us, *even if it is for just a few moments.* If not, all we are doing is distracting ourselves again. Distraction comes from reaction – we don't like what is going on and we want to get away from it as fast as we can. But as we explored earlier, reaction only fuels what we don't like, keeping us cut off from a true and abiding connection with the only moment that matters – now.

Practicing the Steps

We are so used to doing the exact opposite of what we are exploring here. We are skilled masters at reacting and distracting. So, if you are like most people, you haven't been used to checking into exactly what is happening in your body. At the beginning it can be helpful to bring your attention into these three areas where feelings and their corresponding sensations are most likely to be:

❖ The first is the head, neck and shoulder area. What to look for are raised shoulders, clenched jaws, dizziness, throbbing temples, pressure behind the eyes, shooting pains along the side of our heads, dull ache in the forehead, sore tongues, a burning between the shoulder blades, etc.

❖ The second area is the chest. Here people often describe a lump in the throat, a heavy pressure on the chest, a tight band of tension that makes it hard to breathe, sharp pains, shallow breathing, a racing pulse or heart palpitations.

❖ The third area is the belly. This is *Feeling Central*. Almost every feeling you will ever have will be registered here on some level. People describe both butterflies and fists of tension in their stomachs, tight bands across the lower pelvic region, sharp pains, explosive pressure, empty holes right around their belly button, sinking sensations right below their stomach, intestinal cramping and queasiness.

As you begin your check-in, pause for a few seconds in each area and see if there is any tension there. You don't need to make a big production out of this. Stay in each area for no more than a breath or two and notice what is going on. When you have practiced this enough, you will be able to see immediately what part of your body is holding tension.

When you have touched on all three areas, go back to the place that felt the most constricted and allow your attention to rest there for a couple of breaths. *As the sensations receive your non-judgmental attention they can let go, for it is in openness that things can move.* This release may feel like a physical opening or a warmth that comes from the locked energy being released. *Sometimes this wave of letting go will expand and fill your whole body with a cascading warmth and joy.* Even if you feel nothing release, your attention is laying the foundation for future releases. Let's try it now:

After you read this exercise, close your eyes and take a few deep breaths to focus your mind. As you settle in, add a short pause at the end of the in-breath and at the end of the out-breath. As your mind quiets down, bring your attention to your body and ask the question, "In this moment, what am I experiencing?"

Be curious about what sensations you are experiencing, allowing your attention to be like a flashlight that is searching your body. Somewhere in your body is a pocket of tension. Check in with the three main areas and when you find the place where it is the easiest to recognize the tension, let your attention settle there. As you allow your attention and the tension to meet, exactly what you are experiencing will become clearer.

Don't rush this. Allow the sensations to come to you. Then name to yourself what is happening there. To amplify your curiosity, go deeper in your naming. There may be tingles, warmth, pain, throbbing, tickles, aches. Be patient. Know that even though you

221

> *may not be able to feel it, the tension is beginning to release under the light of your attention.*
>
> *If the tension is still there, open this area with your in-breath as if you were blowing up a balloon. As you breathe out, say a long slow ahhhhh and let go. Then ask yourself, "For this moment, can I let this be?" Let that question soften any remaining resistance so that you can fully be present for whatever is there.*
>
> *When you feel a sense of spaciousness about this experience, then ask yourself, "Right now, what do I truly need?" Listen to the deep knowing within you that knows what needs to be done to bring peace into your life. If nothing comes clear, know that these questions are working their magic.*
>
> *Now let go of paying attention to this area of tension and place your attention on all of the sounds of Life around you – the music of birds, the hum of voices, the sound of cars. As you relish them for a few moments notice that there is a big difference between being caught in the struggles of your mind or being present for Life the moment it appears out of mystery. When you are ready, open your eyes.*

Each of the six steps is powerful in its own right and can be used just by itself. Or you can use them together as we have explored. When using the six steps, it is important to remember the three questions:

☆ *In this moment, what am I experiencing?*

☆ *For this moment, can I let this be?*

☆ *Right now, what do I truly need?*

You can use the Open-Ended Questions in the Six Steps when nothing is clear, you don't want to let anything be, or you don't have a clue about what you truly need.

★ *What is asking to be seen?*

★ *How can I bring compassion to this?*

★ *What is the way through this?*

Remember, these questions are asked to
the deep wisdom within you. The beauty
of these questions is that you don't have

> *Attention heals.*

to know what you are experiencing; you don't have to be willing to accept
what you are experiencing; and you can even be too confused to do anything. When you are that contracted, these questions will work for you
underneath your everyday awareness. With these questions, you don't look
for an answer, but you can expect one! In the right time and in the right
way, the answer will live you.

These are the tools of alchemy, tools that will heal and transform you to
your core. Don't be fooled by their simplicity. *Giving our undivided attention to a place of constriction in our bodies, opening up a space around it
and then asking for help from the deep knowing within, is what lasting
healing is all about.*

Remember, attention heals. What happens when you have had a bad day and
somebody truly listens to you? You lighten up! The same is true for the
contractions in your body. Every moment you *respond* rather than *react* you
lessen the power of your patterns and eventually they are transformed under
the light of undivided attention. You then have a greater choice about what
you are going to focus on in your life. *Responding* rather than *reacting* also
taps you into the wellspring of wisdom within you that is much smarter than
your mind and will unfailingly guide you every step of the way.

In time these steps will become automatic. When you turn toward your
experience, your curiosity will be immediately drawn to the exact area that
needs your undivided attention. In just two or three breaths you give it the
attention that it needs in order to open again, and then you see clearly what
needs to be done to bring it back into balance. The energy that was formerly
caught in tension and the energy that was used to block this tension from
your attention are now freed back into the free flowing energy field that it
comes from and you are available again for the fullness of Life.

Let me give you an example from my life:

As I am writing this I am working on giving space to some very unpleasant
sensations. Because of osteoporosis I am on hormone replacement therapy,
and what a roller coaster ride that is! I woke up with something that felt like
menstrual cramps this morning and my mind immediately went into reaction
mode. "Oh, fudge farts. This is going to be a challenging part of an already
full day."

Recognizing the tension that comes from reaction, I took a few deep breaths
and brought my attention to the sensations in my belly. Allowing the light of

my attention to recognize the cramps rather than turning away from them cut through the reactive mode that was making it all worse by contracting my muscles. I then took a few moments to explore what I was experiencing there, discovering that the cramps weren't as bad as I thought, now that I was paying attention to them.

As I described to myself exactly what was there, the muscles around my belly began to relax. With my breath I opened up space in my belly and then asked, "For this moment, can I let this be?" Immediately I felt very tender with myself. This allowed me to loosen my grip on the experience, recognizing that it was a temporary storm of sensations that was moving through me and the more I gave it space, the quicker it will move.

As my belly softened under the light of my spacious attention, allowing the trapped energy to move, the contractions went from sharp pulses to a dull ache and my whole body felt much more alive. I could now focus on the rest of my body, which actually felt quite good. It brought me back to the joy of *being alive*.

My mind that had been caught in reaction to the contractions was now experiencing gratitude for the gift of *being alive*. I didn't even need to ask the question, "Right now, what do I truly need?" for it was very clear that I needed to simplify my day. As I was typing this into the computer later on in the day, I realized I had hardly been aware of any contractions during the day. That is the power of bringing our attention to whatever we are experiencing, giving it space to *be* and then listening for what would bring peace.

When There is No Release

You will come across holdings in your body that won't let go immediately with the light of your open and focused attention. Know that your willingness to be present for them and to ask the questions – even if it is for just a moment or two – is taking you down the pathway of your healing. We will explore more deeply in *Treasure Hunting With Feelings* what you can do when you come across pockets of tensions that are not ready to let go. Until then, you can open a field of contraction by moving your body. This is one of the most skillful choices you can make when you ask the question of the Fifth Step: "Right now, what do I truly need?"

Movement is such a powerful healing force. Watch the wind dance. It loves to move. Watch water as it cascades and crashes, laps and whirls. All of Life is in constant movement. And the pockets of tension in your body want to move too. Remember, whenever you are caught in an old energy pattern in your body, your mind or your emotions, it is just free-flowing and alive energy that has become restricted.

> *When you are contracted, little movements can go a long way to opening up contracted places.*

Movement can be as simple as deep breaths, as healing as cleaning the house or as liberating as getting outside. It can be as wild as putting on some music and dancing or it can be as gentle as lying on your side and rocking your body back and forth with your hand over your heart. When you are contracted, little movements can go a long way to opening up contracted places. After all, the mighty Columbia River started as rivulets from the snowfields of lofty mountains.

Running, massaging, dancing, singing, hiking, gardening, playing with your dog, yoga, stretching – all of these move energy. It is amazing what just a ten-minute walk will do to move things through, leaving you more connected and clear. If you can remind yourself, especially when you are really contracted, that movement moves things – changes your experience of your body, your mind and your heart, bringing you back into the joy of being open again – you can dramatically shift your experience of Life with just a little bit of movement.

For simplicity, let us explore some techniques that can be done right here, right now without needing to go anywhere else. They all reopen the field of our bodies. One of my favorite ways to invite a pocket of tension in my body to begin to move again is to exaggerate it. This was what we did when we explored breathing in *Skills of Being* on Page 154. On an in-breath, we tighten our whole body and as we breath out, we let it all go, melting back into Life. You can do this with individual parts of your body that are tight and you can do it with your whole body. The reason this works so well is that muscles literally cannot hold on to tension that is exaggerated.

If your body needs more than just a few deep breaths along with some exaggeration, stand with your feet at least two feet apart. Then put your hands together and raise them above your head. Then, just as if you were chopping wood, very forcefully bring your hands down between your legs as you say as loud as you can, "Ha!" Do this a number of times, allowing your *Ha* to come from as deep in your body as you can. This really gets things going.

Another way to open ourselves again is to use a very powerful breathing technique called the *Breath of Fire*. In this exercise your main focus is on the out-breath. Let's try it after you read the following paragraph:

> *During your next out-breath, pull your belly in with a snap, forcing the air out of your lungs. Then relax your belly and let the in-breath come naturally. Then snap your belly again to begin the out-breath and relax the belly on the in-breath. After a couple of practice breaths, begin to speed up the pace of your breath so your breath sounds as if you are a train engine going faster and faster. Remember, the power of this breath comes from focusing on the out-breath. Be careful with this breath. Most people are not used to getting this oxygenated and it can make them dizzy. If you become light-headed, stop for a few moments.*

Singing is also a great way to get energy moving again. Sing favorite songs, silly songs, inspirational songs. You don't even need a song or even need to carry a tune. You can chant a vowel sound like *ah,* letting it resonate in your chest and opening any constriction there. You can chant the sound *oh,* giving it a deep tone so that it can open your belly. The sound of *ai* that moves into an *eee,* causing your neck muscles to pop out, opens your neck and throat. The sound of *ah* or *eee* chanted in the higher ranges can open your head.

In whatever way you choose to move your energy, it is important to do this *after* you have brought the light of your attention to whatever you are experiencing – even if it is just for a few moments and even if you can't recognize what is going on. You can make tension go away with these techniques, but if you aren't cultivating the willingness to be present for it – for at least a moment or two – it will keep on coming back in order to be fully transformed.

And if you can't move – either your body doesn't allow it or you're just too contracted, smile. It is amazing what a smile will do to your flow of energy. A smile understands that on some level this is no big thing. After all it is just trapped energy, a kink in the flow of aliveness that you truly are.

If none of these works, it just means that the pattern is not ready to let go. Most likely the feeling that is showing up as these sensations needs your attention too. We will explore in the next chapter how to use the light of your attention to transform even the deepest of feelings. Until then, know that *your willingness to be available to the sensations in your body is making it safe for the feelings to reveal themselves to you.*

Checking In Throughout The Day

Being compulsive is about numbing out. Checking in and telling ourselves the truth of what is really going on is about waking up. To practice this simple technique throughout the day keeps us current with ourselves. It brings us back into what is really going on. This can help immensely, not only in keeping us away from the need to be compulsive, but also in training our minds in curiosity so that when a wave of compulsion does come, we can be present for it, gathering the treasures that it is always bringing to us.

It is helpful in the beginning to practice checking in with yourself when your emotional body is quiet and your compulsion is far away. *As you do quick check-ins throughout the day, you are training your mind to be curious about what is happening right now rather than always trying to change* what is. You can take a breath and ask the question, "In this moment, what am I experiencing?" while watching TV, at a business meeting, or while riding on a bus. You can ask the question when you are brushing your teeth, waiting for the doctor, driving in the car, getting a massage, at the theater, or falling asleep at night.

Then you can name to yourself what is happening. Every time you name to yourself what you are experiencing, you have created more space around the experience, for in that moment *you are relating to it rather than being lost in it*. Again, if nothing becomes clear to you, know that just asking yourself, "What am I experiencing?" is retraining you into curiosity.

If you discover something that is tightening your body, mind or heart, breathe into it and ask if you can let it *be* for just this moment. In that moment you are not fueling the experience through your reactions. Then ask to hear exactly what it is that you need to bring balance back into your life. Remember, the deep Wisdom at the heart of Life is with you every step of your way and is waiting for the opening of a request for help.

Practice these six steps when you are calm and centered. Then they will be available to you whenever you notice even the slightest bit of contraction coming into your life. They will cut through even the oldest of fears and the deepest of beliefs within you, leaving you connected to yourself and to Life.

As we learn to be curious about everyday sensations, eventually we will be able to use these six steps before, during or after a wave of compulsion. If we add even just a moment or two of pure attention to

> *Being compulsive is about numbing out. Checking in and telling ourselves the truth of what is really going on is about waking up.*

exactly what is going on inside of ourselves, we will literally be untangling the web of convoluted ideas and boxed up feelings that cause us to be compulsive in the first place. And without even noticing it, our deeply grooved pattern of compulsion will begin to heal.

Core Ideas in Treasure Hunting 101:

❖ Telling the truth is the art of letting go just for a moment of all the images you carry about how you are *supposed to be* and, instead, reporting to yourself what is *really happening.*

❖ It is called Treasure Hunting because, hidden in the sensations, thoughts and feelings we have habitually run from, there always lies a treasure.

❖ All of the struggles in your head show up as contractions in your body. These contractions are messengers from the deepest and wisest parts of yourself. They come bearing information and insights that will help you unravel the web of reaction that fuels your compulsion.

❖ You are not being present for sensations and feelings in order to get rid of them. You are being present so that they can let go, for it is in openness that things can move.

❖ Giving your undivided attention to an uncomfortable experience in your life, opening up a space around it, and then asking for help from the deep knowing within is what lasting healing is all about.

❖ When we use the Six Steps, we can begin to see what we need to transform with our undivided and compassionate attention.

The Six Steps

1. Re-center with Breath

2. Bring Curiosity to Your Experience

3. Name What You Are Experiencing

4. Create Space Around the Experience

5. Listen to the Wellspring

6. Open to Life

✦ TREASURE HUNTING WITH FEELINGS ✦

What we have been exploring is the art of experiencing what we are experiencing so that what is going on in our lives can be transformed through the healing light of our compassionate attention. For awhile, working with the physical sensations of our lives may be all we can do. That is enough. *Don't rush this.* Moments of asking yourself, "In this moment, what am I experiencing?" and then being present for a lump in your throat or a knot in your stomach are steps on the path that is taking you back to yourself. And if you can't let it be, that is okay. Just the willingness to ask the questions, "For this moment, can I let this be? will loosen the constriction. Even if nothing becomes clear when you ask the question – "Right now, what do I truly need? – that question is working for you underneath the level of your everyday awareness, awakening your inner wellspring.

Now that we are becoming more aware of what is happening in our bodies, it is time to learn how to be present for the feelings that are creating these sensations and that are fueling our compulsions from underneath our everyday awareness. There are four basic categories of feelings that are asking for our undivided attention.

1. The first is *anger*. It comes from not getting what we want. It can show up as irritation, frustration, hatred, jealousy, rage, criticism, self-judgment, annoyance, resentment, antagonism. These feelings cause us to want to strike out against Life.

2. The second is *fear*. It is about getting what we don't want. It can show up as free-floating anxiety, unease, panic, alarm, trepidation, apprehension, dread, terror, shame. These feelings cause us to pull back from Life.

3. The third is *despair*. These feelings come from a sense of nothing ever working out. They can show up as unfulfilled longing, hopelessness, helplessness, sadness, despondency, grief, sorrow. These feelings cause us to want to give up on Life.

4. The fourth is *aliveness* and *openness*. We are afraid of the openness that is required to live from our authenticity. We are so familiar with struggling and being contained that too much openness, too much joy, spins us out of control and back down again into the world of contraction.

To come into a healing relationship with these feelings, we need to get to know them. This is not about collapsing into them. This is about meeting them, giving them the non-judgmental attention they need to heal. We will use the Six Steps we explored in the last chapter, amplifying them in order to meet the feelings that are fueling our compulsions:

1. The First Step will be used in the same way we did in the last chapter, working with our breath to re-center ourselves.

2. The Second Step will be used in almost the same exact way as in the last chapter, but as we cultivate the ability to be present for our experience, this step becomes a doorway for our feelings to reveal themselves to us.

    We begin by asking the question, "In this moment, what am I experiencing?" just as we did in the last chapter. This question grounds us in our body, taking us out of the whirling mind that is always trying to understand, fix or run away. As we fine-tune our ability to bring our attention into our bodies, *this makes it safe enough for whatever feelings are there to make themselves known.* Because we have been developing a relationship with ourselves *as we are* rather than as we think we should be, many feelings will not only become clear; they will also respond to our undivided attention, moving through us without contracting our mind, body or heart.

    If it isn't quickly evident what you are feeling, keep your attention on the restricted area in your body and ask this question in an Open-Ended way – "What is asking to be seen?" You can also ask, "What am I feeling right now?" Let the feeling develop like a polaroid picture. If nothing comes clear, you can go to either the fifth step and ask, "Right now, what do I truly need?" or the sixth step and simply place your attention elsewhere. If you get stuck on any of these steps, simply go to the default question, "What is the way through this?" and know it will work for you underneath the struggles of your mind.

There is another level of feelings that most of us become aware of only when we are stretched to the max. It is these feelings that are the core fuel of our compulsions, operating from underneath our everyday consciousness. Since they usually require more than a few minutes of our undivided attention in order to be healed, we need to amplify the third, fourth, fifth and sixth steps.

3. In the Third Step, if feelings come clear, we will name to ourselves what we are experiencing. We will then learn how to deepen our ability to *relate to the feeling* rather than being lost in it through the statement, "I see you. I'm here."

4. It can be difficult to be with many of the feelings that are fueling our compulsions, so we will deepen the Fourth Step by exploring how to open the space around a feeling by bringing compassion to it. This is what the question "For this moment, can I let this be?" is all about. It makes enough space in our experience so that our hearts can open.

5. When we ask, "Right now, what do I truly need," we will amplify this Fifth Step by exploring the two different types of wise choices we can make in order to give our feelings what they need.

6. And finally, we will use the Sixth Step in much the same way we did in the last chapter, opening the field of our attention beyond the struggles of our mind, body and heart in order to reconnect with the fullness of Life as it is happening right here, right now.

Since the way we use **The First Step** and **The Second Step** in dealing with feelings is almost identical to the way we used them with sensations in the last chapter, we will not repeat those steps here. (Please refer to Page 216) In the following section, we will work with the **Third** through the **Sixth** steps, exploring how we can amplify them in order to heal the feelings that fuel our compulsions.

The Third Step: "I see you; I'm here"

Through a deep breath or two, and then asking the question, "In this moment, what am I experiencing?", we turn our attention toward our immediate experience, becoming interested in what is happening right now. As we allow ourselves to be curious about an area of contraction in our bodies, *the feeling that is causing the tension in the first place may reveal itself.*

Remember, most of the tension in your body is guarding parts of yourself that you are resisting. Also remember that primarily what these parts need is the light of your undivided attention. As you focus on the sensation it can become clear what feeling it is expressing. You can then give your attention to the feeling, exploring it in the same way we explored sensations. What does it feel like? If it is fear, is it an overall anxiety or a dark knot of dread? If it is anger, is it fiery and explosive or just a slow burn? Remember, there is no need to judge, analyze or deny what is there. Be willing, at least for a moment or two, to simply be present for your experience.

If a feeling is clear, describe it to yourself in as much detail as you can. As you are naming what you are experiencing, you are developing a part of

> *The feelings that fuel your compulsion have been waiting your whole life for you to mature enough to respond to them rather than reacting.*

yourself that is not lost in the feeling. This is a major step in healing, for what your feelings need more than anything is your ability to be present for them. *The feelings that fuel your compulsion have been waiting your whole life for you to mature enough to respond to them rather than reacting.*

A skillful way to deepen your response is to say to whatever feeling is there, "I see you. I'm here." As you say this, you have taken another step out of the feeling and are giving it your non-judgmental attention. The power of this statement is that it creates the willingness to be compassionate with this contracted part of yourself.

Let us take the lump in your throat again. As you make contact with the tension in your throat, telling it that you are here for it, waves of sadness may show up, or maybe tears. Along with this may come the feeling of being very alone, or maybe of being a failure. Don't second-guess what happens. Whatever needs to show up will be there. Stay present for the feeling by saying, "I see you _____. I'm here." Fill in the blank with whatever sensation or feeling you have discovered.

It may seem that just giving it the light of our compassionate attention is too simple but its effects are profound. What happens to you when somebody simply bears witness to your experience without any desire to judge or fix you? It's quite magical. As you feel recognized and heard, something inside of you begins to open again. This holds true for your feelings. When you step out of the normal mode of denying and dominating and instead, meet the truth of your experience in a non-judgmental way, things begin to move and transform.

When you get this close to what you are experiencing, you may have a few moments of getting lost in the feeling. When you notice you are struggling again, come back to being the witness. Remember, these are very young parts of yourself that need your undivided attention. They don't need you to get lost in them, losing your perspective. They need you to see them and give them non-judgmental acceptance.

It is important to understand that *we are not paying attention to the sensations and then the feelings in order to make them go away.* That is just more of the *same old, same old* that we have been doing forever – "I don't like it and I will try to get rid of it." There is only one problem with that. It doesn't work, at least not on the level of healing we are truly longing for.

And, as we have all discovered, when we try to get rid of a contraction, whether it is physical, mental or emotional, it has a tendency to return!

What we are doing here instead is making it safe enough *for the feeling to let go*. By giving the constrictions in our bodies and emotions the full light of our non-judgmental attention, the contraction that is inherent in any pattern of tension can let go, returning again to the free flowing energy of a whole and alive person.

Also, you will have times, just like with sensations, that you do not have a clue about what is going on. That's okay. Just the willingness to be curious for a few moments is powerful. Then, after you have brought your attention toward yourself with the question, "In this moment, what am I experiencing?" you can ask the Open-Ended Question, "What is asking to be seen?" If nothing reveals itself after resting there for a few moments let the question go and it will work its magic.

Be patient. We are retraining our knee jerk reaction to run away. In the beginning this happens much like a Polaroid picture developing where your attention is the developer. Don't rush this process. If nothing happens, it is okay. *Your willingness to turn toward your experience is making it safe enough for your feelings to reveal themselves when they are ready.*

There is a great example out of my life that will demonstrate how powerful it is to notice and then bring your non-judgmental attention to the sensations happening in your body, allowing the feelings that are fueling them to reveal themselves.

In my early years of awakening, and usually when I was very tired, I would feel great frustration if somebody took my turn at a four way stop or cut in line before me. I would fume and fuss in a self-righteous way. Of course, this did nothing for my peace of mind.

Then one day I finally became curious. What is so upsetting to me? The next time I noticed this feeling of righteous frustration was while standing in line at the grocery store. I was feeling very rushed and the grocery store clerk was flirting with the customer before me and taking her sweet time about it. There was a knot in my stomach that felt like it was going to explode. In my pre-curious stage, I would have simply reached over to the display by the check out stand, picked up a couple of candy bars and added them to my

> *Your willingness to turn toward your experience is making it safe enough for your feelings to reveal themselves when they are ready.*

> *Initially, you don't have to stay with feelings very long if you aren't ready to. Just a moment or two in the beginning is enough to start opening the doors to your healing.*

grocery cart (all the while unmercifully judging the grocery store clerk and maybe even giving her a few ugly looks as I left.)

This time I became curious instead. Since I had lots of time (it didn't look like this was going to be a short session of flirting), I closed my eyes and took a few deep breaths. I then made contact with the knot in my stomach. As I acknowledged this knot and allowed my attention to rest there, I heard a very young voice inside of me say, "It's not fair! I'm important too." In a flash, I realized that this was the part of me that had grown up in relationship to an older, very dominant sister. I always had to be second in everything. This part of me was vigilant for the *Big Sister of Life* that would shove her out of line or take her place again.

This was definitely one of my boxed-up feelings because my mind's immediate response was one of shame. "Such a childish response," it said. But I was present enough to remember that this was just a very young part of myself, and the rage that it carried was really about all of the *second bests* that happened when I was little. Until this day at the grocery store – except for moments when this part would flare up and make a mess of my life – this feeling had been boxed-up inside of me since I was very young.

I told this part of me that I saw her and I was here for her. Immediately the cloud of rage lifted and the candy bars didn't look interesting at all. I was even able to be present for the grocery store clerk and in fact thanked her (quietly inside of myself!) for flirting long enough for me to meet this part of myself.

This enraged one still comes, especially if I am overly tired and find myself in a new situation. But I have given her a name. It is *Sib* (for sibling rivalry) and even before the thoughts in my head, it's that particular knot in my belly that signals to me that she is here. I say "Hi Sib. I see you. I'm here." and most of the time the constriction passes right through me.

The wonderful thing about being present for feelings is that initially you don't have to stay with them very long if you aren't ready to. Just a moment or two in the beginning is enough to start opening the doors to your healing.

As we have explored throughout this book, the healing power of attention is transforming.

At times this can feel scary, for it is the opposite of how we have been trained – to resist, run away and deny. And even though resistance may bring us a temporary break from the deep unease inside of ourselves, the unexplored feelings in our lives don't go away. They sit there inside of us like a low-banked fire waiting for the tiniest bit of wind to flare them up again into a conflagration of struggle and compulsions. Creating a relationship with them instead is the doorway to freedom.

The Fourth Step: "For this moment, can I let this be?"

The feelings that fuel our compulsions were buried deep inside of us at a time when we had no other way to deal with them. And without us even noticing, they run us from underneath our every day awareness, causing us to live from our *I am not knots* that show up in our mind, body and heart. Because these feelings are so young, they often won't lose their power over us until they are met with the vast spaciousness of our hearts. In the fourth step we have been using the question, "For this moment, can I let this be?" to cultivate the acceptance that is needed in order to give our feelings the spaciousness they need to heal. For if we truly want to heal something, we need to accept that it is there.

In that acceptance, we can then bring compassion to these feelings we formerly hated and feared. At the center of all great religions is the knowing that the heart is the place where everything is truly healed. From respected writers, great spiritual leaders, inspiring poets, and all the children of the world, we are reminded that mercy, kindness, understanding, compassion and love are what Life is all about. The reason why heart energy is so powerful is that it doesn't hate or fear what it focuses on. Instead, it allows whatever is happening to be exactly as it is, and in this spaciousness and inclusion, things are transformed.

Because it is so easy to hate and fear the feelings that are fueling our compulsions, there may be

> *If we truly want to heal something, we need to accept that it is there. In that acceptance, we can then bring compassion to these feelings we formerly hated and feared.*

many times in the beginning where we absolutely don't want to allow a part of ourselves to be here. That is the time to ask the Open-Ended Questions – "How can I bring compassion to this?" or "How can I not struggle with this?"

Besides asking these questions in an Open-Ended way, there are some things we can do to awaken our natural inclination toward compassion and understanding. As we reawaken our heart, we can then know the power of allowing something to be. It is the spaciousness and mercy that comes from letting something be that transforms even our deepest holdings back into the joy and peace that we long for.

Let us explore two ways we can keep opening our hearts:

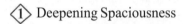 Deepening Spaciousness

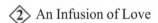 An Infusion of Love

Deepening Spaciousness

There are some feelings within us that we have hated and feared for so long that it is almost impossible for us to see them without feeling a strong urge to reject them, running as fast as we can in the opposite direction. Usually these are the ones we have hidden deep within the basement of our body, the ones we are absolutely ashamed to let anybody know that we feel. And we aren't just afraid of what other people may think about the full range of feelings within us. We are also afraid of letting *ourselves* see the truth of our experience. There is a part of us that feels that if we let *ourselves* know we have unacceptable feelings, we may die of the shame.

There is a wonderfully freeing truth that can help you immensely in healing all of the boxed up feelings inside of you: *you are not original in the depth and breadth of crazy, vengeful, whining, terrified, petty, overwhelmed, prideful, larcenous, and all-around unpleasant thoughts and feelings that you experience.* In just *being alive* you have, at one time or another, felt the full range of feelings that are possible for a human *being*, all the way from pure victimhood to murderous rage. If you doubt that you have ever felt mad enough to want to really hurt someone, watch a two year-old when somebody thwarts him or her! Then remember that at one time you were a child.

So the truth is that we're all nutty as fruitcakes. But that is okay. Can you feel the deep breath that comes from accepting the full range of feelings within you? *This is not permission to act upon them. This is permission to acknowledge that they are there. The truth is that you are far less likely to act upon these thoughts and feelings when you can accept the truth of their existence.*

This acceptance is one of the most powerfully transformative things you can do. When you give something space to be, you allow it to move and change. Giving something space is so powerful that if a feeling is not responding to your attention, it is probably because there is still a part of you that doesn't want it to be here. Big surprise! The reason you boxed up your feelings was because you hated and feared them! So why wouldn't there be a part of you that would resist acknowledging them.

In order to truly make space for a feeling (remembering that the ones that most need this spaciousness are the ones you have most deeply hated and feared), you need to understand that every single feeling you have is as valid as the Earth turning on its axis or winter unfolding into spring. It doesn't matter if the feeling that you are meeting is illogical or inconvenient. It doesn't even matter if it is irrational. The deep ones usually seem that way if we try to understand them in relationship to what is going on now, rather than what was happening when they were boxed up.

You also need to understand that giving a feeling space to be isn't about allowing it to take over your life. *It is about allowing the feeling to be there without becoming lost in it.* It is the difference between feeling angry and saying, "Ahh, anger."

We take a huge step into the healing we long for when we realize that if we keep on resisting these old feelings, we will stay stuck to them like glue. If we truly want to heal something, we need to *accept that it is there*. We need to give it space to *be*. This puts us into the level of consciousness that is beyond *right* and *wrong*, *good* and *bad*. This spaciousness is the neutral place that does not fuel anything by denial or active resistance. The ability to truly accept what is happening right now is exactly what all the boxed up feelings are really longing for inside of us. That is why we have been talking so much about non-judgmental acceptance.

To understand how powerful spaciousness is, all we have to do is look closely at Life. Life loves space. It is four light years to the nearest star in our galaxy. That means it would take light over four years to get to that star, and the next galaxy is over 150,000 light years away! Quantum Physics has shown us that atoms are mainly space, as well. And a bowl or a cup works because of space. There

> *Giving a feeling space to be is about allowing the feeling to be there without becoming lost in it.*

> *The way out of the prison cell of resistance and reaction is to give whatever we are resisting the freedom of space.*

would be no music without the spaces between the notes.

We can recognize the healing power of space in other areas of our lives, as well. Take a cramp for example. If we tighten down, it hurts more. If we go toward the experience instead, allowing the muscles to relax, the pain moves through like an ocean wave rather than a knife tearing up our leg. The same is true emotionally. If someone is very angry and we give them space to vent, letting them know we understand, the storm clouds move through much more quickly.

This is such an important step in healing our feelings for we are deeply programmed in its opposite – fight or flight. We either freeze in the face of these feelings or we run. Both of these modes close down the energy around the sensation or the feeling and this effectively slows down any healing. It even causes whatever we are resisting to grow and we find ourselves at the mercy of monsters we have built through our resistance. *The way out of the prison cell of resistance and reaction is to give whatever we are resisting the freedom of space.*

Giving our sensations and feelings space also gives us space to explore them. Imagine holding something unpleasant in your hand, clenching and wringing it thoroughly in order to crush it out of existence. First of all, you can't see what it is you are resisting. Also, when you open your hand, it is still there (in a more mutilated state!) But if you open your hand fully, you can now really see what you were contracting around. You can become familiar with it, exploring its depth and breadth, gathering the information you need in order to heal. And when it is time, with just a subtle tilt of your hand, you can let it go. That is the gift of space. *What flows the most hurts the least.*

To deepen spaciousness, there are two different things we can add to our healing skills. The first is our dear friend the breath. The second is the statement, "It's okay you're here."

The Power of Breath

Deep breathing is an invaluable friend in staying spacious. Just as it is known that breathing techniques can help a woman while she is giving birth, the same is true as we are giving birth to ourselves. This is why we spent so much time on Open Breathing. It is a powerful tool in this process of returning to ourselves for it can keep us spacious in so many ways.

The most basic thing you can do with breath is keep on breathing as you are exploring your body. Because turning toward what we are experiencing and exploring it with curiosity and compassion is so new to most of us, it is easy to hold our breath. To add even one deep breath is very freeing.

There are also two breathing techniques you can use to actually bring space to the feeling:

The first is an amplification of the balloon breath we did on Page 126. As you take in a deep breath, gently expanding this area of contraction from the inside out, you imagine that you are infusing this area with deep tenderness and care. Then on the out-breath you imagine all of this contraction melting like ice does in the presence of the warm summer sun.

The second breath technique is to imagine your breath moving in and out of the area where the feeling is. If you have never done this before and it feels a little hard to do, imagine a nose on your skin right in this area. Then see your breath coming in and out of that nose, opening up a space around the feeling. You can also breathe into this area exactly what you feel that this feeling needs – love, acceptance, understanding, warmth. As you breathe out you can imagine all of the tension being expelled out of that area by your breath.

A client of mine whom we shall call Cynthia had an experience that reveals everything we have talked about so far – the power of paying attention to the sensations and the feelings that are present; the healing that comes from giving them permission to be; and the power of breath to keep the space open for healing.

Cynthia had a boss who was very difficult. She not only felt shame in the presence of his unrelenting criticism, but also felt very isolated and alone. Everyone else in the office was terrified of him and of losing his or her job. So it was every person for him or herself. Cynthia tried to please him. She then tried to ignore him. When neither of these worked and with no relief in sight, she decided that since she wasn't able to stop being such a wimp (her words), her only option was to quit her job.

When Cynthia and I started working together, she was assaulted over and over again by tension headaches and was caught in an addictive cycle with pain medication. One day she showed up for a session with a full-blown headache. After some deep breathing, I invited her to bring attention to the

> *Whenever you find yourself unclear or even stuck, just a few deep breaths and an invitation to simply be curious about what is happening will keep your attention spacious so the healing can continue.*

headache through the question, "In this moment, what am I experiencing?"

Because it was such an intense pain, it needed more than a few minutes of attention. I asked her to amplify her attention by being curious about exactly what type of headache it was. Feeling the pulsating quality mainly on the left side of her head, along with the stabbing pain behind her eye, she began to *relate to* the experience rather than *being lost in it.*

Her whole relationship with her headache began to change. Rather than a solid, impenetrable wall of pain, she experienced a variety of sensations, all moving and dancing through her head. The more present she was, the more the muscles in her head relaxed. This happened because she was no longer resisting the pain. In this spacious relationship her whole *being* felt lighter and her experience of the pain diminished.

I then asked her to live in the question, "In this moment, what am I experiencing?" with the rest of her body. As her attention settled in I asked her to report what she discovered there. After some more deep breathing, what revealed itself was an overall tension that came from being relentlessly but often subtly attacked on a daily basis.

Attending to this guarding, exploring how it felt inside of her, she then noticed a knot in her stomach that felt dark and scary. As she had some difficulty staying with the sensation, I invited her to do the balloon breath in this area. This immediately relaxed her whole body, opening space around the knot. I then asked her to be curious about exactly what was going on in this area, describing to me what the knot felt like. Being this curious about it took her from *reaction* to *response,* and she became fascinated.

She described the quality of this tension in her stomach as dense, its color as dark, and its texture like a whirling vortex. As she got this close to a place she had run from her whole life, it was important to remind her that, for these few moments – and in the safety of our time together – *it was okay that these sensations were here.* Whenever she found herself resisting, I invited her to keep on opening around the experience with her breath.

As she stayed with this knot in her belly, the fear that was showing up as these sensations began to revel itself. The deep pool of self-rejection lying in her belly and the terror that she would never get her life *right* became clear.

With great relief she kept on saying to the shame and the terror, "I see you. I'm here." It was easy for her now to breathe tenderness into the deep fear in her belly. She said she could dramatically feel the feeling soften. For the first time since this feeling was boxed up inside of her, it was being heard in the way it needed to be in order to heal.

All through this process, we worked with open breathing for the breath kept her body and mind spacious around the experience. *Whenever she found herself unclear or even stuck, just a few deep breaths and an invitation to simply be curious about what was happening kept her attention spacious so the healing could continue.*

This was different than anything she had done before. *She wasn't just talking about her feelings nor was she just feeling them. She was meeting them. She was experiencing them but she wasn't lost in them.* Formerly unwilling to experience the headaches and the feelings that were fueling them, she had stayed contracted and this contraction had fed both her headaches and her compulsion.

We broke this vicious cycle by a small but powerful shift from resistance to the willingness to experience the truth of what was happening inside of her, giving it space to be there. As she learned how to *respond* rather than *react* to these feelings, her headaches became a signal that the feelings of inadequacy were close and needed her attention. As she was able to be present for her headaches, over time the feelings that were causing them diminished and her need for the pain medication became nonexistent. She was also able to take care of herself now in wise and skillful ways.

◆ It's Okay That You're Here

Another powerful thing to do to give feelings the spaciousness they need in order to heal is to say to a feeling, "It is okay that you are here!" This is different than "I see you. I'm here." This one is about letting the feeling know that you recognize it and that *you are here for it*. The statement "It is okay that you are here" is about *giving the feeling permission to be.*

To let a feeling know that it is okay that it is here works like magic. It works on even our very young, very stuck feelings. Think of what happens when a friend lets you know that it's okay for you to be exactly as you are. What a relief! Our feelings feel the same kind of relief when we are present for them in this way.

We are conditioned that we have to *do* something with our feelings in order to get them to change. That is exactly what we do with our loved ones – we feel we have to fix them, change them, let them know how they need to be

> *As we let go of the
> story in our heads,
> we can then be
> present for our own
> experience.*

different. But over and over again you will find in healthy relationships that both people have learned how to listen to their partner, accepting them for exactly who they are. In fact, the quickest way to effect change in a relationship is to allow the person to be exactly where they are! The same is true for our feelings.

There is a story that I would like to share that reveals the power of letting our feelings know that it is okay that they are here. It is one of the most powerful healings I have seen in a short period of time:

The family of a friend who had been diagnosed with an inoperable brain tumor called me as they were concerned about him. There were other medical things that could be done for the tumor, but he had retreated to his bed for two months, hardly eating or drinking anything and not wanting to live. After the phone call I flew back east to work with him.

I stayed with the family for 5 days and every day he and I would spend hours exploring all the feelings that were coming up inside of him. He had had a very intense spiritual life, but he chose to focus on transcendence. By this I mean that his belief system said a successful spiritual life was about making contact with a higher self and leaving all of this mundane earthly stuff behind. This had never brought him the peace that he longed for; it also had not given him any skills for working with the great initiatory process called illness.

For the first two days, we worked with the deep sadness of possibly leaving his family, the despair of feeling like he had never fulfilled his life purpose, his deep self-judgment, and the fear of the unknown. As we explored all of these, he was able to see each of them from a different perspective, and he felt quite relieved. Rather than fighting where he was in his life, he began to open to it and was experiencing quite a bit of peace.

But he would get tripped up around his anger, most of which was projected upon his wife. No matter how spacious he became through the work we were doing together, at times when he would come into her presence the light would go out of his eyes and his whole body would tense up in resistance. The first few times it happened, he didn't have any willingness to be curious about this feeling at all. Whereas he had been able to explore the other ones, around anger it all became *her fault*.

I knew this feeling needed to vent and be heard. As I listened, I waited for an opening, and when it came, I asked him to turn his attention within and report to me what was there. He could feel a tight knot in his belly. I asked him to stay with it as I shared with him the power of simply bringing attention into the sensations in his body. We also talked about how all of these sensations were simply boxed up feelings from his childhood.

By asking the question, "In this moment, what am I experiencing?" he was able to let go of the story around the anger, the story that kept him lost in the idea that this anger was all his wife's fault. *As he let go of the story, he could then be present for his own experience.*

As he stayed with the knot in his belly, exploring it with deep curiosity, he began to be able to feel the rage that was creating this knot. I kept on repeating to him that it was okay that it was here and that it had been trying to get his attention his whole life. He began saying to the rage, "It is okay you're here," and for the first time in his adult life, he was actually present for this rage. His heart began to open, and with tears rolling down his cheeks, he clearly saw that these feelings had been boxed up inside of him at a very early age, only to control his whole life.

What then came to him was an image of himself as a young boy, right before he had to hide this feeling deep within. He could feel his aliveness, his exuberance and his joy. Then he watched as the fear he had of this rage (especially in relationship to a step brother that was 6 months older than he) caused him to close down so tightly that he lost sight of his joy.

As we talked together later on that day, he said he now realized that his whole life had been lived in relationship to this rage. He could look at almost all of the decisions he had made and see that many of them came from the need to keep this rage at bay. But now death was looming on the horizon and he was running out of options for running away.

Two days later, right before I left, his anger got triggered again so deeply that his body was shaking. He asked me to come to his room where he lay down on the bed in order to clearly feel what was going on in his body. After working together for the past five days, he could easily turn his attention toward his body, find the knot of energy that was his rage, and give it his undivided attention. He was able to stay with this feeling longer than ever before, exploring it in depth. Much to his amazement, the waves of rage began to turn into waves of love. He was lying on his back and tears of joy were streaming down both of his temples. Every once in a while he would say, "I always thought I had to do something with it."

This is a man who had tried every therapy he could think of. Now he was simply giving the feeling his undivided, non-

> *All the energy we have spent keeping our feelings boxed up is now available for the joy of living.*

> *As our feelings get a moment or two of undivided attention without our falling into identification with them, they will begin their transformation back into free flowing energy.*

judgmental attention, allowing it space to be. And the energy encapsulated in that feeling was transformed back into joy. He had finally awakened to the power of simply telling himself the truth of what he was experiencing, giving it the space to be and then letting it know that it was okay that it was here.

On the day I left, he told me that this was the first time in his adult life that he really wanted to live. He also said he had more energy than he could remember having for a long time. Of course! All the energy he had spent keeping the rage boxed up was now available for the joy of living. I called and talked to him a week later. He said that the process was still continuing, and he was able to meet the feelings that were arising with curiosity and compassion. His family also reported to me that he was eating and drinking now, and was spending more time with them.

The statement, "It's okay you're here," is all about giving the feeling permission to be. And as we have seen with my friend, this permission is transformational. In my own life, when very deep feelings appear, I still at times will have a knee jerk reaction of resistance. But this causes such tension in my body and mind that very quickly I notice I am resisting again and creating more pain. That tension signals me to remember that it is okay that I am feeling what I am feeling. I then say to the feeling. "It is okay that you are here." I immediately drop out of my struggling mind, my belly begins to soften and my heart begins to open, giving the feeling the space it needs in order to heal. Such relief! Such joy!

As our feelings get a moment or two of undivided attention without our falling into identification with them – saying, "Ahh sadness" rather than feeling engulfed in sadness – they will begin their transformation back into free flowing energy. It is much like ice melting into water and then heating up into steam so that it becomes one with the atmosphere again. As the tension around our boxed-up feelings lets go, the feelings begin to melt and eventually they evaporate into free-flowing energy. Granted, some deeper feelings need a lot of space in order to transform. But moments of meeting feelings throughout the day are where the work happens in the long run.

An Infusion of Love:

Besides giving our feelings the space to be, they also respond deeply to an infusion of love. Most of these feelings have roots in deep fear. The word afraid comes from the root word *frai*, which means *beloved, precious, at peace*. When we add the prefix *a*, which means *away from*, the word afraid means *being away from the state of feeling beloved, precious and at peace*. To give our feelings an infusion of love is to give ourselves again the experience of being beloved, precious and at peace. We can also become free. For if we can love whatever comes into our lives, moving beyond *reaction* and into *response*, what we are struggling with loses its power over us.

One of the most startling moments of my healing came after spending the better part of a day in a state of anxiety. And I was really disliking what I was feeling. My voice of wisdom finally got a word in edgewise and said, "This resistance is not making you feel any better. Why don't you make it okay that you are feeling what you are feeling?" Just like the light bulb going off above somebody's head in a cartoon, I felt a flash of insight. All this feeling wanted was permission to be! I then knew that I could *love myself for feeling scared.* My heart opened to how vulnerable I felt and immediately the very uncomfortable feelings of fear began to turn into waves of joy.

This is the power of infusing our feelings with love, for the heart is where all true healing happens. Every single one of our feelings simply wants to be recognized and loved. But there are some feelings we have that are so young and so scared that they are easily spooked. These are the ones that need a deep and nurturing love in order to become free, and it takes a number of infusions of love for them to truly understand that you won't reject them again. These are the feelings that will teach you that you can't let go of anything you haven't embraced.

Jack Kornfield tells a poignant story about a woman who discovered, through health challenges, the power of infusing whatever she was experiencing with understanding and mercy. When I heard this story, I wrote it down word-for-word in my journal, for it moved me deeply. It reminded me how to touch my feelings with my own heart

This woman had spent her life struggling with a

> *My heart opened to how vulnerable I felt and immediately the uncomfortable feelings of fear began to turn into waves of joy. This is the power of infusing our feelings with love.*

degenerative disease that caused pain and weakness. Her whole relationship with her difficulties was *not this* – "I don't want this;" "I don't deserve this;" "I don't need this." It kept her lost in perpetual war. She meditated to ease the pain and with the hope that it would go away.

At a meditation retreat, after having been lost for hours in struggling with the pain, *she finally let go of her resistance* and with a truly open attention, saw that she had spent her entire life trying to get away from it. She hated her pain and she hated her body. She deeply wept for how little love she had shown her body. *She decided that if the work given to her was to sit with a body in pain, she would bring to it all the tenderness and mercy she could.* As she embraced her pain, she discovered a peace that she had never known.

There are four different things we can do to meet the contracted parts of ourselves with our heart.

ⓐ One of the most powerful tools I have discovered for embracing a feeling is saying to the feeling inside, "It's okay. I understand." Over the years, my experience has been that these formerly hated and feared parts of ourselves are grateful to finally have, not only our attention, but also our compassionate understanding.

ⓑ The second heartfelt thing you can do is to imagine a little child experiencing the same feeling that you are having right now. Then ask yourself what you would do for them. Whatever you would imagine you would do for them is exactly what your feeling needs from you. You then give to yourself what you have discovered.

ⓒ The third thing you can do to open your heart is to physically let the feeling know that you are there. Children love to be held and rocked. It brings them a sense of safety and connection that is especially needed when they are scared or overwhelmed by Life. The same is true for the boxed-up feelings inside of us. They respond to physical acts of kindness.

ⓓ The fourth way to touch your feelings with the healing of compassion and mercy is to breathe them straight into your heart.

Let us explore each of these tools so you can see how to use the power of touching your feelings with your heart.

ⓐ "It's Okay. I Understand"

My sister was visiting from Los Angeles at the same time my son was visiting. And even though I love both of them with all of my heart, there were three people living in a small house. We were also visiting a lot of different family members and I still had to work.

Needless to say, it was a very full time. I also was building a meditation pond in my yard, a project that started out very small and quickly mush-roomed into a huge undertaking. After a whole week of struggling with trying to build a water filter, at the end of a very busy day and right after I discovered my roof was leaking, I got a call saying I had been building the wrong filter and I needed to start from scratch again. Not only did I have to go out and buy all new supplies while throwing the old ones away, I had to call my neighbor and ask for more help, which brought up an old fear of being a bother.

Upon hanging up the phone I froze in overwhelm. Even though I have experienced this place thousands of times in my life, I couldn't say exactly what I was feeling. All I knew was I was hurting and wanted to run away from my life. This was always the place where I would eat and eat and eat. Instead I went into my room, sat down and closed my eyes. Taking a few deep breaths I began to ask the question, "In this moment, what am I experiencing?" Letting my attention settle in my body, I began to feel tightness in my chest that felt like a vise around my breath. As I named what I was experiencing, it let go a little and it became easier to breathe.

As my attention became sharper, what I noticed was a dropping sensation right below my chest, the same feeling I would have had if I were on a scary roller coaster ride. As I stayed there, the feeling of overwhelm became clearer. I heard the words that went along with it: "This is too much. I'll never figure my way out of this. I need a break and I can't get one so everything is going to get worse."

I knew it was important to allow this feeling to be there, for if I fought it, it would only get worse. When I asked if I could let it *be*, all I got was resis-tance. I took a few deep breaths and then asked, "*How* I can I let this be here?" Quickly it became clear that what this feeling needed was under-standing and mercy. I began to say, "I see you and it is okay that you are here."

As the feeling of overwhelm felt heard and accepted, the despair that was underneath it welled up. It was so deep it needed more than just my recognition of it. It needed to be touched by my heart. It was a very young feeling and it wanted to know that it wasn't alone. So many, many

I began to say, "It's okay. I understand." I wasn't saying these words to an idea or a memory. I was saying them to the actual feeling in my body, a feeling that had been frozen since my childhood.

times in my life when it had risen to the surface I had run away from it as fast as I could, abandoning myself when I most needed myself. I began to rock back and forth, saying at the same time, "It's okay. I understand." I said it over and over again and it brought up very healing tears.

I wasn't saying these words to an idea or a memory. I was saying them to the actual feeling in my body, a feeling that had been frozen since my childhood and had been triggered by everything that had been happening that day. Slowly, as I stayed there giving this feeling my non-judgmental attention, much like the sun coming out from behind the clouds, I came back to myself. I felt such joy for being able to be that present for feelings that I had run away from so many times in my life.

I then went back into the living room to be with my sister and my son. My son said later, having experienced me in this overwhelmed place many times when he was growing up, that he had never seen me move through that feeling so quickly.

You can shorten the journey back to yourself by using these simple words – "It's okay, I understand." Your feelings have been waiting to hear them for a long time.

ⓑ Taking Care of The Child

It is a profound moment in our lives when we realize that *the deep feelings we have run away from inside of ourselves are very young and in need of our help.* It can dramatically aid the opening of our heart to imagine what our response would be if a child was feeling this feeling. This helps to cut through our judgment and resistance to having the feeling in the first place so that we can be present in the way it needs in order to heal.

The best way to do this is to imagine a child who is hurting and then discover what it needs to feel safe. It can either be an imaginary child like we explored in the chapter on *Loving Ourselves From the Inside Out* or we can remember an actual experience we had as a child where we were feeling exactly what we are feeling right now. In both instances, as we make contact with the image of a suffering child, we can ask the question, "What would I do for a child who is experiencing exactly what I am experiencing right now?" This is another way to ask the Third Question, "Right now, what do I truly need?" It allows us to see clearly what is needed in order to bring balance back into our lives.

A great example of this comes from Cynthia's session (which we explored on Page 239 in *The Power of Breath*). In this session, she was able to see that the feelings she had been experiencing with her boss went back to her childhood. It reveals what happens when we connect with the truth of how young these feelings are and then are able to touch them with compassion.

> *What would I do for a child who is experiencing exactly what I am experiencing right now?*

As Cynthia was willing to make space for this very scared part of herself that was sure she would never be *enough*, I asked her to imagine a little child who was having the same experience that she was. As sometimes happens when I suggest this, she remembered a specific instance from her childhood. She was hiding in her closet with her body curled up into a little tiny ball as her father stormed around the house in a rage.

For the first time in her adult life, she was able to feel – in her body – the terror she experienced over and over again with a rageaholic as a father. And for the first time ever, someone met that little child in the closet exactly in the way she needed to be met when her father was raging. And that someone was Cynthia herself.

Her heart opened in deep tenderness for this wounded one inside of her whom she had been trying to run away from her whole life. She began saying the statement, "It's okay that you're here. I understand." Then it naturally turned into a wonderful flow of healing words: "I am here. I am here now. I know you had to suffer this terror all alone. I know you have waited your whole life for me to see you and understand. I am now here. I understand."

She then went to the Third Question, asking what she needed to do when this feeling showed up in her life. What came bubbling up into her consciousness was that she needed to remember to be present for this vulnerable part of herself. So Cynthia took a picture of herself as a child to work and put it on her desk. This helped her to stay current with her feelings throughout the workday.

For Cynthia, meeting this feeling was life-transforming. With her heart finally open to one of the most hidden parts of herself, she was no longer caught in its web. Because the feeling of terror was listened to and understood, it could let go and merge again with the free flowing energy that is Life. Because her heart had finally touched it, this feeling never again dominated her life like it used to. She left that day glowing in radiance.

She was also thrilled when she discovered that on most days, her boss no longer bothered her. The part of herself that formerly believed she wasn't *enough* was no longer easily hooked by his criticism. With healing clarity she saw that he had come into her life so she could see on the *outside* the discounting voices she had lived with on the *inside*. Rather than reacting to him, she was now able to see the fear that caused him to be so cruel. What amazed her most was that because she was no longer living in reaction to him, his attacks let off and eventually he began to share his pain with her!

Cradling the Feeling

It is powerful to recognize the feelings that are moving through us, and it is even more powerful to talk with them, giving them the understanding and support that they need. There is another thing we can do that can have a profound effect and that is to respond with our body in a way that evokes deep compassion in every cell of our *being*.

There are a number of ways to do this. One of my favorites is to hold a hand out, palm up and allow it to fill with all the love you can imagine. Then you bring the hand to the area in your body where you are experiencing this feeling and cradle it in tenderness. You can also hug yourself with both arms and say any of the mantras that we have explored: "I see you, I'm here;" "It's okay you are here;" "It's okay. I understand."

In order to cradle a feeling, I have also been known to sit down, put both of my arms around myself and rock back and forth, back and forth, all the while saying to myself, "It's okay. I'm here now. It's okay." When I was first meeting my feelings and a feeling that showed up was so deep that it was terrified of even my loving attention, it was through rocking that I let it know that I am here. I have brought the most terrified parts of myself out of the corners of the basement through this technique. Sometimes I even needed to put a heating pad on my body and enfold myself in a quilt before the feelings felt safe enough to reveal themselves.

A wonderful tool for developing the capacity to be present and embracing a feeling rather than reacting to it is the *As Is, I'm Here* meditation from my book *Belonging to Life*. Let us explore it in the following exercise:

> *After you read this exercise, close your eyes and discover the circle of your breath, bring your hand to the area where the feeling is and touch it as tenderly as you would a little child. Then say silently to yourself, 'As is, I'm here'. The 'As is' is spoken on the in-breath in order to cultivate the willingness to allow yourself to be exactly as you are in this moment. It is the art of letting go of struggling with whatever is, and moving into the release that comes from letting it be. Then say, "I'm here" on the out-breath, allowing whatever is there to know that your intention is to be present for it.*

The two halves of this mantra cultivate both a keen curiosity and the capacity to meet whatever we discover in the vast regions of our heart.

◆ Heart Breath

There is a powerful way to work with your breath that can not only meet with compassion the most contracted of feelings within you; it can also transform the world. This is my version of an ancient Buddhist practice called Tonglen. Let us explore this practice now.

Once you have read through the exercise, begin by closing your eyes and allowing your attention to rest on the rhythm of your breath. As you settle in, let your breath deepen, bringing a sense of spaciousness inside of yourself. You can add the pauses at the end of the out-breath and the in-breath to intensify your experience, if you wish.

Now bring your attention to the center of your chest and remember the warmth and the radiance that we breathed into ourselves in the Ball of Love meditation we explored on Page 119. Breathe in and out of your heart area for a few minutes and let this ball of light expand and glow with warmth and love.

Now bring your attention to any physical or emotional pain that you may be experiencing somewhere in your body. Feel as specifically as you can the sensations that are appearing as this pain. If you can't find any pain, imagine a pain you have had in the past. Then just like a vacuum cleaner, on the in-breath pull whatever you are focusing on straight into the healing radiance of your heart. See it dissolve just like ice dissolves in the warmth of the sun. If you like to visualize, you can imagine it as dark smoke being pulled into your heart and then being transformed into pure light.

On the out-breath, send waves of radiant warmth from your heart into the area that is in pain. Stay with this breath for awhile, breathing your pain into your heart and then sending clear, radiant light back on the out-breath. If you want to, you can also send the opposite quality into your pain. If you are experiencing fear, send courage on the wave of your out-breath. If it is anger, send compassion. If it is confusion, send clarity. If it is despair, send the knowing that you are not alone.

When this feels complete, bring into your mind's eye another

> *person on the Earth that is experiencing the same pain that you*
> *are. It could be a child, a friend, a loved one or even a stranger.*
> *Realize that, just like you, they are suffering and long to live from*
> *the healing of the heart. Again, just like a vacuum cleaner, breathe*
> *their pain straight into your heart. Let it be touched by the trans-*
> *forming energy of this radiant light. On the out-breath imagine*
> *waves of warm, loving, compassionate energy flowing from your*
> *heart to them. See them being transformed right before your eyes.*
> *When you are done, open your eyes.*

This is one of the most powerful tools I have ever come across in my journey back to myself. It not only transforms our pain by touching it with our hearts, it transforms us by reminding us we are not alone in our pain. When we are in pain, whether it is physical, emotional or mental pain, we have a tendency to implode in ourselves, only making matters worse. This contraction cuts us off from the very energies that can heal us. When we can remember all the other people in the world that are caught in struggle too, the pain we are experiencing becomes less *my* pain and more *our* pain.

This meditation is so powerful that you can do it not only with individuals but also with groups. What would it be like if you breathed in all of the hatred and fear that is fueling the terrorists in our world, sending them love in return? It is one of the most powerful things we can do for the healing of this planet. You can do this with politicians, with batterers, with orphans and widows, with all the children of the world. Know that in the continuous field of connection that is Life on the planet, your breathing in the pain of the world and breathing out compassion and healing makes a difference.

All of the techniques we have explored that can transform our feelings back into the free flowing aliveness that they came from can be boiled down to just two words *it's okay.* These words move us back into our center where we know, from the core of our *being* that no matter what is happening in our lives, *it is all okay.* Everything that happens to us is a part of our journey back to ourselves. And at the truest of levels, *it is all for us.* It is all okay. This doesn't mean that it is necessarily pleasant. We will meet all sorts of challenging, scary and very unpleasant experiences on our journey back to ourselves. But these words allude to the truth that there is a greater process happening. Even the deepest of challenges are opening us in a way where we can again know a deep and trust-filled relationship with ourselves and with Life.

These two little words – It's okay – cut through the reactive cycle of frustration and fear that kept on fueling her compulsion, and the glow of her okayness is wonderful to see.

The statement "It's okay" isn't alluding to the content of what is going on. Instead these words are about *transforming our relationship to what is going on.* They take us out of our struggling mind so that we can calm down. They clear the static out of our lives so we can truly listen to what is happening, connecting again with our wellspring of deep knowing that will unfailingly guide us through the ups and downs of Life. These two words are the foundation of our new relationship to our feelings – "It's okay. I'm here." "It's okay you are here." "It's okay. I understand."

The experience of a young woman I have been working with reveals the power of these words *to change our relationship to what is going on.* She has been bulimic for a number of years and is also a diabetic. The combination of bulimia and diabetes can be lethal. So it wasn't okay that she was bulimic. But when her entire relationship with her bulimia was "This is not okay," she got caught in a downward spiral of struggle, a struggle that the bulimia was winning. Having tried everything else, she finally admitted herself to a two-month treatment program, only to begin binging and purging a short time after she returned home. In the program, she had recommitted to stopping her compulsion. Of course, this only made it worse in the long run.

She came to me in desperation, truly feeling that since she had tried one of the better-known treatment programs in the country and it had *failed*, she would never be free. We began working together on a consistent basis and after a month of learning the skills, her compulsion began to slow down. A couple of months later, the only time the urge to binge and purge came was after she had been in a high stress situation – often having something to do with her family. As I taught her to become very curious about what she was experiencing before, during and after these storms, she began to see what was fueling her compulsion.

The urge to be bulimic was still there. After all, it had taken years to fully develop this compulsion and it will take a while to dismantle it. All of the feelings that fueled it were still there but they were easier to work with when she remembered to let go of struggling with what was going on. Whenever any of the old patterns showed up in her mind and heart, she would simply

253

say, "It's okay" – whether it was the idea that she wasn't doing something *right* or her waistband felt tight or she was afraid of being rejected by her boyfriend. The more she said these words, the more she saw that her whole relationship with herself and with Life had been that things were *not* okay!

These two little words cut through the reactive cycle of frustration and fear that kept on fueling her compulsion and the glow of her *okayness* is wonderful to see. Now she rarely throws up, and when she does, she can quickly find her center again. In one visit she shared her amazement at the power of these two words, especially since practically every single one of her friends from the eating disorder treatment program was still throwing up on a daily basis.

If you find a moment where feelings are moving through you with such power that it is difficult to remember anything we have explored together, just take one deep breath and say, "It's okay." If everything is calm, you can still use these words. They can become a talisman, reminding you that this moment is exactly as it needs to be and everything is all right. The power of adding these two words into your life is enormous. I have given talks based on just these two words and people have come up to me afterwards and even contacted me weeks, months and years later. They want to share with me how deeply these two words have changed their lives.

Ultimately, *it's okay* opens the door to our heart. When cultivating an openhearted relationship with our feelings, it is important to remember that this is a process. We have closed our hearts to ourselves for many years and some of our boxed-up feelings are very, very locked up and hidden far away. That is okay. Each time we can touch them (our feelings) with our hearts, even for a moment or two, they melt a little more, coming out of the dark and into the light.

The Fifth Step: "Right now, what do I <u>truly</u> need?"

As we have explored, all throughout this book, you have an inner radar that is a part of the wellspring within you that knows exactly what to do in any given situation. It knows when to say yes and when to say no. It knows when to stop and when to go. It knows how to eat, exercise, work and play in ways that bring balance to your whole being. Because most of us have been caught in struggle a good deal of our lives, we have lost contact with this deep inner knowing.

As you live in the Third Question, "Right now, what do I <u>truly</u> need?" you reawaken this inner radar. This re-awakening allows you to trust your own gut knowing that can identify better than anybody else what the appropriate choice is for you in any given situation. Not only that, every day you are a different human *being*. You have lived a little longer, growing more

> *As you live in the question, "Right now, what do I <u>truly</u> need?" you reawaken your inner radar, allowing you to trust your own gut knowing which can identify better than anyone else what the appropriate choice is for you in any given situation.*

deeply into yourself. Thus, the needs of every wave of compulsion can be different. There are no pat answers on the journey to healing. This is why questions are so important and why the question, "Right now, what do I <u>truly</u> need?" can be such help.

At the beginning, you may not hear a thing. Ask anyway, for every time you do, you energize your inner radar. The more we ask it, the clearer we get. It is like the silt in a glass of water. As it begins to fall to the bottom, the water gets clearer. As we open the space of wisdom through this question, choices that are for our highest good become clear to us.

It is helpful to know that wise choices come in two different flavors – what I call *Ha choices* and *Ah choices*. The *Ha choices* come from the firm and benevolent *No* that we all have within us. The *Ah choices* come from an open and tender heart. You can get the flavor of these choices by saying these two words out loud. *Ha* is short and clipped. *Ahhhhh* is long and soft.

To understand how to use these two seemingly opposite choices, we need to remember that working with the feelings that fuel our compulsions is like working with a two year-old. A skillful parent knows that there are times when the child is acting out because it is scared, and all it needs is a few moments of pure attention and some deep hearted understanding. This is an *Ah choice* and we have explored it deeply all throughout this book. Most of the feelings that we will meet on our journey back to ourselves are in desperate need of the wise heart that is inherent in this kind of choice.

A skillful parent also knows that there are times when the child needs boundaries and some very clear directions. This is a *Ha choice*. It may be just saying to the child "That's enough." Or they may need a time out in their room. This is true for our feelings too. There does come a time in our journey when we can say to a feeling or to our compulsion, "No. We are not going there."

> *As I learned to open my heart to the full range of the feelings that moved through me, my feelings began to trust that I truly saw them and understood. Then, and only then, did they begin to trust my 'No.'*

This is a new kind of *No*. Formerly our *No* was *against* what we were experiencing. We either hated or feared what was going on and wanted to get away from it as quickly as possible. This *Empowered No* is not against anything. It is a wise and benevolent *No* that is for the good of the whole. Just like with a two year-old, when parents can see what is going on without reacting to it, their *No* has authority and the child recognizes this.

In working with these two types of choices, always go to the *Ah choice* first. Pull on all of the skills that we have explored on how to keep your heart open, both in this chapter and in the chapter on *Loving Yourself From the Inside Out*. Then if you feel that it is appropriate to put some limits on your feelings, do so buy calling upon your empowered *No*.

For myself, I had to work for quite a while to truly open my heart to the deep feelings that fueled my compulsions before I could say a skillful *No*. When I said "No" before I had touched these feelings with my heart, it only made it worse. *As I learned to open my heart to the full range of the feelings that moved through me, my feelings began to trust that I truly saw them and understood. Then, and only then, did they begin to trust my No.* I felt that when I finally discovered my empowered *No* that I had truly taken my power back from the web of thoughts and feelings that had run my life.

So the question, "Right now, what do I truly need?" is tapping us into the field of wise and kind choices. It can be asked directly to whatever feeling you are experiencing by saying, "What do *you* need right now?" The more connected to your feelings you become, the more you recognize how desperately they need us to be there for them. They respond deeply to our willingness to ask them what they need and the willingness to listen for a response.

This Fifth Step taps you into the deep inner knowing that is always with you. But sometimes you may not be able to listen and or even be interested in listening. This will happen many times on this journey back to yourself. In these types of situations you can ask the Third Question in an Open-Ended way – "What is the way through this?" Remember, this is the default question. This is the one you always ask when you aren't sure of what to do. It works even if you are still lost in doubt and confusion.

Listen as deeply as you can. If nothing comes and you feel in need of some clarity on what to do right now, ask yourself what a friend or loved one would do if they were in this same situation. You can also go back to the Lost Child meditation on Page 118. to see exactly what it is that you need. If it is still not clear, imagine asking the advice of one of the people you admire most in the world

It is also helpful to imagine what you would be doing if you were doing the exact opposite of what you are doing right now. If you are feeling quite closed, go outside and take a walk. If you are moving at a frantic pace, take a break. If you are judgmental, cultivate your heart.

Remember, this Fifth Step taps you into a wisdom that is much greater than what your mind can come up with all on its own. Keep asking and know that the questions are working for you.

The Sixth Step: "This is it!"

After we have met our feelings and given them whatever they need – even if all we can do is just a moment of recognizing that they are there – one of the wisest choices we can make is the Sixth Step. The Sixth Step is a great guide for what to do when you ask the question "What do I truly need?" because most of the time, after meeting our feelings what we need to do is place our attention elsewhere.

With this Sixth Step we rediscover two essential things that happen in healing:

❖ The first is that we do have the choice about where we are going to place our attention.

❖ The second is that the struggles that we pay attention to in our minds, bodies and hearts are just a small fraction of what is going on in this moment of our lives.

We don't have to stay caught in the never-ending story in our heads and all of the reactions it breeds in our bodies and emotions. Instead, we can open the field of our attention and rediscover Life, with all the joy and wonder that is available right here, right now. We can open the field of our attention and realize that we are alive! Our hearts are beating. Our breath is rising and falling. Our bodies are glowing with the gift of Life.

In some deep and profound way, all of the struggles of our lives – especially compulsions – are a part of a process that is bringing us back into a deep and abiding connection with the only moment that matters, *Now*. The key word in the Sixth Step is *open*. As we become more present in this process,

> *Life is happening right here, right now, and this is the only moment that matters.*

sometimes we will be able to just let go of all of our struggles and *open* to the newness of Life, here and now.

Other times we will need to consciously cultivate opening, lifting our attention from the narrowness of our struggle and placing it onto something else. We can walk, dance, bake, sing, bike, sit quietly in the garden, read a good book, rent a funny movie or call a friend. Gratitude also opens us again and so does generosity, especially the generosity of *being* there for another person.

Remember – our old patterns have a momentum that has been built upon for days, months and even years. But when we see how our struggles cut us off from the pure joy of *being alive*, it becomes easier to let them go and bring our attention back to the fullness of Life right now, with all of the joy that is waiting for us here.

The second thing to remember is that we should only do this step after we have done at least one of the other steps. To try to open ourselves without at least a few moments of responding to our contraction just fuels the cycle of reaction. But after we have met our experience, even for a moment or two, we can use this energy that was caught in struggle for living.

Everything we have explored in the first five steps clears up the house of our *being*, unboxing our feelings, opening the doors and windows and even cleaning up the basement. Then in the Sixth Step Life says, "Let's live! These are just old feelings that are moving through us. Don't hold on. Let them through like a cloud dances across the sky." We then can again fully engage with the wonder and the joy of *being alive*. Remember, our natural inclination is toward joy.

I am constantly delighted to discover that no matter how deeply my mind and heart may be struggling, when I use the Six Steps in order to be fully present for my experience, there is nothing in my old story of struggle that can ensnare my attention, drawing me into a tightening spiral of struggle. Not only that, no matter how many challenges I may be experiencing, I can now easily return to the fullness of Life, right here, right now.

I had a day last week when everything in my life fell apart – the computer went on the fritz, my pond started leaking, my eye was swollen shut, my back was excruciatingly painful and some funding I thought I had fell through. And yet I was glad for this depth of craziness, for it showed me that even when everything is really chaotic, with the Six Steps I didn't need to get lost in the struggles of my mind.

It also reminded me how to cherish my imperfect life. Every time I asked the question "Right now, what do I truly need?" it was clear that what I needed to do was not fight the process and instead bring my attention back into the fullness of Life as it is right now.

There is a statement that can help define the difference between being caught in our story or being fully present for Life. The statement is, "This is it!" It reminds us that this moment is a gift. These three words say that everything that *has happened* in our lives belongs to the already lived. And everything that is *going to happen* isn't yet here. They remind us that Life is happening right here, right now, and this is the only moment that matters. One day we won't have any more moments so let us be fully present for the ones we are given.

These words reconnect us with the living adventure that is the river of Life. This river isn't always likable, but it is much more painful to stay closed than it is to open. As a Moody Blues song says, "It is easier to stay than to turn around and run!" There are times that my mind resists when I invite it to let go of struggling. It is like a rebellious two year-old who doesn't want to be present for the living moment of Life. When it says, "Why would I want to be present for a headache, or a noisy room or a whining child?" I remind it that resisting only makes it worse. I also remind it that resistance cuts us off from everything we truly long for – the fullness of Life that is waiting for us, right here and right now.

I have a wonderful statement that works like magic on my rebellious mind. I say, "This moment is where the good stuff is!" And usually this does the trick, inviting my mind out of reaction, back into being fully available to my own living adventure.

The invitation is to pause for a moment, let go of all of your ideas about Life and be fully present for wherever you are. See the space you are sitting in. Hear the sounds of Life all around you and within you. Feel the pulsating, aliveness of your body. Be here. This is the living moment of your life.

What To Do When Feelings Persist

It is important to remember that it does take time to heal the core feelings that run our compulsions. We have hidden them deep and run from them hard for many years, often many decades. But sometimes there is not enough space in our consciousness to see nor is there enough mercy in our hearts to meet the feelings that are cascading through us, and when we ask the three questions –

☆ In this moment, what am I experiencing?

☆ For this moment, can I let this be?

☆ Right now, what do I <u>truly</u> need?

– nothing is clear. We may not even want to ask the questions.

A skillful thing to do in this situation is to ask for help. No words can express how central this is to lasting healing. In fact it could be said that *all of the challenges in our lives are given to us in order to confound us enough that we have to ask for help.* When you finally understand that help has always been waiting for your request, and when you see how much easier your life becomes, you will wonder how you ever lived without asking for help in this way.

One of the simplest and most powerful ways to ask for help is to use the Open-Ended Questions:

★ What is asking to be seen?

★ How can I bring compassion to this?

★ What is the way through this?

It would be useful to reread the part on Open-Ended Questions in the chapter on *Living In Questions* beginning on Page 166. This will help you to remember that you are living a very specific process, one where no matter what is happening in your life, it is a part of your journey back to yourself and the Intelligence that gave you your challenges in the first place is always close at hand.

It is also extremely helpful to move the energy that is showing up as these feelings. There are two ways to do that.

◇1◇ Moving the energy

◇2◇ Giving Feelings a Voice

◇1◇ Moving the energy

As we explored in the last chapter, getting our bodies moving can be very helpful. It is now reported that for milder cases of depression, a 10-minute walk is more effective than antidepressants! Movement can so quickly and powerfully change our experience, and yet when feelings are running us, we can have a lot of resistance to moving.

An experience from my life shows how healing it is to get physically moving. It happened one morning when I woke up in despair. I was in the middle of a very busy time in my life and at the same time a dear friend of mine was dying. My mind was tired enough that I didn't have the energy it takes to sit with this formerly very scary guest. And yet I knew that in order to not

> *The challenges in our lives are given to us in order to confound us enough that we have to ask for help.*

be engulfed by it, I needed to *respond* rather than *react*. I considered staying in bed for awhile, cuddling with myself. Sometimes that is very appropriate, but my wisest part recognized that on this occasion it would cause me to freeze more.

As I listened to my body, I knew it wanted to physically move. But this despair, being very contracted and very young, wanted to stay frozen like a deer freezes in the presence of a hunter. 49.999% of me wanted to stay behind the prison walls of despair. 50.001% of me wanted to open again. With resistance screaming in my head, I got on my exercise bike and began to peddle. For the first two minutes I wanted to stop and hide. Then the energy began to move. Oh, the bliss of that ride! Waves of energy flowed from the top of my head to the tip of my toes. And the joy that came from having opened rather than having closed was so delicious!

Physically moving our bodies is not the only way to move energy. It can also be done by allowing someone to hold you and, without words, to simply be there. If no one is around, you can hold yourself. One of my favorite gifts to myself when I am feeling vulnerable and overwhelmed is to make a nest of my bed, putting on multiple layers of comforters and burrowing down deep inside.

We can also move through exaggeration. If you get into the sense of play that exaggeration is, it can be a lot of fun. If I am mad, I love to yell and scream and rant and rave in my car. I work on getting the yells to come from deep within my body and boy does that feel great. If I am feeling overly responsible, I love to go to my neighborhood park and swing.

If I am judging myself, I will sometimes go to the mirror and say, "Oh boy you really screwed up didn't you," with a little twinkle in my eye. I then go on and give myself a list of supreme screw ups around the most ridiculous things – "You drank out of the wrong side of your tea cup this morning! You even put on your left shoe before your right. And besides that, you didn't hang up your towel perfectly!" I think you get my gist. It is all in the name of perspective, for *being truly alive* is about screwing up part of the time

> *Being truly alive is about screwing up part of the time!*

(and some days it is even more than that!)

Even though a good deal of the time moving energy is very freeing, when we are contracted we all carry an inclination to stay closed. From the prison of contraction, opening looks very, very scary. So each of us has our own brand of resistance to moving when we freeze again. I used to be afraid of going outside when I felt particularly frozen. It was just too much space! As I began to honor my fear of going outside when I was contracted, I became willing to push its boundaries a bit and I found it to be so freeing. I now can go outside even when I am sad or afraid and I find that rather than contracting, I become more spacious.

Listen to yourself as to whether moving the energy is appropriate. It is your inner radar within that will tell you what needs to be done. Every time it will be different. Be willing to push the envelope of your resistance just a bit and watch what happens. If what you do causes you to resist even more, be gentle. It is okay to let yourself stay frozen. In just the recognition that you are too scared to move, you have moved your energy by touching yourself with your heart!

Allowing Feelings a Voice

With a feeling that threatens to take you over time and time again, it can be skillful to allow this feeling a voice. This is more powerful than we can imagine. Michael Meade, a very skillful leader in the men's movement, takes groups of men that are fighting with each other – such as inner city youths and local business people or Catholics and Protestants – and invites them into a room together.

At first it is nothing but fireworks, but it is astounding to watch Michael include every single person's point of view. He gives each one of them a voice and through his example teaches everybody in the room that every person's view is valid and necessary. By the end of a weekend together they all become bonded in a way that they couldn't even begin to imagine before. This same thing works inside of us. *Every part of us needs a voice, and when all of the parts are recognized and heard, we become more whole within ourselves.*

One of the ways you can allow the different parts of yourself a voice is to write to them and allow them to write back to you. You can reread the

> *Every part of us needs a voice, and when all of the parts are recognized and heard, we become more whole within ourselves.*

section on *Engaging with Our Compulsions* (Page 44) where we explored writing letters to our compulsion. Now that you can see that it is feelings that are fueling your compulsion, you can write letters to these feelings and allow them to write back. You can amplify your feelings with different colors of pens like blue for sorrow and red for rage. You can also do this by writing letters you never mail to people you need to speak your truth to. This can be so healing, especially around rage.

If writing is not your mode, you can speak the truth of what you are experiencing. One way to do this is to call a friend who knows how to listen and let your feelings have a voice. Have you noticed how good you feel after having been with a person who really listened to you? That is because through this listening, the place where you were stuck got acknowledged and heard so it could begin to move.

The core feelings that fuel your compulsion may be so young that you need a professional *listener* to give you what we explored in this chapter – undivided attention, wise listening, understanding and mercy. This was what happened for me. I so hated and feared the core feelings that I had run from my whole life that somebody outside of me needed to accept them first before I could accept them myself. As I was listened to, I learned how to listen to myself. Eventually there came a time where, whenever I was feeling vulnerable and overwhelmed by Life, I would automatically reach for my own compassionate attention rather than food.

There is a wonderful system of listening to yourself called Voice Dialogue. It is based on the truth that each of us is made up of many parts, and in order for us to become whole, these parts need to be allowed a voice so they can become a respected part of who we are. You can either learn this on your own or you can go to a professional who is trained in this kind of listening. Either way, the books and tapes by Hal and Sidra Stone, the creators of Voice Dialogue, are excellent tools for learning this system.

In this section we have explored how to bring the light of our compassionate attention to all the feelings that are fueling our compulsion. Many of them will dissolve under the light of pure attention. And the ones that don't will

> *Every time you meet a feeling, even if only a brief time, it loses a little more of its power over you.*

usually dissolve under the light of understanding and mercy. For feelings, just like people, become healthy and balanced in the face of non-judgmental attention. It is important to not push the river. There are times to go toward a feeling and there are times to move away. Many of the feelings that are asking for our attention are very, very young and it is essential to respect their timing.

Know also that at the beginning, a moment or two of meeting will probably transform a more surface feeling but probably not the deeper ones that are fueling your compulsion. *But every time you meet a feeling, even if it is for only a brief time, it loses a little more of its power over you.* As you learn how to be truly present for a feeling, you are giving it exactly what it is longing for, your undivided attention. *For it is not in changing, getting rid of or denying our experience that we will know the peace we long for. It comes from being in direct relationship with it.* As Robert Frost, the eminent American Poet once wrote, "The only way out is through."

Staying On the Path of Healing

All the skills we explored will eventually help you to transform your boxed-up feelings back into the field of aliveness that is your birthright. On this path back to yourself, don't dive into the core feelings right away. That would be like going to the gym and starting with the 100-pound weights. All you will do is pull your *muscles* of frustration and despair. Start treasure hunting with the more everyday experiences of your life – asking the questions when it is just an ordinary day and your compulsion is nowhere to be found. This will strengthen your ability to be curious and compassionate and will remind you to not do your life alone. You will then be able to be truly present for yourself when you are compulsive.

A dear friend of mine, who has been reading the drafts of this book and working with the skills, shared a story the other day that describes what I am talking about. Her 11 year-old daughter belongs to a circle of friends that have been together for years. At each of her birthday parties, my friend would set up a treasure hunt for the girls. When they were six, the clues were really obvious – go to the stereo in the living room and there the treasure would be, sitting out in the open. As they got older, the treasure hunt became more challenging but not more frustrating. Since the girls had been *practicing* treasure hunting for years, their capacity to listen to the clues and be very curious about what they were pointing to increased along the way. My friend also said that you could watch their developing minds rising to the challenge.

When she was relating this story to me, she said that this is exactly what happened to her. When she began to *treasure hunt* her own life, it took her a while to be curious about her compulsions. She had been so trained, like all of us, to react and control. She first had to start with little things – her irritation at the length of the stoplight, the slight headache at the end of a busy day. She then began to be able to ask the three questions in the middle of her daily challenges. Finally she was able to be truly present for herself when she was compulsive, and wise choices became much easier to make.

As you *treasure hunt* in your life, it is important to understand that there will be times when you will be able to incorporate all six steps in an instant. Other times you may need to explore only one step, and for only a moment, before you need to distract yourself. Or you may find yourself spending over an hour with just one or two steps. Time does not matter. Just the willingness to turn toward yourself in curiosity and just a moment of opening your heart takes you another step into your healing.

You will also have times when you use these skills in order to try to stop an uncomfortable experience. That is a common human reaction. It will soon become clear that the quickest way through the maze of thoughts and feelings that fuel your compulsion is to be very curious and deeply compassionate about whatever you are experiencing right now.

All of the steps we have explored can stand alone by themselves. They can also be mixed and matched so you can find your own pathway through the web of compulsions, into your true empowerment. You may have the kind of mind that likes to follow the guidelines. They have certainly proven to be effective. Or you may have the kind of mind that likes to pick and choose. Trust yourself. It can be useful at this time to go back and reread the section on *Working With the Questions* (Page 187). There is a lot of good information there that can keep you on the road to healing for the long haul.

You can also discover your own ways to compassionate attention. Just ask the question, "How can I bring curiosity and compassion to myself?" Or you can ask, "How can I *respond* rather than *react*?"

> *Don't rush this. What we are talking about here is a healing process. It does take time, and it is worth it.*

Don't rush this. What we are talking about here is a healing *process*. It does take time. And even though it takes time, it is worth it. Imagine living a life in

> *Imagine living a life in which you truly trust and love yourself. Imagine living a life in which your struggles, rather than sending you down into an ever-tightening spiral, awaken you more fully into Life.*

which you truly trust and love yourself. Imagine living a life in which your struggles, rather than sending you down into an ever-tightening spiral, awaken you more fully into Life. That has been my experience. I used to live in a black ball of struggle. I was a bundle of reaction filled with negative thoughts and overwhelming feelings. No wonder I tried to eat myself into oblivion. *Remember, our core compulsion is to struggle – we try to do Life rather than be Life. And all of our other compulsions are an attempt to numb out from this struggle.*

For myself, the ball of struggle became tighter and denser over the years until I didn't want to live anymore. But slowly, using everything we are exploring in this book, I began to spend more and more time out of this black ball, living in the spaciousness of being fully connected to myself and to Life. I now live in that spaciousness most of the time and only rarely visit the black ball. And every time I do, because I am willing to be curious, I return to spaciousness with deeper wisdom and more love.

So let all that we have explored be seeds planted in your consciousness. Don't make what we have explored in this chapter into a *have to*. Let the seeds grow in their own time and in their own way. You will then become like a new shoot that has grown for a long, long time up through the dark winter soil and has now found the light. As it is not yet spring, some days will still be very cold and some days will carry the riotous promise of spring. In order to allow the new green shoots of your healing to blossom into the fullness of who you really are, don't force things. Your deep inner knowing knows how to allow your life to unfold until, in your own time and your own way, you fulfill your promise, giving your true beauty and essence to the world.

Core Ideas in Treasure Hunting With Feelings:

❖ In order to heal your feelings, you need to come into relationship with them. This is not about collapsing into them. This is about meeting them, giving them the non-judgmental attention they need to heal.

❖ There is a huge difference between *feeling* a feeling and *meeting* a feeling. In *feeling* a feeling you can get lost in the middle of it. *Meeting* a feeling is about standing with the feeling and giving it the attention and understanding that it needs in order to be transformed into free flowing energy again.

❖ The deep feelings within you that you have run away from for a long time are very young and in need of your help.

❖ Your willingness to turn toward your experience creates safety for your feelings to reveal themselves.

❖ Feelings are only too painful to bear if you turn away from them.

❖ The safest thing you will ever do is meet your feelings.

❖ Being present for your feelings for even just a moment or two begins to release them back into the free flowing aliveness they came from.

❖ The three statements – "I see you. I'm here." "It's okay you are here." "It's okay.; I understand." – dramatically heal your feelings. Your feelings have been waiting for a long time to hear them.

❖ When you arrive at the Sixth Step that says, "This is it!" you can begin to engage with the wonder and joy of being alive.

❖ As you return to yourself and to Life, you become Life celebrating itself.

✦ TREASURE HUNTING ✦
WITH COMPULSIONS

We are now ready to bring all that we have learned into the great teacher of compulsion. The short version of what we have explored is: Take a breath; ask the first two Check-in questions; breathe into what you discover, giving it your compassionate attention so it can transform back into the free-flowing energy of aliveness. Then ask the third Check-In question, awakening the wellspring of deep knowing within you. If the Check-In questions don't work in your situation, use the Open-Ended questions or combinations of both.

This section is about amplifying that process, drawing upon everything that we have explored together so far. Let us first do a quick synopsis.

When we were born, we were wide open to Life and we lived in the house of our *being*. We were at home inside of ourselves, comfortable in our own skins. We trusted ourselves; we trusted Life. Because we were open to the living adventure of our lives, our eyes sparkled and our bodies tingled with the pure joy of *being alive*. We hadn't yet bought into the belief that we needed to be any different than we were in order to stay connected to ourselves and connected to Life.

But slowly, as the circumstances of our lives scared, overwhelmed and disappointed us, we pulled back, tightening our bodies, holding our breath and dimming our radiance. As we contracted, we boxed up all of parts of ourselves that we felt were unacceptable and hid them deep inside. As we left the world of *I am!* for the world of *I am not/I should be*, we closed the curtains and locked the doors of the house of our *being,* filling our bodies with *I am not knots.* Retreating to the attic of our minds, we took on a story of what Life *should be* and who we *ought to be*, cutting ourselves off from a deep and nourishing relationship with ourselves as we are and with Life in its fullness.

> *As we left the world of* I am! *for the world of* I am not/I should be*, we closed the curtains and locked the doors of the house of our* being, *filling our bodies with* 'I am not knots.*'

Whenever the boxed-up parts of ourselves made a prison break and came knocking on the attic door, we learned how, with great alacrity, to shove them back into their boxes through denial, distraction and disconnection. We became masters at living very far away from ourselves. When this didn't work, compulsion became our friend. It numbed us out so that we could survive, for we didn't yet have the skills that were needed to meet the seemingly unacceptable parts of ourselves.

Compulsions also gave us a hint of the joy that we knew when we lived in the whole house of our *being*. Because it wasn't the real joy that comes from being connected to ourselves and to Life, it was easy to get lost in *more, more, more*. But it was never enough. Eventually, the price we paid for taking care of ourselves in this way became greater than the help we received.

Living in reaction, we became caught in a vicious circle – taking care of ourselves through compulsion, hating ourselves for doing so, trying to stop, only to have this fuel another wave of compulsion. Living in contraction, we lost trust in ourselves and in Life, totally forgetting the joy of living in the full house of our *being*.

This is where many people are caught, fighting forces that actually become stronger when they fight them and then feeling like a failure for being unable to control them. And even though at times they may be able to control their compulsions, this doesn't bring them the peace that they long for because they are still disconnected. They have forgotten how to live in a deep and abiding relationship with themselves and with Life.

How do we step out of disconnection and struggle, back into the house of our *being*? How do we learn how to *respond* rather than *react* so that we can open back into Life again? Let us look at some of the most important points we have explored:

❖ *Compulsions are not the enemy.* If we think so, we get caught in endless war, fighting these forces that are much stronger than our attempts to control them. Rather than being the enemy, they are a survival system that has taken care of us until we could learn how to be present for ourselves. Compulsions aren't here because we are weak-willed ninnies, helpless in the face of powerful urges that are trying to destroy us. These forces that confound and confuse us are here to awaken us – to open us back into a deep and abiding relationship with ourselves and with Life that nourishes us to our core.

❖ *Compulsions come straight from the longing at the heart of Life for us to reconnect with who we truly are.* We will be given the exact set of circumstances in our lives that we need in order to come out of the attic of the mind, back into the house of our *being*. Compulsions are one of the greatest teachers in this shift from contraction to connection. Because they are more powerful than any of our attempts to control them, they push us, prod us and cajole us into *responding* rather than *reacting.* They will refuse to go away until they have taught us how to be curious about what we are experiencing and compassionate with everything we discover.

❖ Lasting healing happens when we can be present for whatever we are experiencing in this moment. Whenever we are compulsive, instead of turning *away*, this is the time to turn *toward* our experience. Rather than *managing* our experience, this is the time to *engage* with it, giving whatever is there the light of our compassionate attention. *We are not responsible for our compulsion and all that comes with it. We are responsible to it.* This means that the essence of healing is the under-standing that ultimately we don't need to fix our compulsions nor do we need to change them, hate them or fear them. What we need to do is *be present* for them and touch whatever is there with our heart.

❖ The gift of compulsions is that they bring close to the surface everything inside of ourselves that is asking for our compassionate attention. When we meet what we are experiencing with curiosity and understanding, our boxed-up feelings lose their power to fuel our compulsions and control our lives. Also, the energy that was bound up in our old patterns is freed back into free flowing aliveness that we truly are.

❖ As we reconnect with ourselves, instead of our familiar mode of struggle, we experience an ever deepening joy and an abiding trust in ourselves and in Life. Eventually we come to know and live again from the entire house of our *being*, connected to the wellspring of deep knowing within. This is the greatest gift compulsion has to bring to us – to reunite us with our own wellspring that is connected to the Creative Intelligence at the heart of Life. This great and wondrous Intelligence that beats our heart and breathes our breath then becomes our partner in this marvelous adventure called Life.

The Three Questions:

In order to see what our compulsions are here to teach us, we need to become more interested in what is happening inside us than we are in getting lost in our compulsions or trying to control them. This curiosity will ulti-mately untangle their web and bring us the healing that we long for.

The Three Questions that are woven into The Six Steps hold the keys to doing this. They retrain our reactive our minds so we can *see* and *be* with *what is.* They also tap us into the deep knowing within that will guide us every step of the way on this journey back to ourselves.

Before we take the questions into our compulsions, let us review the essence of each one.

☆ *In this moment, what am I experiencing?* This first Check-In Question dips the finger of our attention into the river of our experience. It transforms our curiosity into a high-powered flash-light, exploring exactly what is happening right now. If we can see the truth of what is going on, then we can heal it.

★ *What is asking to be seen?* When we cannot see or don't want to see what we are experiencing, we can go to the Open-Ended version of this question. With this question, we ask for help from our deep wisdom in seeing what is going on inside of us.

☆ *For this moment, can I let this be?* This second Check-In Question is about moving from *reaction* to *response*. Whatever we are experiencing is a part of the living process of our lives. Healing isn't about getting rid of it. It is about *opening* to it. This question allows us to step into the river of our experience with a curious mind *and* a compassionate, understanding heart.

★ *How can I bring compassion to this?* When we cannot accept our experience, let alone open to it, we can go to the Open-Ended version of this question. This question asks for help in bringing the healing of mercy into that which we have formerly denied and resisted, for it is in the heart that all lasting healing happens.

☆ *Right now, what do I <u>truly</u> need?* This third Check-In Question awakens the wellspring of deep wisdom within us that knows what will bring balance into our lives. It reminds us to truly listen to ourselves in a keen and focused way so that we can make wise and kind choices in our lives.

★ *What is the way through this?* When we cannot listen to ourselves, or when we are too caught in struggle to do anything at all, we can go to this Open-Ended version of the Third Question. This is our default question that we use at any time, especially when nothing else is working. It makes space for our deep wisdom to support and guide us. Remember, Open-Ended Questions create a vacuum in the universe and into this vacuum our answers will come.

We will first look at how we can bring these questions into the different phases of compulsion. We will then explore the things we can do no matter where we are and no matter what is happening with our compulsion. These two sections are meant to be a synopsis of all that we have explored together and hopefully will become handy references for when you find yourself caught in your compulsion.

The Wave

Let us look now at how we can apply these three questions to our compulsions. To do that it is important to see that most compulsions come in waves and that there are three phases to a wave – the end, the middle and the beginning. We will begin with the end of the wave for that is the easiest place to learn the art of engagement. We will then explore the middle of the wave, the part where the boxed up feelings that are fueling our compulsions are most evident. And finally, we will explore the wave just as it begins. It is here that we can relearn how to make kind and skillful choices that empower us to our core.

- ◇1◇ The end phase is after the wave has moved through. It is a treasure trove of information that can allow us to take our power back from our compulsion.

- ◇2◇ The middle phase is when we are fully engulfed by the wave, usually losing clarity, connection and mercy. This is the place where we can meet and heal the core feelings that are fueling the wave of compulsion.

- ◇3◇ The beginning phase is when the wave is just beginning to build. This is the time where we have the most choice about where we are going to put our attention. As we learn more about our compulsion and how it operates, rather than following it like children follow the Pied Piper, this is the time when we can relearn how to make choices that are for our highest good.

Let us look at each of these phases in depth and see how we can best use The Three Questions, along with The Six Steps.

◇1◇ After The Wave Has Passed Through: Breaking The Spell

Because we have been so unconscious around our compulsions, the temptation to fall into them and pull the covers over our head is very strong. So asking ourselves to begin to be curious about what is going on when the wave is building or after we are fully lost in it can be difficult at the beginning. It is when the wave has passed through and the cravings have subsided enough that we can peek our head out of the covers and see what is really happening.

After the wave has passed through, we need to:

    a.   Be truthful with ourselves about the price we pay for being compulsive.

    b.   Break the spell of the heavy states of mind which arise in the wake of a wave.

⬥a The Price We Pay

After a wave of compulsion, rather than tapping into the wealth of information that is waiting for us there, we usually stay in reaction, losing the opportunity to recognize the price we pay for taking care of ourselves in this way. We all know that compulsions cause havoc in our lives, but we use this information to try to get ourselves under control. After a wave of compulsion has passed through, we usually pull ourselves up by the bootstraps and declare that *now* we will be in charge. "Never again will I allow my compulsion to get the best of me," we declare.

For a time we feel a sense of power as we start another diet, dump the pills down the toilet, throw all the alcohol away, cancel our internet provider, promise to end our workday at 5:00 PM or cut up the credit cards. But there comes a day, if we haven't yet allowed ourselves to recognize and *feel* the price that we pay for taking care of ourselves in this way, that the urge to fall into our compulsion resurfaces stronger than any resolve we may have mustered.

To take a breath and ask the question, "In this moment, what am I experiencing?" in the aftermath of our compulsion allows us to see, *and finally feel* with great clarity, the heartache that comes in its wake. This is true whether it is the rages of a food hangover, the anxiety that dogs us when we can't ever get to the end of our To-Do list, the penetrating and pervasive smell of cigarettes, the price our family and social life pays for us being a workaholic, or the despair we feel when our credit card is

> *The question, "In this moment, what am I experiencing?" turns your attention into a flashlight, highlighting what is happening.*

denied – *the short-lived satisfaction of our compulsions isn't worth it.* Even if we do get a small bit of peace, we can finally see that it doesn't last! There are easier, kinder and more lasting ways to take care of ourselves, ways that enhance our lives rather than leaving us struggling and disempowered.

We begin by asking this question about the sensations happening in our bodies, for that is usually where we will be able to most clearly see the price we pay for our compulsions. The question, "In this moment, what am I experiencing?" turns your attention into a flashlight, highlighting what is happening. Whatever you discover there – headache, tightness in your throat, acid stomach, difficulty breathing – describe it to yourself. Get as specific as you can. Remember that the power of naming something is awesome. *In that moment you are relating to it rather than being lost in the middle of it.*

If feelings show up, name them too – anxiety, sadness, dread, irritation. Every moment you can be present for the habitual patterns of sensations and feelings in your body that come on the heels of your compulsion, you lessen the power of your compulsion. In the chapter on *Loving Ourselves From the Inside Out* under "Listening to Yourself" (Page 115), you can review how to be truly fascinated by what is going on in your body.

If food is your compulsion, notice what it feels like in your body to over-eat. Does your heart pound? Is there a bad taste in your mouth? Is your stomach upset? What happens to your emotions? Do you hate being in your body? Are you lost in despair? Be as curious and as real as you can.

If drinking is your way, explore what it feels like to wake up with a hang-over. How does your body feel? How does it change your emotions? In what ways does it make the next day more difficult? A powerful way to break the spell of over-drinking is to ask a friend or loved one to video tape you when you have had too much to drink. It is quite a wake up call to see yourself under the influence.

If it's over-shopping, notice that the wonderful feelings don't last very long – both the warm, cozy feeling of being in the store and the thrill of your new purchases. Especially notice what it feels like when you recognize how much money you spent. Also be truthful about the subterfuge that goes along with over-spending – hiding from yourself and from your loved ones exactly what you are doing. How does this hiding and lying make you feel?

To amplify this *weather reporting*, you can write down what you discover, either in an *Awareness Diary* or in free flowing writing. You are not doing this to change anything. You are doing this so you can see what is going on.

You can be truthful with yourself about any compulsion. For example:

> *To see what is going on after the wave has passed through can show us that our compulsions never bring us what they promise.*

- ❖ Sexual – What is it like to wake up with a stranger in your bed?
- ❖ Cigarettes – What about the smell on your clothes, the constriction in your lungs or the ostracism from society?
- ❖ Busyness – What happens when, after seeming to be on top of your life, you crash and burn again, or the panic comes from not getting everything done?

Whatever your compulsion, you pay a heavy price for taking care of yourself in this way, a price, that when you finally acknowledge it, is never worth it.

To see what is going on after the wave has passed through can show you that *compulsions never bring you what they promise.* In fact, they do the opposite. It can also be helpful to make a list. Write down in as much detail as you can what you are experiencing. When compulsions are knocking on the door, it is so easy to forget the price that you pay for taking care of yourself in this way. When you have a list available, a list that can remind you that compulsions don't give you what they promise, you have some more help in making wise and kind choices.

Once you have a list, it can also be helpful to share it with a friend or counselor. It is essential that they are someone who won't judge you if you fall into your compulsion again or try to use this information to make you stop being compulsive. They are simply there to bear witness to your truth. The reason it's so powerful to share your truth is that when somebody listens to you, you can begin to listen to yourself. This brings you out of the fog of denial that tries to convince you that compulsion will truly give you what you want.

If your heart is open enough, you can also look in the mirror and be clear about the exact price you pay for your compulsion. This must be done with copious amounts of kindness. For it is kindness that can cut through self-judgment and allow you to meet yourself fully in that moment. In that meeting you can recognize that you are worthy of a kinder way of taking care of yourself.

To pay attention to the price we pay for riding this circle of disempowerment over and over again is the first ray of clarity on our pathway back to ourselves. Just a little bit of attention begins to break the vicious cycle of going to our compulsions for help, being devastated by them, promising to never do them again, only to get seduced and then falling into the self-hatred and despair that fuel the next cycle of compulsion. When compulsions cast their spell again, promising that if we follow them they will give us all the comfort and peace we long for, we can remind ourselves of the price we will pay for believing what they say.

◆ Breaking the Spell

When a wave of compulsion has moved through it leaves us vulnerable to some of the core feelings that fuel our compulsions – fear, self-judgment, and despair. Let us take an in depth look at each of these, for if we can see how they operate, we can become free from their spell:

❖ Fear:

Can you recollect the fear that comes after a wave of compulsion? It usually makes itself known when the numbing aspect of compulsion wears off and you realize that "Oh no. I have done it again!" There is both the fear that you will never be free of your compulsion and the fear of the consequences you will now have to live.

Fear can contract you so much that all you want to do is crawl back into your compulsion. If over-eating is your compulsion, you may experience the fear of gaining weight. If you have a type of compulsion where nobody knows about it, then the fear of being found out will come rushing in. If your compulsion affects your health, the fear of what will happen to your body can be paralyzing.

To run from our fear only makes it worse. *Meeting our fear is where the healing is.* This invitation to meet our fears can bring up more fear or it can bring freedom. As Eleanor Roosevelt once said, "You gain strength, courage and confidence by every experience in which you really stop to look fear in the face."

If you are whirling and spinning in a web of confusion after the wave has moved through, it is most likely that some level of fear is there. The question "In this moment, what am I experiencing?" can focus your jumbled mind so it can see what is going on. Then if you find fear – maybe the free floating anxiety that

> *To run from our fear only makes it worse. Meeting our fear is where the healing is.*

276

restricts your chest, or the ball of dread that lives in your belly, or the band of tightness in your head that signals trepidation – name whatever you discover.

> *Anger is usually there because you are afraid in some deep part of yourself*

Stay with it as long as you can – *relating to it rather than being lost in it.* If it works for you, talk to it. This is a very young part of you that needs somebody to acknowledge it, just as children need somebody to acknowledge their fear of the dark. The more present you are for it, the more it will dissolve, leaving spaciousness and clarity in its wake. If you can't be with the fear, be with the fear of being with the fear. It does take courage to turn around and meet our fears, but as Mrs. Roosevelt reminds us, standing with fear brings healing.

If you find yourself very angry, the anger is usually there because you are afraid in some deep part of yourself – afraid you won't get what you need. The anger is trying to protect you. It also distracts your attention from whatever fear you are experiencing. Anger that is resisted becomes either very explosive or turns inward into corrosive shame. To open to anger is very freeing. As we learn how to feel it without using it for attack, it can become a very alive and pleasurable experience. As our anger is freed up, we can then work with the fear that is always there underneath it.

❖ Self-Judgment:

It is so easy to judge ourselves for being compulsive. We are trained from when we were young that being compulsive is evidence of our weakness and our willfulness. And so we judge ourselves, not seeing that this judgment helps to keep our compulsions going.

The most dramatic story I ever heard about the power of judgment to fuel our compulsions and the power of mercy to heal them came from a woman I was counseling a few years ago who was a chronic over-eater. She was able to take a huge step in her healing when she was able to transform her relationship with her mother who was in the later stages of diabetes. Her mother was at the point where her legs were going to have to be amputated. And even though her health was fragile from the diabetes, this woman still smoked.

Her mother's smoking would bring up judgment in my client that bordered on the level of fury. She felt that her mother should have been smart enough to give up smoking years ago. Because she didn't, my client felt that her mother was to blame for everything that was happening inside of her body.

> *Compulsion is a powerful force from within that is bringing enough discomfort into your life so that the only option left to you is to pay attention and meet whatever you discover with an open heart.*

This fury not only put a wedge between the two of them that was causing great heartache, but it was also keeping my client caught in a struggling mind, fueling her compulsions without her even being aware of it! Part of my work with her was to help her to see that this searing self-judgment for her mother was exactly how she related to her own compulsions.

Eventually she realized that her mother had done the best that she could with the level of understanding that she had, and rather than anger, she began to feel compassion. Their relationship became dramatically better; so much so that she finally told her mother how mad she had been and how she now understood. When she did this, her mother began to cry. She told her daughter that she was that mad at herself too, feeling that she was a total failure for not being able to stop her smoking. She also shared how tormented she had been by this self-judgment. No wonder she needed to keep numbing herself out!

This was an important moment for my client. She finally saw what we had been talking about – that what you try to control only controls you, keeping you caught in a never-ending circle of disempowerment. She was also able to see how important it was to meet compulsions with compassion and mercy. As she met her mother with mercy, she learned how to do this for herself, and her urge to be compulsive dramatically lessened! And when the mother received compassion rather than judgment for her inability to stop smoking, she was able to stop!

To access compassion, it is important to remember that you did not tumble down into your compulsion because you are stubborn, weak willed or have *screwed up* again. *Compulsion is here because it wants to teach you how to reconnect with yourself. It is a powerful force from within that is bringing enough discomfort into your life so that the only option left to you is to pay attention and meet whatever you discover with an open heart.*

After a wave of compulsion has moved through can be one of the hardest times in our lives to become merciful with ourselves, but it is also one of the most powerful. Because self-judgment can be so seductive, we can use the Second Question to begin to break its spell – "For this moment, can I let this be?" or "For this moment, can I bring compassion to this?" You can even get more specific with this question by asking, "Can I meet myself with understanding and mercy?" The energy of these questions is all about kindness and compassion. They can circumvent our knee jerk reaction to meet our experience with judgment and shame.

If your heart is closed tighter than a drum, you can ask the Open-Ended Question of, "How can I bring compassion to this?" Because this is an Open-Ended Question, it is asking our deep knowing to help us to meet ourselves in understanding and mercy. Feel the relief that you don't have to figure out how to do this!

You can also explore the skills under "When Your Heart Is Closed" in the chapter on *Loving Yourself From the Inside Out (*Page 118*). The Lost Child Meditation*, the *Ball of Love Meditation* and the *Voice of Kindness* can, each in its own way, open your heart again so that self-hatred cannot get a foothold inside you, fueling another wave of compulsion.

❖ Despair:

After a wave of compulsion passes through, the other core feeling that can engulf us is despair. One of its core voices is, "This is hopeless. I will be caught forever." Although this may be harder to let go of than self-judgment, it is still a non-truth. Nothing ever lasts – neither our difficult experiences nor our joyful ones. They are all a part of a river of experience that is heading back to its source. And the difficult ones are not here because we have *screwed up* or because God has fallen asleep on the job. The challenges in our lives are openings rather than closings. They are doorways into the healing that we long for. As Albert Einstein once said, "Within every difficult experience lies an opportunity."

To dismantle the experience of despair, you need to realize that you are a growing and continuously changing process. As you unfold, you are being molded and shaped by powers that are much greater than you. You are like those breathtakingly beautiful trees along the Washington coast that are sculpted by the great forces of nature. If you watch a limb being torn off in a wild storm, you may feel despair that the tree is being marred in that way. But over time you can see that it is this *pruning* by the forces of Life that gives the tree its unique beauty. You too, just like the windswept trees along the coastline, are being molded and shaped by powerful forces, and one day you will recognize the perfection of yourself exactly as you are.

> *The whole purpose of compulsions is to narrow down our options so we finally discover that there is truly something bigger than us in charge that is with us every step of the way.*

Another standard voice of despair is "It is bigger than I am. I will never be able to stop this.*" Both of these are true.* Compulsion *is* bigger than any of your attempts to control it. Thank God! *And you are not the one who can heal it. The whole purpose of compulsion is to narrow down your options so you finally discover that there truly is something bigger than you in charge, and this Presence is with you every step of the way.*

There will be times after a wave of compulsion has moved through when you are not interested in discovering the price you pay for being compulsive; or your mind and heart are too jumbled to work with fear, self judgment and despair; or it is all so confusing that you don't have a clue about what is going on. This is the time to use the Third Question, "Right now, what do I truly need?" This question points you into the direction of listening to the wisest part of yourself that knows how to bring balance back into any situation in your life.

If the mind is too foggy to see what would be the most healing thing to do or even if it is too resistant to listen, you can ask the Third Question in an Open-Ended way – "What is the way through this?" This is our default question and is extremely helpful in working with whatever shows up inside of us after a wave of compulsion has moved through. For just a moment or two you can let go of struggle and truly ask for help.

Again, you don't have to get an answer or even know what you are asking this question to. This question is like a ray of sunshine breaking through the stormy clouds on a dark winter day. It points to the truth that something bigger than you is in charge of your life and is waiting for the opening of your request for help. The sun may shine for only a moment, but that one moment reminds you that even though the cloud cover is thick, it doesn't stop the *sun* of support that is always with you. So let the question set things in motion even if you don't feel a thing.

② During The Wave: Meeting Feelings

As you break the spell of compulsion by paying attention after a wave has moved through, allowing yourself – without judgment – to fully feel the effects of following your compulsion again, one day you will find yourself in the middle of a wave and all of a sudden become aware of what you are doing. The story I recounted earlier about sitting on the couch with ice cream in my lap and a whole row of cookies set out on the back of the couch was the first time this happened to me. It was like waking up out of a dream and, without judgment, becoming very curious about what I was doing.

This is such a powerful time in a wave of compulsion. Here you are running away as fast as you can and, at the same time, you are running toward an imaginary cessation of your pain. With the information you discovered by paying attention after the wave has moved through – that it never brings what it promises and instead it makes you feel worse – you can stop running away and turn to meet yourself instead.

There are two things we can give ourselves at this time – the curiosity to see what is going on and the healing of compassion.

Seeing What Is Going On

The first step in meeting these feelings is to see what is going on. This isn't just *thinking about* what is going on. This is actually *experiencing it.* Turning toward yourself in this way is how you can begin to heal. With the light of your attention you can meet the feelings that are fueling your mad dash to numbing out.

Remember the Wicked Witch of the East in the film version of *The Wizard of Oz*? She had such power over everybody's life – until Dorothy discovered that no matter how scary the witch was, she dissolved when Dorothy threw water on her. That is the same power our attention has when we can bring it to whatever we are experiencing – especially in the middle of a wave of compulsion. Our attention begins to dissolve whatever is there like water dissolved the witch.

Imagine yourself in the middle of a wave of compulsion – maybe you are eating a large pizza on your own and rather than feeling better you are feeling more despair. Or possibly you are lost in your To Do list, absolutely furious at the line at the post office because it isn't going to let you get everything done. Or it could be that you are lost in an x-rated web site and it isn't bringing you the high that you were looking for.

In these situations everything is becoming more uncomfortable inside of you. Then imagine the question, "In this moment, what am I experiencing?" waking you out of the dream of reaction just like the light bulb turns on above the head of a cartoon character. Through this question you become fascinated about what is happening. That is a moment of being able to see exactly what is going on, and it is this curiosity that breaks the ever-tightening cycle of compulsion.

> *In looking, you will be able to recognize that whatever is fueling your compulsion is close to the surface and is asking to be met.*

In the beginning you will probably

> *Once that door is open just a crack and you feel the relief of being present for yourself – even if you are upset, angry, overwhelmed, afraid or sad – it all becomes workable.*

only be able to be present for a moment or two, for the urge to run away is deeply programmed. A moment or two is extremely potent. Just the willingness to be curious is powerful in and of itself. It allows the dust of reaction to settle so you can begin to see what is really going on. And in looking, you will be able to recognize that whatever is fueling your compulsion is close to the surface and is asking to be met. Even if you can't pause and be curious, know that simply asking the question has brought a moment of consciousness into your compulsion.

If nothing comes clear when you ask the question "In this moment, what am I experiencing?" you can ask it in an Open-Ended way – "What is asking to be seen?" For whenever we are compulsive, there is something that is fueling it and it needs our attention. As you ask this question, it is skillful to pause for a moment, and if a sensation or feeling reveals itself, pay attention. If it doesn't, let it go, knowing that the question will work its magic. Over time all of the feelings that fuel your compulsion will reveal themselves, not to be fixed or analyzed or understood, but to simply and powerfully be seen and transformed in the light of your compassionate attention.

A close cousin to the question, "What is asking to be seen?" is "What am I resisting?" It is evident that whenever we are in the reaction of compulsive, there is something we don't want to see. By asking to see what it is that we are resisting, the mind becomes curious rather than reactive and the chances are greater that the part we have been resisting will reveal itself. If it doesn't, let the question go and it will signal Life that you are learning how to listen.

Meeting our feelings through these questions reweaves a bond of trust. It is important to understand that healing our compulsions is much like healing a relationship where you had a major falling out. Neither one of you trusts the other. You don't trust your compulsion because it has caused so much heartache in your life. And it doesn't trust you! The only relationship you have had with it has been one of domination and annihilation, a relationship that *never* included listening. These questions are all about listening and will eventually take you to the place where you are not afraid to experience what you are experiencing.

So whenever you find yourself in the middle of a wave, the most important thing to do is to ask a question. If you dive right back in, that's okay. You didn't learn how to walk overnight and you won't learn how to respond to your compulsion overnight either. At the beginning this one little step may not seem to make much of a difference, but moments such as these have a power and a momentum of their own. They begin to open a door back to yourself. Once that door is open just a crack and you feel the relief of *being present* for yourself – even if you are upset, angry, overwhelmed, afraid or sad – it all becomes workable.

ⓑ The Healing of the Heart

The second step to healing the deep and hidden feelings that fuel a wave of compulsion is to meet them with understanding and mercy. Whatever you discover in the middle of a wave of compulsion – even if it is the unwillingness to discover anything – will respond to the question "For this moment, can I let this be?" This question adds spaciousness and non-judgmental awareness to the process. And if everything is too stirred up to even contemplate letting your experience *be*, you can go to the Open-Ended Question of "How can I bring compassion to this?"

Relearning how to be merciful with the feelings that fuel our compulsion breaks the self-judgment that keeps the cycle going. A feeling may be irrational and very scary, but it loses its power when we can *see* it and then *be* with it, even if it is just for a moment or two. Yes, these are powerful forces, but they are not more powerful than our ability to *respond* to them. The only reason they seem like such monsters is that we have resisted them. Now that we are listening to them, their power to engulf us will be greatly reduced.

The mantras we explored in *Treasure Hunting With Feelings* can also help immensely in giving our feelings the understanding and mercy that they need. "I see you. I'm here," lets the feeling know that you are willing to be with it. Because these feelings can so easily retreat back under our awareness or flare up and engulf us, the mantra, "It is okay you are here," stabilizes the lines of communication between you and the feeling. The mantra "It's okay. I understand" can melt even the most angry and terrified feeling inside of you. These words can be wonderfully soothing for our feelings at the same time they put a doorstop in our heart when it may want to slam shut again. Our heart may still close, but it can't close all the way under the influence of these two powerful words.

> *You are not trying to make your experience go away. You are giving it the space that it needs in order to let go on its own.*

283

Whatever you use to *respond* rather than *react*, these techniques are about giving the feeling space to *be*. Remember, you are not trying to make your experience go away. *You are giving it the space that it needs in order to let go on its own.* It may take awhile before whatever you are experiencing feels safe enough to let go as you support it with your full attention. As you do this, you will discover that right behind that feeling is a wide-open space, a place where everything is okay again.

It can also be helpful to reread the chapters on *Treasure Hunting*. Start with the one on *Sensations* (Page 212), for in the beginning feelings can sometimes be overwhelming. As you learn how to be with the tight fist in your belly or the uncomfortable sensation of tension all over your body, the feelings that fuel these sensations can make themselves known. Remember, what they are asking for is to be seen, heard and loved.

The feelings that fuel our compulsions have been waiting a long time for us to grow up enough so that we can do what we are talking about here – relating *to* them rather than being lost *in* them. And they have definitely been waiting our whole lives for the understanding, tenderness and mercy that will allow them to dissolve back into the free flowing aliveness that they came from.

What to Do When Nothing Is Clear

You may be so lost in your compulsion that you don't even want to see what is going on, let alone listen and respond. This is when the Third Question, asked in an Open-Ended way, truly reveals its power. Asking, "What is the way through this?" taps you into the core wisdom of Life and can be very healing in the middle of a wave of compulsion. Even just a moment of surfacing out of your compulsion and asking this question is a step down the path of your healing.

If you don't feel connected to the question, reread the part on Open-Ended Questions on Page 176. It will remind you that you are not alone. The Force at the heart of Life that breathes you and brings forth mighty oak trees out of tiny acorns is always with you, waiting for a request for help. If it is hard to hold the space that Life truly wants to help, ask for help in trusting that help is there.

Where there is awareness, there is choice, and where there is choice, there is freedom.

If you are still deeply caught in the grips of your compulsion or you have a compulsion that directly affects your ability to pay attention such as drugs and alcohol, you may not yet be able to ask a question or be present for yourself in the middle of a wave of compulsion. If so, you still have the beginning and the ending of the wave that are full of important insights and information. There will come a time for you too when *being present* for yourself is much more interesting than getting completely lost in a wave of compulsion. You will then be able to meet the feelings that are fueling your compulsion as they are happening.

◇3◇ As the Wave Begins to Build: Empowered Choice

Most of us are either not aware that we are falling into a wave of compulsion until we are completely lost in it or we don't want to acknowledge what is happening. But as we become curious, respecting and listening to our compulsions when they show up, we become attuned to their rhythms. It is then possible to wake up and be present for a wave just as it is beginning. This is the time when we have the greatest influence – the greatest possibility of making choices that are for our highest good. For *where there is awareness, there is choice, and where there is choice, there is freedom.*

Besides working with the questions, there are three other ways we can work with our compulsions at the beginning of a wave:

- ⓐ Say "No"
- ⓑ Give Options
- ⓒ Choose Your Compulsion

ⓐ Say "No"

There is a point when we have gotten to know our compulsions well and we have met enough of our feelings with our heart that we have earned the right to say "No" to the urge to be compulsive when it arises. After all we explored around how detrimental it is to try to dominate our compulsions, this may seem confusing at first. It will clear up when you understand that this is a different *No* than most of us have experienced in the past. An *Empowered No* is not *against* anything. It is *for* the good of the whole. It comes from a deep place of empowerment within us rather than from the reactive mind.

The old type of *No* comes from feeling hatred and fear toward our compulsions, hoping that if we can dominate them, they will go away and leave us alone. The controlling mind uses it to try to make us behave. And as we have all discovered, this doesn't work in the long run.

> *An Empowered No is not against anything. It is for the good of the whole. It comes from a deep place of empowerment within us rather than from the reactive mind.*

The *Empowered No* comes from the very center of our *being*, "We don't *need* to go there," it says. It comes from inside of us (where our deep knowing guides us) rather than from the top down (where our head tries to legislate our actions.) It is very clean and clear, and because of that, it has a much different feel to it. Its truth rings like a clear bell throughout our *being*.

We have to earn the right to an *empowered No*. Because our old type of *No* tried to dominate our experience, we empowered a very stubborn and rebellious part of ourselves. We say, "I am not going to be compulsive!" and it says, "Oh yes we are!" That is why there have been so many times that we have felt a deep determination to never be compulsive again, only to have the urge flare up and roar through us like a wildfire. Whatever we tried to control, controlled us.

This Rebellious One is ultimately a very healthy part of us. It says, "I won't let go until you begin to listen." Every time we listen to ourselves rather than running away, we not only untangle the web of compulsions; we also gain the respect of our Rebellious One. In this listening, the Rebellious One – whose only option to lessen the pain of our lives had been to numb out through compulsion – begins to see that we are maturing. It recognizes that we are learning how to be present for ourselves and make choices that are for the good of the whole. It can then, and only then, begin to respect our empowered *No*.

And believe me, even though the Rebellious One can be truly unbearable at times, opposing our highest intentions, when we discover our empowered *No*, it is so glad to have somebody else on board. It is like an abandoned child who has had to be completely in charge of its own life. Finally an adult, in the form of our *empowered No*, has assumed responsibility. The child, after some fussing and fighting, feels great relief.

I once knew an eight year-old boy who was as obnoxious as the Rebellious One within me used to be. He was being raised by a single parent, and he ruled the roost to the point of being almost intolerable. The first time we were alone together, he started out being as obnoxious with me as he was with his mother. Rather than reacting, I simply set very clear boundaries with him. And these boundaries were not done through raising my voice or my hand. They were done through a very firm and steady look. After that, whenever he and I spent time together, he was as loving and balanced as a young boy can be.

When he realized that he could trust that I would be clear about what was appropriate and what was not and that he could see that my *No* was *for*

> *The Rebellious One is ultimately a very healthy part of us. It says, "I won't let go until you begin to listen."*

him and not *against* him, he went back to being a delightful little boy. He, just like our compulsions, needs somebody on board who knows how to kindly but firmly set limits. And when there finally is an adult in charge, even though our compulsions (and little boys) may resist at the beginning, they are secretly relieved to have boundaries that they can trust.

The *empowered No* that I used with the little boy is the kind of *No* our compulsions can respect. It is understanding, but it is also firm with the rebellious part that just wants to be compulsive. And our no is respected *because we have cultivated the respect of that which we are saying no to!!* Because I have gained the respect of my compulsion, most of the time it can listen to my *No*. And it is a source of never ending joy that I can make wise and kind choices in my life.

❖ **Discovering Our "No" Through the Three Questions**

There may be times, even after living and practicing our empowered *No*, when we temporarily lose sight of it again. All that means is that there is something that needs to be met inside of us before there is space for a clear and empowered *No*. In many instances, with the help of the three questions we can free things up and make it easy to follow the choice of an empowered *No*.

I had an experience on September 11th, 2001, that highlights what we are talking about. When I turned on the television that morning and learned about the terrorist attack on the World Trade Center in New York City, I stood there in stunned disbelief as wave after wave of grief roared through me. Almost immediately the phone began to ring. Rather than being present for my own experience, I became present for other people, which at that time was appropriate. I went on to work with people individually and then led a group.

After the last person left, I immediately felt the urge to eat and eat and eat. For the first time in ages this feeling was so strong that the idea of going to the grocery store was very seductive. I immediately asked for help by asking my favorite version of the Third Question, "What do I need to do that is for my highest good?" Out of the fog of reaction came the knowing that the only reason I wanted to fall into my compulsion was because there was something burbling within me that needed my attention.

From an empowered place I was able to say to myself, "No, we aren't going to the store." The Rebellious One inside of me said, "Don't mess with me. We're going." Even though I was sitting on the fence, I was able to remind the Rebellious One that this only prolonged matters, making everything more painful in the long run.

Remembering that the wisest thing to do was to get curious about what was going on inside of me, I sat down in the chair on my front porch. I then asked, "In this moment, what am I experiencing?" What was most evident was the overwhelming urge to eat. As I was present for it I then asked, "What am I resisting?" Immediately I could feel the fingerlings of grief that had been ignored earlier in the day. "Can I let this be so I can be fully present for it?" was my next question. This question connected me to my heart, and because my feelings do trust my willingness to allow them space to be, the grief welled up within me. I cried and cried tears of grief for the Earth, for all the human beings who had died and for the people who had lost friends and loved ones on that tragic day. I even cried for the terrorists, for they had to be deeply wounded themselves in order to plan and celebrate such an act.

Those tears were so cleansing, opening a vast space of compassion and mercy within me. From this clear and present place the wave of compulsion met the shore of my heart and simply faded away. I was then able to be truly present for all of the people that I worked with for the rest of the day.

❖ Where Our Empowered No Takes Us

The more we work with our empowered *No*, the more we discover one of the most healing things a human *being* can discover – that we can mature to the point where we have choice about what we are going to pay attention to in our lives. And the core choice to be made is whether we are going to pay attention to the stories in our heads and all of their favorite struggles or come back into the fullness of Life as it is happening right here and right now.

Because compulsion won't let go until it teaches us how to *see* and *be* with what we are experiencing, it retrains us to use our minds as we did when we were young – to make contact with Life as it is right now. This contact is about tasting what we taste, feeling what we feel and seeing what we see. In other words, it is about experiencing what we are experiencing. And this is what, in the deepest parts of ourselves, we are truly longing for whenever we are compulsive.

That is what happened for me that day on my porch as I was feeling the grief of the terrorist attacks. After I opened to my grief, I raised my eyes and saw the autumn leaves beginning to turn gold. I heard the music of the waterfall in my pond, and I watched the

> *Our compulsions are trying to bring us to a connection with Life beyond our own individual struggles.*

play of the squirrels in my yard. I was fully *here* for Life. I realized with an even deeper commitment that this was my gift to Life, especially to the many people who lost their lives on that day. They died because of human beings who were lost in their story of struggle. In these moments of my life, where I have moved beyond my own struggles and reconnected with Life, right here, right now, I was a part of the healing of our troubled planet.

If I could free myself from the struggling mind, then so too could others. As more and more people do this, eventually humanity itself will wake up enough to reconnect with the spectacular gift that is Life and recognize how precious it is. This is what our compulsions are trying to bring us to – a connection with Life beyond our own individual struggles.

The more we wake up to Life, the more our own struggles, rather than being something to struggle with, become a wake up call. When we notice any kind of contraction – tightening our bodies, holding our breath, wanting what is not here, not wanting *what is*, feeling the urge to be compulsive – all of these become a signal that we have gotten caught again in the attic of our mind and we have a choice about whether we will stay there. With just a simple recognition of what is going on and then a remembering that we don't have to limit ourselves to this old story, we can bring our attention back into the fullness of Life and the fullness of who we truly are, right here and right now. The joy of coming home to this moment and to Life is a million times greater than any fleeting joy that compulsion can bring.

◆ Give Options

This new kind of *No* isn't the totally blanket, non-negotiable *No* that we used to use. If we can feel a clear *No* and yet there is also a pull to follow our compulsion, this is the time to look at skillful options. Let us imagine that 75% of our self feels the empowered *No* but the rest of us wants to get lost in our compulsion. When we are this close to stepping away from our old behavior, this is the time to ask the question, "Right now, what do I truly need?" Again, this is listening for what you *need*, not what you *want*. Your compulsion is trying to take care of a part of you but, as we have learned, when we take care of ourselves through compulsions, we always pay a price. Asking for clarity on your most valid needs opens a doorway to your

289

deeper knowing so you can listen for how you can take care of yourself in a way that brings balance rather than upset.

Remember, whenever you are compulsive, it is not the compulsion that you are wanting. You are trying to get to the temporary peace and connection that compulsion brings to you. How can you get that peace and that connection in a skillful way? That is what the question, "Right now, what do I truly need?" is all about.

Most of the time when you are this close to not following your compulsion, the wisest choice is to place your attention elsewhere by doing something else. Through this you begin to learn that you have the choice about what you are going to pay attention to in your life. You also learn that there is so much more going on in Life than just your struggles. You can transform this urge to be compulsive through physical movement, through writing, through speaking your truth, through singing, dancing, washing windows and even through gratitude and generosity. So, rather than following your compulsion, you can give yourself options – other more skillful things that will take care of what the compulsions were trying to take care of.

You can take this question, "Right now, what do I truly need?" deeper by changing it to "What do *you* truly need?" You ask it directly to whatever experience you are having right now – a headache, a vise of anxiety in your chest, a ball of anger in your belly. This question not only focuses your attention, it also signals the feeling or sensation that is grabbing you that you are willing to listen to what it needs. Through this listening, the feeling will get the attention and spaciousness it needs in order to calm down again.

Take a moment to remember a time in your life where you were overwhelmed, scared or angry and imagine it deeply enough that you can feel it in your body. Now imagine a person whom you deeply trust saying to you, "I am here for you. What do you need?" If you let this person in, your body will immediately soften, the intensity of the feeling will lessen, and your heart will begin to open, too.

> *Know that when you are sitting on the fence, it is because there is a part of you which truly believes that being compulsive will make you feel better.*

That is exactly what our feelings need and we very rarely give this to them. We are so far away – resisting, hating, and fearing them – that we have never contemplated the possibility of giving them the gift of our undivided attention – of listening to what *they* need. Once you learn how to listen through the magic of these questions, your feelings will trust you more, and rather than needing to rebel at the limits you feel are appropriate, they will respect your empowered *No*.

At the beginning you may not have a clue about what you need, but know that every time you ask, you are awakening your inner radar. Even if you ask them and then immediately dive into your compulsion, the questions will be working for you, making it a little easier the next time to listen to your own deep knowing. As you work with them, you will discover that they will begin to live you, bringing clarity, insight, wisdom and nourishment in their wake.

❖ 50/50

Sometimes only 50% of our self will be feeling an empowered *No* and the other half will want to follow the urge to be compulsive. This is the time where the work we have done with noticing the price we pay for being compulsive can help us immensely. When you are sitting on the fence, it is because there is a part of you which truly believes that being compulsive will make you feel better. You may not even be aware of this but it is there nonetheless.

With the information you have gathered by paying attention after a wave of compulsion has passed through, you can remind yourself that it doesn't make you feel better and that may do the trick. Or your compulsion may come roaring back and say, "Leave me alone. All I want to do is go into oblivion." It is important to not use force at this critical moment. Instead, what I say is, "Yes, I know that you truly feel that this will help but I remind you that it doesn't make us feel better, and it will surely make us feel worse." Remember, your compulsion is trying to take care of you. It is a lumbering beast on automatic pilot. But it is a beast that can be educated.

When I am at this point, I like to remind myself how good I will feel if I don't follow my compulsion, and my Rebellious One, just like a lumbering beast with a puzzled look of understanding, will often say, "Oh yeah, that's right." But I don't just leave it high and dry. I usually give my urge to be compulsive another option. I go back to what we explored in the last section by asking for help in seeing what would be the kindest choice. Some of my favorites are warm baths, brisk walks, swinging on my swing, talking to a friend, or crawling into bed with a

Whenever you are compulsive, it is never the object of compulsion that you are longing for. What you are longing for is a nourishing and sustaining connection with yourself and with Life.

good book.

When you are sitting on the fence, it also helps to remind yourself that whenever you are compulsive, it is never the object of compulsion that you are longing for. It is something much deeper than that. What you are longing for is a nourishing and sustaining connection with yourself and with Life. You don't have to figure out what it is. Simply ask your deep knowing within to clarify this for you. At first you may not hear a thing, but Open-Ended Questions will prepare the groundwork that is needed in order for you to begin to truly listen to yourself.

The day I realized that it was never my compulsion that I was truly longing for was the day my daughter got married. If you have ever experienced this, you know what a wonderful but extremely stressful time this is.

At the end of the day, I headed straight to the refrigerator and, in blind reaction, started eating right off of the shelves. I hadn't done this for years! Next I took some things out of the refrigerator and started making a plate, and as I did so, I began to calm down and ask the question, "In this moment, what am I experiencing?" Without the least bit of judgment I noticed what I was doing and immediately said to myself, "I understand. It has been a very high energy day with a lot of joy and a lot of challenges. And you are trying to take care of yourself through eating."

The urge to eat was like a cornered animal at that point, and I knew I needed to be very gentle. I said, "Yes, you can eat all of this, but I remind you that tomorrow you will feel quite rotten." I was far enough along in cultivating an understanding and respectful relationship with my compulsion that it was able to hear me. The next time I looked down at the plate of food, it didn't have the power over me that it had just a few moments ago.

I then asked, "Right now, what do I truly need?" The first option I thought of was what I call deep comfort. All I needed was a quilt, an open heart and the willingness to take care of myself in a way that is kinder than through my compulsion. I said to my compulsion, "Let's go snuggle on the couch." Much to my joy, it let go of its grip and I was able to choose that option.

I threw the plate of food away, took off my wedding clothes, and got into my favorite pajamas. I then grabbed my big fluffy quilt, wrapped myself in it and lay down on the couch. As I put one hand over my belly and the other over my heart, I began to gently rock. I immediately felt a nourishing connection

> *Slowly the Rebellious One lets go of its grip in the face of our willingness to work with it.*

with myself. In this safety, I was able to recognize the fear that had been festering all day long underneath my ordinary awareness. I could see that this was what the Rebellious One had been trying to take care of through numbing out with food. My heart then opened, and I was back into a kind and healthy relationship with myself.

❖ Negotiation

Sometimes when I offer another option, there will be some grumbling going on inside. "I don't want that," says the Rebellious One, "I want my compulsion." There is no accident it sounds like a two year-old. That is how young our urge to be compulsive can get. This is where negotiation works well.

The place I discovered the power of negotiation was around exercise. For most of my life, I was in relationship with exercise just like I was in relationship with my compulsions – I was demanding and dominating. I would either exercise in ways that were really boring or I would exercise to exhaustion, only to have all of my *have tos*, *got tos*, and *shoulds* foster their opposite, *I won't*!

So for years I didn't exercise. Because this wasn't helping my health and because all of my attempts to muscle myself into submission had failed, I began to create a relationship with my Rebellious One. I realized it wouldn't even consider the smallest of exercise programs because I had been such a demanding and dominating taskmaster. Now I exercise on a daily basis and do it with great joy. My path back to exercising began when I saw that following my Rebellious One was just shooting myself in my own foot! Of course, I started small and spent a lot of time noticing and reminding myself how good I felt after I exercised.

Slowly the Rebellious One let go of its grip in the face of my willingness to work with it. Every once in a while it will try to take over again and rebel against any exercises. If reminding it that exercising will make us feel better doesn't do the trick, I negotiate with it. I say, "Let's only do 15 minutes on the bike today." And that usually works. But there are still times when it isn't going to listen to any negotiating whatsoever. And those are the times I say, "Okay. Let's not exercise today." The more I negotiate and listen, the more consistent my exercise becomes! In fact, exercise is now pure joy rather than a chore.

I was then able to transfer this ability to negotiate to my compulsion. There are times when my compulsion can't listen to my empowered *No* and it isn't interested in any other option other than to be compulsive. I now can negotiate with it. I may say, "I understand that you are absolutely certain that you need to be compulsive. Rather than a whole chocolate bar, how about having just a bite or two and really savoring it, letting it melt in your mouth?" And a good deal of the time, because I have cultivated a kind and respectful relationship with my compulsion, it can still listen to me at this point and will be amenable to negotiation.

There are times when I forget and push myself too far – both around exercise and my entire life – and the Rebellious One will let me know in no uncertain terms that I am getting out of balance again. In so many ways my Rebellious One and I are now partners in the journey of awakening. Rather than having to follow it down the path of making unskillful choices, I listen to it and then ask myself, "What do I need to do that is for my highest good?"

Choose Your Compulsion

Sometimes an Empowered No is nowhere to be found. All we want to do is crawl into our compulsion and get lost. In addition, our attempts at exploring what is going on and offering options or negotiations fall on deaf ears. All is not lost. *For whatever we are experiencing, there is a reason why we are experiencing it. It is part of our path back into a deep and abiding relationship with ourselves and with Life.*

Remember, we are not compulsive because we are weak willed ninnies at the beck and call of urges that are out to get us. We are compulsive because there is something we need to see, to embrace, to heal in order to become conscious human beings. So when a wave does come, it is here for a reason.

When a wave of compulsion doesn't dissipate upon the shore of your curiosity and instead looks like it is going to crash right on top of you, one of the most powerful things to do is to *choose your compulsion*! You literally say to yourself, "I choose to be compulsive." Even though this may seem crazy at first glance, I assure you it is one of the quickest ways to take your power back from your compulsion.

Why is this so powerful? Remember what it used to be like at the beginning of a wave of compulsion before you became curious? You wanted your compulsion but you didn't want it. It was like driving down the road of Life with one foot on the accelerator and one foot on the brake. Most of the time the compulsion won because you fueled it through your resistance. Compulsions thrive in resistance! From little urges they grow into big monsters when you try to fight them. You shift the energy when you say, "I choose this!"

Choosing his compulsion was the doorway for a client I worked with a number of years ago. His core compulsion was alcohol. It was the way he tried to take care of himself after a full day at work. He often had resistance to going home and being with wife and four children! He could easily be overwhelmed by the intensity of it all and found he could hide in the soft haze of a few drinks. But soon a few drinks were not enough and over-drinking began to invade his life.

> *Compulsions thrive in resistance! From little urges they grow into big monsters when you try to fight them. You shift the energy when you say, "I choose this!"*

The more he distanced himself from his family through alcohol, the more the family would try to get his attention, often through fighting and confrontation. The more the family struggled at night, the more he would drink and the more he would drink the more struggles there would be. He didn't know how to get out of this ever-tightening spiral. It was when his health deteriorated to the point that the doctors told him that he should cut back on the drinking that he came to me.

We worked with becoming aware of the price he paid by taking care of himself this way, and then we worked with becoming curious about exactly what was fueling this urge to over-drink. He was able to see that one of the main fuels was his self-judgment. His inner conversation was full of self-shaming ideas, making it very unpleasant to be himself. One of his favorite judgments was that he was too selfish. It didn't matter that he worked in a service-oriented job and that he brought home the only income. All that mattered was that he called himself selfish for drinking. With venom dripping off of his words he told me once, "I am so selfish when I drink, for I am putting my needs above the needs of my family." When he spoke this, his whole face changed, transforming into a dark cloud of self-loathing.

When he understood that this so-called selfishness was just an old survival system that was in place because he didn't know how to take care of his overwhelm any other way, his heart began to open again. He could now work with his compulsion rather than always struggling with it. As his compulsion calmed down through his curiosity and compassion, he began to learn how to take care of himself in ways that allowed him to keep his center, even at night with the family.

As he expanded his capacity to *see* and *be* with himself exactly as he was, he began to feel his empowered *No*. He wasn't using this a*gainst* his drinking. He was using it *for* the health of himself and his family. He experienced more and more nights when he didn't need to drink. At times his drinking would flare up again, and every time it did, he learned something new.

295

During a crisis at work he had a two-week spell where the Rebellious One took over again and all he wanted to do was drink. The urge was so strong that it wouldn't respond to any of the skills he had been learning. At first he was freaked out. "Oh, no! It has come back again and I will never be free of it." When he came to see me, we worked with that fear. As he got some space around it, he remembered that *even though the urge to drink was very strong, it was not stronger than his ability to be curious about it.*

We then began to explore the idea of choosing this period of compulsion. I watched his whole *being* change from disempowerment to empowerment. He could see that as long as he fought with it, he lost himself in the struggle. As soon as he said, "I choose this," his attention was free from struggle, and he could again be curious about what wanted to be healed inside of him through this period of compulsion.

Now that he was centered again in his own process, he felt that the most important thing he could do was work with the question, "What do I need to do or be in this situation that is for the highest good for both myself and my family?" He let this question go and allowed it to work its magic from underneath his everyday awareness.

The next day, while absentmindedly raking leaves in his yard, it came to him with deep clarity that it was more important to him to be with his family than it was to isolate inside of himself through his drinking. This wasn't something that he was going to try to *do* in his life. This was a deep knowing within him that felt right and true. Along with this came his empowered *No* again where he was able to say "Yes" to a balanced and healthy life.

When he shared this with me, he was a bit perplexed at the same time that he was thrilled. He said that for the two weeks leading up to this revelation from within, his inner experience had been that if he didn't follow the urge to drink, he would be unable to live. The urge was that urgent. And yet now, even when it came through that strongly, when he said "Yes" to it, he could then easily say "No" with a ring of truth that the compulsion absolutely heard. And rather than falling into a black void, he felt more alive. He was amazed and thrilled at the power of both his new *Yes* and his empowered *No*. So was his family!

> *Choosing your compulsion isn't giving in to it. It is holding the intention to be curious about what is going on.*

Choosing your compulsion isn't giving in to it. It is holding the intention to be curious about what is going on. Curiosity that starts at the very beginning of a wave of compulsion is a wide-open, spacious curiosity. It is a fascination about what you can learn, as you consciously go through a wave of compulsion.

> *When you hold the intention to be spacious and curious throughout a wave of compulsion, there is always something you can learn.*

To enter a wave of compulsion in curiosity is a little bit like having gone out with someone for over six months and all of a sudden discovering they have a scar on their nose. It is just amazing to you that you have never noticed that before. You didn't notice because you weren't really looking at this person. The same is true with your compulsion. You haven't been taught to pay attention. When you hold the intention to be spacious and curious throughout a wave of compulsion, *there is always something you can learn.*

Every once in a while, when I am very tired and my life is very busy, I will come to the place where I just need to comfort myself through my compulsion. I then yield to it, but remind it I will be as present as I possibly can throughout the wave. When I go through it with deep curiosity, I always learn something more about myself and about my healing. Because of this, I have long times without even a hint of a compulsive urge. Also, my waves are much smaller than they used to be (a couple of bites of a food that isn't good for me rather than a whole package) and their duration is shorter too.

There is another empowering gift that comes from choosing your compulsion, and that is giving yourself the best. Let's say food is your compulsion. Rather than fighting the urge, say to yourself that you can eat whatever you want with no guilt and no restrictions. Remember, this permission can dramatically minimize the urge to be compulsive. Do this mindfully. Ask yourself what do you *really* want to eat. Think of what taste, texture and temperature you want to experience. The chances are that if you eat what you truly want, you will end up eating less. Then when you do eat, be present for the experience. Really taste what you are eating. Really enjoy it.

If the voice that says you are bad for pleasuring yourself in this way pipes up and tries to rain on your parade, tell it that what you are doing is okay. We have been so trained to hate ourselves for being compulsive that we rarely enjoy our compulsive times! And often our urge to be compulsive is trying to take care of a deep need for comfort. So choose the highest quality of your compulsion that you can think of and then open to it. It is amazing what you will discover.

Meeting ourselves before, during and after a wave of compulsion is not a logical, systematic process. Sometimes you will be able to be present at the beginning, sometimes only in the middle and sometimes not until after the storm has blown through. And you will go through cycles and levels of each one of the parts of yourself that were boxed up inside of you. Some days will be easy and some days will be more difficult. At times it can be scary and overwhelming as you turn toward your experience, and sometimes it will bring some of the greatest joy you have ever known.

Remember, to stay in control and manage your feelings through compulsion (and trying to manage the compulsion itself) is to live in a low-grade fever of struggle, never discovering the healing that you long for. To meet and transform your experience through the healing light of attention and mercy is to experience at times the fever of purification. But this fever is cleansing and healing.

At Any Time

Let us now explore some of the other things you can do no matter where you are in a wave of compulsion. Each of these may look like the smallest of things – almost insignificant – and yet they are powerful beyond words. As someone once said, "Great things come in small packages." This is certainly true for each of the gifts we can give to ourselves around our compulsions:

◇ Ask For Help

The belief that we are alone is at the heart of the suffering that human beings experience, and it shows up dramatically around compulsions. Our attempts to control our compulsions only enhance our sense of isolation and the corresponding belief that we, and we alone, can free ourselves from our heartaches. It could be said that one of the reasons compulsions arise is to bring us up against the wall of control over and over again until we begin to get a glimmer that there really is something bigger than we are in charge.

We are not dancing the dance of Life alone. There are forces much wiser than we are that are with us every moment, every hour, every day. Our forgetting thistruth doesn't eradicate it. Just as the sun doesn't go away when it is cloudy, the truth that we are not alone never goes away. It is just covered over by the clouds of our forgetting.

The power of asking for help is that it temporarily parts the clouds by opening a doorway where the wisdom and support that is waiting for an

> *To meet and trans-form your experi-ence through the healing light of attention and mercy is to experience at times the fever of purification. But this fever is cleans-ing and healing.*

opening can come in. Just like a stuffy room only needs a little opening for fresh air to come in, the forces at the heart of Life can work with even a momentary request for help in the middle of the challenges of our lives. Asking for help is powerful. Jesus alluded to it when he said, "Ask, and it shall be given you; seek and ye shall find; knock and it shall be opened unto you. Everyone who asks, receives; and every-one who seeks, finds."

With Open-Ended Questions, you have a simple and direct way to ask for help. They don't cloud the process by getting your struggling mind involved. You ask and then let the ques-tion go, allowing it to work for you. And of all the Open-Ended Questions, "What is the way through this?" is the most basic. It is our default question. It truly takes efforting out of the equation for it is asked directly to the powers at the heart of Life. With this question, for a few moments you are letting go of trying to do it all by yourself and are acknowledging that something is there waiting to help you.

Two of my other favorite ways to ask for help in an Open-Ended way are: "What is Love's wisdom in this moment?" and "What do I need to say, do or be that is for my highest good/the highest good of everybody concerned?" After years of working with this last question, it all boiled down to just two words, "Show me." Whenever I say this, I am saying to the Intelligence at the heart of Life, "You have given me this challenge and I am open to your wisdom and support in moving through it."

We need to remember that we are asking for help in a new way. This is not the beseeching, demanding request for help that we are used to. Instead, we ask for help and then let it go, knowing that our question will do its work from underneath our everyday consciousness. Sometimes the answer will come immediately and sometimes it will take longer, for answers come in the time and in the manner that is for our highest good. *But be assured that an-swers will come.* So be willing to ask and keep on asking. The help that is always there for us simply awaits the opening of a question.

> *We are not dancing the dance of Life alone. There are forces much wiser than we are that are with us every moment, day.every hour, every day.*

◇ Breathe!

Breath is a magical tool that is always with you no matter what is happening in your life. If you become connected to the deep and powerful healer that is your breath, everything in your life becomes much easier. Breath is all about reconnection. Whenever you are compulsive, you are not hungry for your compulsion. You are hungry for connection with yourself and with Life. Breath provides this connection through opening what has been closed, calming what has been turbulent, and clearing what has been cloudy.

The most basic of breaths is just one deep breath. If you added these throughout your day the chances of the confusion of compulsion taking you over would be a lot less. And even if it does, breath can keep you open so that you can gather all the treasures that lie hidden in a wave of compulsion.

Besides the deep breath, we have explored other ways to use the breath to keep the process of healing moving along:

- ❖ The *Balloon Breath* to open up a physical or emotional space that is contracted. (See Page 126.)

- ❖ The *Deep Natural Breath* in order to calm the mind. (See Page 133.)

- ❖ The *Breath of Fire* to clear things up. (See Pages 225-6)

- ❖ The *Ha Breath* to open up emotions. (See Page 225)

◇ Be Merciful

One of the core reasons that we have been cultivating the ability to be curious is so that we can be present enough to touch ourselves with the healing of our own heart. As Saint Exupery's beloved character the Little Prince said, "It is with the heart that one sees rightly. What is essential is invisible to the eye (mind)." Healing is about meeting ourselves with understanding and mercy, and no matter where we are in a wave of compulsion, what we truly need is mercy. Just saying the word *mercy* over and over again can have a very healing effect. This opens a space around whatever we are experiencing. If this word is not enough, reread the section on *Meeting Ourselves in Our Own Hearts* at the end of the chapter on *Loving Ourselves From the Inside Out* (Page 107).

Here are some other ideas and techniques that can help in opening your heart again:

❖ Forgive your compulsion. It has been trying to take care of you.

❖ Forgive yourself for being compulsive. It is not a defect. It is a doorway.

❖ Be a self-judgment sleuth. See what your shaming voices are doing, rather than believing what they are saying.

❖ Imagine what you would do for a child who is experiencing what you are experiencing. Then give whatever you discover to yourself.

❖ Imagine what someone who really loves you would say or do for you and then give this to yourself.

❖ Know that your perfection includes your imperfections!

❖ You are enough!

❖ Open your heart to how closed your heart is to yourself!

❖ Acceptance is magic.

❖ Accept whatever is happening in your life. It is okay. You are okay.

❖ You are worthy of love.

❖ Live in the question, "What is the kind choice here?"

❖ Live in the question, "How can I bring compassion to myself?"

❖ Look at yourself in the mirror and wink!

❖ See all your feelings as little children in need of your understanding and mercy.

❖ Use the 3 statements: 'I see you. I'm here.' 'It's okay you are here.' 'It's okay. I understand.'

❖ Breathe tenderness into your pain.

❖ Rock yourself

❖ Bring your hand to your heart.

❖ Practice the Heart Breath on Page 251.

◇ Live in Questions

Live in questions! Live in questions! Live in questions!

Enough cannot be said about living in questions. With the Check-In Questions you can lift the clouds of reaction, open the prison gates of your heart and begin to listen to something deeper than your reactionary mind. With Open-Ended Questions you can tap into support and clarity, no matter what is happening in your life.

Remember, you aren't asking questions to figure anything out. With the Check-In Questions all you are doing is inviting yourself to be present for exactly what is happening right now in a compassionate and curious way. With Open-Ended Questions you are unlocking the door to a wisdom that is greater than you.

The wonderful thing is that you don't have to be curious, trustful, calm or even clear in order to ask questions. All you need do is ask. They will work their magic from underneath your everyday awareness.

Play with the 2 sets of 3 questions. Also revisit the list of other questions on Page 185. If none of these questions call to you, live in the question, "What are my questions?" And when all else fails, say the Third Open-Ended Question over and over again – "What is the way through this?" Allow this question to fan the tiny flicker of trust that knows that help is waiting for the opening of your questions.

◇ Thank Your Compulsion

It takes the wind out of the sails of our compulsions when we thank them. Compulsion is just a lumbering beast made out of old patterns and it thinks it has to take care of you in this way. When you thank it, it becomes putty in your hand, for compulsions are just like people; they deeply respond to appreciation. In fact, they lose their power in the face of gratitude.

I first learned the power of gratitude through the story I told you earlier about my mentor thanking the smoker within her every time she lit up a cigarette. For six months she did this, reminding the part of her that wanted to smoke that at the end of the six months they would have a parting of the ways. You may recall that she got bronchitis two weeks before she stopped smoking and never smoked again. That is the power of gratitude.

There is a wonderful Buddhist story I told in my first book, *Belonging to Life,* about Sahka, the ruler of the Devas, that reveals the power of appreciation. While Sahka was out visiting the far reaches of his land, a bitter, potbellied dwarf came to visit the castle. Finding the King absent, he sat himself upon the throne. This was an act of supreme sacrilege. Sahka's followers tried to bully, shame, taunt and scare the dwarf away, but he grew bigger and stronger in exact proportion to the resistance to his presence.

The King was called back from his journey in order to get rid of this unwanted guest. Upon entering the throne room, he draped his robe over the shoulders of the dwarf and knelt in respect before him. With every act of welcoming, appreciation and recognition, the dwarf became smaller and smaller, uglier and more bitter, until finally he simply vanished. The King truly understood that nothing could withstand the power of appreciation and gratitude. This is especially true for our compulsions.

Move!

Who you really are is a field of free flowing energy that at its core is aliveness and joy.

When you are compulsive, you have closed again, contracting into patterns of holding and resisting. Underneath that contraction is the longing to be connected again to the free flowing aliveness that you truly are. Whenever you find yourself contracted, ask the wisest part of yourself how you can open up again. Breathing is the simplest way but not the only one. As we explored many times throughout this book, you can sing, dance, walk, swing, skip, clean the house, shake your body, yell at the top of your lungs.

Remember, when you are contracted there is a part of you that wants to stay that way. It truly feels that staying contained is where safety is. But the truth is that safety comes from *opening* to the process Life is giving you and allowing it to take you where it needs to. So open yourself through movement and see how much better it feels than staying contracted.

Speak Your Truth

Speaking our truth is what the First Question is all about – to experience what we are experiencing. I cannot stress enough how important this is on this journey back to ourselves. Over and over again, I listen to people who are struggling and then find themselves struggling with their struggle and sometimes even struggling with the struggle that they are struggling! What they say over and over again is that stopping for a moment, asking the question, "In this moment, what am I experiencing?" and then speaking the truth of what they are experiencing to themselves, cuts through the story around what they are truly experiencing. There is some part of them, even if they are very unconscious, that knows that acknowledging what is happening is a way out of the maze of struggle.

Some people, in the very beginning of their awakening, may only be able to recognize what is going on for just a moment before they fall back into the

> *Nothing can destroy that momentary awareness of the calm in the middle of the storm that comes from* being present *for yourself as you are.*

struggle in their heads. But that is okay. Remembering and forgetting is a part of the process. Nothing can destroy that momentary awareness of the calm in the middle of the storm that comes from *being present* for themselves as they are. Rather than being caught in the whirling and spinning energy of their old patterns, for those moments they are *relating to* what is happening rather than being lost in the middle of it, and that makes a huge difference.

We can amplify what we discover in two different ways. The first is to write it down. Wherever you are in a wave of compulsion, you can get a pad of paper out, ask yourself, "In this moment, what am I experiencing?" and start writing. Put a pen to paper and let it flow. Nobody is going to look at this. You can burn it right after you are done if you need to. To write this way is the safety valve on the pressure cooker of your experience. Keep on writing down what your experience is right now. You can also keep an *Awareness Diary* that we explored in the section on *Weather Reporting*. This isn't free-flowing writing. This is about keeping track of short statements that tell the truth about what you are experiencing.

The second way to clarify the truth of your experience is to speak it to another person. It can be helpful to set up a contact person in advance – someone whom you trust to listen and not judge, and someone fairly easy to get a hold of. Then, when you discover yourself somewhere in a wave of compulsion, this is the time to call them and speak the truth of what you are experiencing. Remember, they are not listening to help you, to fix you or to judge you. They are simply listening so that you can listen to yourself.

◇ It's Okay

These two little words – *It's okay* – are a core part of lasting healing. When you try to control something, it controls you. When you fight something, it fights back. *It's okay* takes you out of that arena of struggle and calms things down. As you let go of struggling with what is going on, you can begin to see more clearly what you need to do in any situation that will be for your highest good.

So tuck these words in your heart and say them in all situations – when you're feeling tired, frustrated, compulsive, overwhelmed, sad, mad, confused or all of the above. For they can take you out of the struggling mind, opening the doorway into the wellspring of wisdom and love that is always with you.

◇ Help in Remembering

When we are compulsive, the parts of ourselves that don't know how to trust, to connect and to love have taken us over again. That is why at times it can be so hard to remember what we are exploring here. We have been trained in contracting and reacting. What we are exploring here is its opposite – opening and responding.

In order to remember what we most need to remember when we need to remember it, there are two things we can do. The first is to go back through the book and write down the ideas and techniques that call to you. If you have underlined passages, use those. If you haven't, open the book randomly, begin to read, and write down whatever feels right to you on an index card. Through these notes, you will have a written memory of exactly what it is that will help you back to your center and you can tuck them in your pocket or purse, tape them to your mirror, put them on your refrigerator, or use them as book marks.

At times you will come across a card and look at what you have written and it won't make sense in that moment. That is very normal. Even though the part of you that can remember your own truth wrote it down, it may very well be the part that forgets that is rereading it. Even if it doesn't make sense, to reread your own truth will touch you on some level. So don't throw your note cards away. Let them wander around your house, only to pop up and remind you at the most interesting times. I have found my cards in books that I haven't read for years or under the bed when looking for a shoe. I also leave a pile of them beside my bed, and when I need a moment of remembering, I pick one randomly. Because it is a written memory of what has worked for me, these cards always contain some gift – even when I read them years later.

A friend of mine who has been working with the manuscript of this book reads a part of it everyday and then writes down the points that ring true to him on a business card. He then tucks this card in his wallet where he has access to it as he moves throughout his day.

The other thing you can do to help

> *When we are compulsive, the parts of ourselves that don't know how to trust, to connect and to love have taken us over again.*

remember is to write down the three questions and put them in your car, all over the house and even at work. I have put them in the refrigerator, under my pillow, on the dashboard of my car, on my toothpaste, across from the toilet. You can write all three down or just one. Whenever you come across them, pause and ask them internally. And whatever response you get is exactly what is supposed to be, even if it is resistance to the questions!

The Pause That Refreshes

To break the spell of compulsion, it can be very helpful to just pause for a moment, feel your breath and become aware that there is a lot more going on in your life than just the urge to be compulsive. To pause can also remind you that you are a part of a greater process. There are more stars than there are grains of sand on every beach of the Earth! And all of Life dances in such synchronicity that we can time the returning of the morning sun to a millisecond. You are a part of a highly intelligent, highly orchestrated unfolding, and the river of your experience, especially your compulsion, is exactly what you need in order to become a truly conscious human *being*.

Say Good-bye

There does come a time to say "Good-bye" to your compulsion. It is part of a survival system that you needed at one time in your life, but as you rediscover a deep and abiding relationship with yourself and with the wellspring of wisdom and love that is within you, you will no longer need this old way of taking care of yourself. It can be skillful to say "Good-bye." Saying "Good-bye" acknowledges all that your compulsion has given to you and taught you. It also clearly affirms that a cycle has ended in your life.

This *Good-bye* may contain some sadness, for it can be important to grieve the loss of finding comfort and connection in that way. Every once in a while, I remember with fondness the joy of crawling into a whole carton of ice cream. Of course, that does not include the devastation that comes in its wake. But a part of my compulsion was the feeling of being enfolded and loved by the experience of consuming food. And even though the ways I bring this connection into my life now are much richer and more satisfying, I did need to grieve the loss of this old friend, and I needed to say good-bye.

One of the ways you can do it is to light a candle every day for a week to honor your compulsion and, as you do this, thank it for all it has taught you. You can write letters to your compulsion and then burn them. You can buy a greeting card that acknowledges the end of a relationship and then send it to your compulsion at your address. There are many ways to say *Good-bye*. If it is time, hold the intent of *Good-bye* and let it unfold as it will.

Core Ideas in Treasure Hunting with Compulsions

❖ Compulsion is not an enemy that needs to be conquered. It is also not here to destroy us because we are weak-willed or defective. It is a survival system that has taken care of us until we could learn how to be present for ourselves.

❖ Treasure hunting with compulsions works at the beginning of a wave of compulsion, when you are lost in the middle of it, and even after it has passed through.

❖ The price you pay for compulsion isn't worth the temporary benefits.

❖ We finally realize that compulsions never bring us what they promise – peace and comfort – and that in fact, they do the exact opposite.

❖ When we respond to our experience, we are not trying to make the experience go away; we are giving it the space it needs in order to let go on its own.

❖ You usually feel fear and despair after your compulsion moves through; curiosity is the key to transforming your experience.

❖ The vulnerability that fuels your compulsion needs you.

❖ Your Empowered *No* is not *against* anything. It is *for* the good of the whole. It kindly and firmly sets limits that can be clearly understood and heard once you have gained the respect of your compulsion.

❖ You have to earn the right to an Empowered *No*.

❖ You can negotiate and compromise with your compulsion.

❖ We have been trained all our lives to contract and react. It is in opening and responding that we will know the healing we long for.

❖ There will come a time when following your compulsion is no longer interesting.

❖ PS: *Love Is.* Let it in.

✦ FULL CIRCLE ✦

Like all of the great myths that speak about finding lost treasures, what we have explored in this book is a journey, a journey back into a deep and abiding relationship with ourselves and with Life. This takes time and it takes courage. (Courage is a French word that means "big heart"). And as in all the great myths, the rewards far outweigh the rigors of the journey.

Because this book has come into your life, you are on this journey back to yourself with compulsion as your guide. Some days will be easier than others. Some days you will be able to move right through a wave of compulsion and some days not. Some days you will be able to be merciful and some days not. Some days you will use all that we have explored to try to stop your compulsion and some days you will use it to be curious. Some days you will be able to live in the questions and some days you won't be able to even remember them. Some days you will be able to stay with yourself and some days you will need to run. Some days you can pause and remember that it is all a part of a wise and benevolent process and some days you will be filled with doubt and fear.

There will be times when you will feel like you are making lots of progress only to experience the sense of backsliding. But there is no such thing as backsliding! The old adage that Life is about taking three steps forward and two back is just a perception of the human mind. It is all forward progress, even when it seems like everything is all falling apart. Life is a very intentional, highly organized process that is giving you exactly what you need in order to awaken. There will come a time that you will be able to see and to live in the truth that Life can be trusted, opened to and fully lived.

Even though it takes time to unravel the web of compulsion, what we are exploring is really the short cut. Again I refer to the story of the tortoise and the hare. We were like the hare, thinking we could dash to the finish line by managing our compulsions. As we failed over and over, we found ourselves back at the starting line again. In the meantime the tortoise, which is slowly and surely unraveling the boxed-up parts that are fueling compulsions, gets closer and closer to the finish line!

> *Because this book has come into your life, you are on this journey back to yourself with compulsion as your guide.*

Even though it is gradual, and even though it is difficult at times to be present for your experience, it is well worth it! Know that each moment that you turn toward yourself with curiosity and understanding is another step on the path to freedom. Each time that you can open rather than close, even if it is opening around how closed you are, and each time you can *respond* rather than *react* and can connect rather than contract, it is a healing moment.

> *The wonderful thing about healing and being healed by your compulsion is that it isn't just for you. You are a part of the Earth that is being healed, and as you heal, so too does the Earth.*

Without even noticing, there will be longer times between the waves of compulsion and when the waves do come they won't be so overwhelming. You will become more merciful with yourself and others and more trusting in the entire unfolding of your life. The pendulum of experience will still swing from side to side but you will be more fascinated by it rather than being caught in reaction. And the more fascination you discover, the quicker you will be able to respond to a wave of compulsion when it comes.

For all of us, as we relearn how to open to Life, we will forget and remember and forget and remember what we have explored a thousand times. It doesn't matter. It is all a part of the process of awakening. Tens of thousands of people have walked this path before you and have experienced the same remembering and forgetting as you. And tens of thousands will walk after you, aided by your willingness to return over and over again to the life and the challenges you have been given.

Whenever you find yourself despairing, feeling that you have lost your way, just take one deep breath and say, "It's okay." For whether you feel it or not, it is. And if you need a deeper remembering, go out and lie down on the Earth. Feel her holding you as you dance through oceans of space and see her breathing through you the river of breath that is Life. Then imagine the possibility of having a deep and abiding love affair with yourself and with Life. Imagine a life of vibrancy, authenticity, trust, peace and spontaneity that is pure joy to experience. It is possible to be this connected, to be this comfortable in your own skin. *It is possible to trust yourself and trust your life enough so that you are healed to your core. It is not only possible, it is your birthright, and your compulsion, if listened to, will take you there.*

The wonderful thing about healing and being healed by your compulsion is that it isn't just for you. You are a part of the Earth that is being healed, and as you heal, so too does the Earth. The challenges you have been given are challenges that we all experience. The compulsion you have is experienced by presidents and by teenagers. That self-hate you get lost in is felt by great opera singers and by children living on the streets of Calcutta. That despair that overtakes you is experienced by women living in abusive relationships and by world leaders who are trying to make a difference. That fear you know so well is felt by children going to school every morning and by the mothers who are seeing them off. You have been given your compulsion and all of the fear, self-hate and despair that come with it in order to wake up. And as you meet yourself with understanding and mercy, you clear the pathway for every other human *being* to be healed in that way, too.

So be willing to show up. Tuck the words "it's okay" into your heart and then open to your life. Live in questions so that they become a beacon of light on the path back to yourself. Be curious. And over and over again, pause and *open to your life,* however it is in that moment. To be present for our lives is the healing that we long for. Everything we need and everything we truly are is right here and right now.

I would like to leave you with the two poems that I wrote this year as a part of the Christmas gift I gave to all of the people with whom I work. I used the picture of the Earth that was taken from the moon on the Apollo 11 mission and wrote these words on the black velvety space that surrounds the Earth:

> *We are so much more than we think we are.*
>
> *Be still. Listen.*
>
> *Hear the truth of who you really are.*

Then on the back I wrote:

> *It is the human heart that will see that we are all in this together, floating on a tiny blue green jewel through vast oceans of space.*
>
> *It is the human heart that will recognize that Love is the ground of being out of which it all arises.*
>
> *By Love I mean the field of pure potentiality that is the connective tissue of the universe. It not only holds all of Life together; it animates and nourishes every thing from the inside out. This includes atoms, molecules, cells, rocks, panda bears, people and planets.*
>
> *It is Love that will reveal to us how to show up for the path we have been given so that we can become Love waking up to the truth of Love.*
>
> *And it is Love that will give us the courage to be to be who we truly are.*

Mary O'Malley

Author

Mary O'Malley is a speaker, author, group facilitator and counselor in private practice in Kirkland, Washington. For over 30 years she has explored and practiced the art of being truly present for Life, and out of this has evolved a transformational approach to working with everything that keeps us from being present for the living moment of our lives. Through her organization, *Awakening*, she offers the opportunity to experience the center of clarity, compassion and trust within us that can be accessed no matter what is happening in our lives. Her work with individuals and groups offers an invitation to live from the place in which the impossible becomes possible and our hearts soar with the joy of being alive.

Mary is available for speaking engagements, retreats, workshops, phone and in-person counseling. To contact Mary:

email: awaken@maryomalley.com   web site: www.maryomalley.com

phone: 425-889-5937

Diane Solomon

Cover Artist

In 1979 my life turned an abrupt, jagged corner as I faced the accidental death of my 10 year old son. I sat in the stillness of my grief for a very long time. I became ill with a chronic disease. Four years later my cousin gave me a well-worn copy of *What Is Zen* by Alan Watts. I began to heal. As I grew in awareness, I returned to my childhood love of painting. It has been both the source and the end result of the spiritual journey I am on. Each of my paintings is a reminder that here – in this moment – is all the beauty and love we will ever need for awakening and healing.

email: dsolomon@snovalley.com   Web Site: www.inspiredmedicine.com

311

MARY'S FIRST BOOK

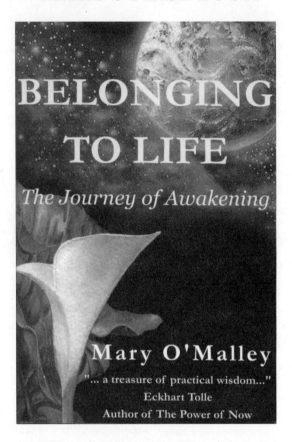

In this book, Mary O'Malley offers an invitation into the rapture of being fully alive in each moment of our lives – the joy of belonging to a greater process and the deep healing of being present in our own lives at the moment each experience appears out of Mystery. She explores how we can cultivate being present for these moments and shares stories, ideas and techniques that invite us into this freeing place that we knew when we were very young.

For most of our existence we have lived in afterthoughts and plans. What we truly desire is direct, intimate contact with life in each moment, the only time that is totally real, truly vibrant and completely alive. It is the place that holds all the love we dream of, where we can again engage creatively with the awesome unfolding that is Life, and where we can remember who we truly are.

To order, please see the contact information on the previous page.